The Character Factor

The Character Factor

How We Judge America's Presidents

James P. Pfiffner

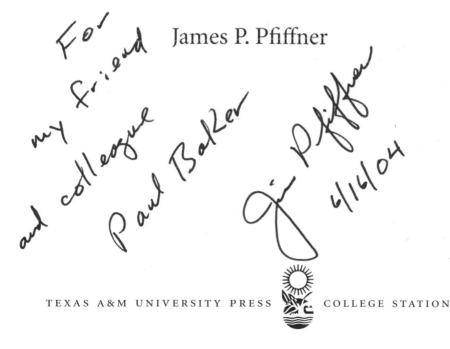

For my friend and colleague Paul Baker

Jim Pfiffner 6/16/04

TEXAS A&M UNIVERSITY PRESS   COLLEGE STATION

The paper used in this book meets the minimum requirements
of the American National Standard for Permanence
of Paper for Printed Library Materials, z39.48-1984.
Binding materials have been chosen for durability.

∞

Library of Congress Cataloging-in-Publication Data

Pfiffner, James P.
    The character factor : how we judge America's presidents /
James P. Pfiffner.
        p. cm.—(The presidency and leadership ; no. 18)
    Includes index.
    ISBN 1-58544-315-8 (cloth)—ISBN 1-58544-316-6 (pbk.)
    1. Presidents—United States—Psychology—Case studies.
2. Character—Political aspects—United States.   3. Political
leadership—United States.   4. Presidents—United States—
Public opinion.   5. Public opinion—United States.
I. Title.   II. Series.
JK516.P48   2004
973.92'092'2—dc22   2003016352

For my wife, Deb Pfiffner,

and our children,

Megan Cyr Pfiffner (1982),

Katherine Courtney Pfiffner (1985),

and Morgan Meehan Pfiffner (1987)

—⁀w⁀—

CONTENTS

PREFACE

In the spring of 1998 members of the Clinton administration found themselves playing roles in a drama that the president had created, but they were not sure whether they were involved in a farce or a tragedy. In truth, the sexual imbroglio the president had created contained elements of both.

The farcical elements resembled an eighteenth-century comedy of manners in which the main character is caught in a sexual affair with a woman not his wife and is greatly embarrassed by the discovery. Clinton's affair also had some far-fetched coincidences reminiscent of musical comedy. The president is brought to court by a woman (Paula Jones) who felt that her honor had been publicly impugned by the author of an article that identified her by only her first name. She claimed that Governor Clinton's rejected sexual proposition to her and its aftermath constituted sexual harassment.

Another woman (Linda Tripp), scorned by the president's lawyer, taped the maunderings of another young woman (Monica Lewinsky) who claimed to have had an affair with the president and was despondent because he was not returning her calls. Tripp tipped off Jones's lawyers, who set a trap by asking the president in a sworn deposition whether he had had an affair with Lewinsky. The president answered in the negative. The judge later threw the sexual harassment case out of court, but the damage was done. The press went into a feeding frenzy; independent counsel Kenneth Starr was hot on Clinton's trail; and the rest made history.

The farcical aspects of the situation were evident because it seemed so petty. That the president would risk his whole administration and legacy for a little sexual gratification was incredible. If the story line had been proposed for a novel, any decent editor would have rejected it; the character motivation and plot would not have been credible.

But important issues were also at stake. Compounding the legal but morally dubious affair, the president was accused of perjury and obstruction of justice. His refusal to come forth with evidence and explanations raised the question of whether the president was above the law and could resist legal inquiry. In a series of legal showdowns courts decided that neither executive privilege nor lawyer-client privilege could protect the president's aides from giving their testimony. Even Secret Service agents were forced to testify about the president's actions. Questions about the president's personal integrity were raised, and it became apparent that he had lied to his family, the public, his closest aides, and members of his cabinet in addition to the judge in the Paula Jones case.

Consequently President Clinton found himself in a tragic situation in the classical sense of the squandering of the potential for greatness because of a character flaw in the protagonist. Bill Clinton was one of the most intelligent presidents and one of the most gifted politicians of the twentieth century. Although he might not have ranked among the great presidents in U.S. history, he had the potential to accomplish much during his two terms in office. But he risked his political legacy and his presidency itself, not to mention his personal reputation and his family, for a few moments of pleasure.

Thus did the character issue again come to the fore in presidential politics. Those who had opposed Clinton all along saw his actions as a natural and even inevitable manifestation of his character. His defenders saw his behavior as an aberration based on a serious character flaw in an otherwise intelligent, talented, and well-intentioned president. The issue of the private lives of public officials was also raised anew. The American public, including pundits and scholars, judged Clinton harshly because of his private sexual behavior. Media standards and public attitudes had changed since the 1960s for reasons discussed in chapter 4, and Clinton was judged by the new standards. But if we want to judge presidential character fairly, we must also consider what we know about the extramarital behavior of other modern presidents.

In contemporary politics the character issue usually implies sex and lies and is used to attack a political opponent. This book takes the character issue seriously. The idea of presidential character deserves to be saved from relativism on the one hand and from cynicism on the other. Relativists would have us believe that moral judgment is hopelessly subjective and that we ought not to judge others' behavior. One variant of the relativist perspective argues that partisanship makes fair judgment impossible; Democrats will blindly defend their presidents, and Republicans will blindly defend theirs. Cynics look at unacceptable behavior on the part of presidents and conclude that "they all do it," so why even bother with trying to distinguish good from bad behavior?

But this book argues that they do not all do it. Yes, some presidents tell lies, but not all lies are equally wrong. Yes, some presidents break their marriage vows, but not all adultery is equally condemnable. This book does not address partisans, hagiographers, or cynics who have already made up their minds. It is rather intended for moderate, reasonable citizens who are capable of admitting that even the best presidents may have character flaws and that even seriously flawed presidents have made important contributions to our polity.

The conclusion of this analysis is that presidential character is not seamless; most presidents have multidimensional characters. That is, presidents can do some things well and others very poorly. There are no summary judgments here that some presidents have "good" characters and other have "bad" ones. The argument is that judging character is subtle and complex. Nevertheless, it is necessary that we as citizens judge our presidents' behavior. Some presidential behavior is admirable and some is unacceptable, and our duty is to weigh both in coming to our own conclusions about how to judge our presidents. This is not easy, but it is not the province only of specialists or scholars; it is the duty of citizens to look at the evidence and make their own judgments.

This book presents some evidence and raises some questions about presidential character. Although I make some moral judgments about presidential behavior, it is not necessary for the reader to agree with them. My main concern is to raise the issues that we ought to consider in making our judgments, not to insist that my specific judgments are correct.

Because common usage of the character issue focuses on negative character traits, this book necessarily examines behavior by presidents that often does not measure up to our hopes. The chapters at the heart of the book focus on presidential lying, marital infidelity, promise breaking, and potentially impeachable behavior. Although these issues entail important aspects of presidential behavior, they are by no means the only or the most important dimensions of our presidents. Good judgment, courage, and effective leadership are crucial to our polity, and any balanced treatment of presidential character ought to deal with them. In order to put the character faults of modern presidents into perspective, the final chapter proposes a way to take a more balanced view, using as examples Lyndon Johnson, Ronald Reagan, and Bill Clinton.

At times I felt uneasy as I did research for the book, combing through the indexes of books in search of evidence for presidential misbehavior. But I concluded that these issues need to be addressed. Charges of presidential lying have been common, and President Clinton was impeached because of his lies. And in light of independent counsel Kenneth Starr's evidence delivered to the House of Representatives and made public in 1998, it is impossible for us to ignore President Clinton's sexual behavior in judging his character. If we judge President Clinton in part by his extramarital sexual behavior, we must examine similar behavior in other presidents if we are to be even handed in our judgments. The point is not to be fair to President Clinton, but rather to be clear about our judgments.

An Overview of the Book

In American politics the problem is that although everyone avers that character is crucial in the presidency, there is no consensus about what constitutes good character. The first chapter of this book emphasizes the importance of presidential character and distinguishes private morality from the moral obligations of presidents in office. It then analyzes commonsense, popular definitions of character and discusses how they apply to politicians.

In chapters 2 and 3 I take up one central aspect of any definition of character: truthfulness and lying. The argument is that most presidents lie at some time while campaigning or in office but that not all lies are of equal gravity. A typology is developed that argues that some lies are justifiable, some are minor, some are wrong but understandable, and some are serious breaches of the public trust. These two chapters present instances of lying by presidents and suggest criteria for judging the lies. The conclusion is that we need to examine the context of any instance of lying in some detail in order to evaluate a president's character.

Chapter 4 examines the question of modern presidents' sexual fidelity. It contrasts an absolutist position that argues that any act of adultery is so morally wrong as to be disqualifying for a president with a perspective that not all sexual infidelities by presidents are equivalent. The chapter considers the sexual behaviors of Presidents Roosevelt, Eisenhower, Kennedy, Johnson, and Clinton in their contexts. It concludes with a comparative evaluation of these presidents' sexual behaviors and the implications for presidential character.

Chapter 5 takes up the issues of consistency and promise keeping. Americans maintain that consistency of vision and purpose are admirable in presidents. On the other hand, in democracies in general and the United States in particular, it is difficult for politicians to avoid changing their policy positions in reaction to changes in public opinion and circumstances. If politics is the art of the possible, overly rigid politicians will not survive long in a democracy. The analysis then shifts to campaign promises that presidents make. We examine high-visibility promises that modern presidents have made, and we then evaluate how well the specific presidents kept their promises in order to demonstrate how we might make such assessments fairly and equitably.

The sixth chapter presents a brief overview of the three major, internally caused, crises in the modern presidency: Watergate, Iran-Contra, and President Clinton's lies about his relationship with Monica Lewinsky. The chapter examines the causes and consequences of each crisis and evaluates each president's culpability for his predicament.

Finally, chapter 7 puts presidential character into perspective by arguing that presidents are complex human beings (as are most people) and capable of admirable as well as deplorable behavior. The analysis then shifts to a balanced approach to understanding the character of three complex presidents: Lyndon Johnson, Ronald Reagan, and Bill Clinton. The positive and negative traits of each are examined in order to show that each had admirable as well as negative character traits. The conclusion outlines a realistic perspective on our expectations of presidential behavior.

The bottom line in this book is the hope that carefully examining the positive and negative dimensions of presidential behavior will lead us to a more realistic understanding of the very human people who have become our presidents. The bad news is that presidents often do not live up to our ideals. The good news is that we consistently find virtuous, if flawed, politicians to lead us in the presidency.

In the course of writing this book over the past several years, I have accumulated many debts due to the kindness and generosity of others who have helped me to think about presidential character. Several colleagues went above and beyond the call of collegiality and read the whole manuscript and gave me helpful comments. I want to thank them for their generosity: Michael Genovese, David Lewis, Robert Pool, Robert Spitzer, and Susan Tolchin. Lou Fisher's careful reading and comments were particularly helpful. David Abshire was generous in allowing me to read the prepublication manuscript of his book, *To Save a Presidency,* about his experience in the Reagan White House. I also want to thank Susan J. Tolchin and Martin Tolchin for letting me read portions of the manuscript of their book *Glass Houses: Congressional Ethics and the Politics of Venom* before it was published.

George Mason has been a wonderful scholarly community for me. I wish to thank Dean Danielle Struppa and Associate Dean Dee Holisky of the College of Arts and Sciences for their work in establishing the scholarly award for which I put together the first version of several chapters of this book. Scott Keeter, the chair of the Department of Public and International Affairs, was generous in releasing me from some teaching, which enabled me to do part of my research. Kingsley Haynes, Dean of the School of Public Policy, and Jim Finkelstein, Senior Associate Dean, did much to enable me to complete this project. Many other colleagues at George Mason helped me with ideas and advice or by reading portions of the manuscript: John Besanko, Brack Brown, Jim Burroughs, Timothy Conlan, Robert Dudley, Jim Finkelstein, Jason Hartke, Peter Henriques, Lois Horton, Don Kash, Scott Keeter, Martin Lipset, Alan Merten, Priscilla Regan, Colleen Shogan, Toni Travis, and Roger Wilkins. Hugh Heclo was particularly penetrating in his questions, comments, and reactions to portions of the manuscript.

Other friends, colleagues, and scholars throughout the country were also generous with their comments and help: Larry Berman, Michael Beschloss, MaryAnne Borelli, Douglas Brook, John Burke, Lou Cannon, Robert Dallek, Chris Deering, George Edwards, Bob Faherty, Al Felzenberg, Booth Fowler, Hugh Gallagher, Fred Greenstein, Stephen Hess, Matthew Holden, Mark Kann, Barbara Kellerman, Paul Light, Cal Mackenzie, Herbert Parmet, Deb Pfiffner, Jeffrey Pfiffner, Megan Pfiffner, Patrick Pfiffner, Dick Pious, John Ritzert, Matthew Spalding, Lee Sigelman, Fred Timm, Jim Thurber, Rick Waterman, Steve Wayne, Kent Weaver, and Joe White. None of these fine people can be blamed for any of my mistakes or misjudgments in the book, and I am particularly grateful for criticisms that I carefully considered but finally rejected. I also appreciate the professionals at Texas A&M University Press who shepherded this book through the production and publication process.

Finally, I wish to thank my wife, Deb, and our children, Megan, KC, and Morgan, for their love and support during the years this book was in incubation.

The Character Factor

CHAPTER 1

Judging Presidential Character

—ɯ—

*Liberty cannot be preserved without general knowledge among the
people who have the right to that knowledge and the desire to know.
But besides this, they have a right, an indisputable, unalienable,
indefeasible, divine right to that most dreaded and envied kind of
knowledge—I mean of the character and conduct of their rulers.*
—JOHN ADAMS, 1765

In American partisan politics, the character issue is most often raised with
negative connotations to imply doubt about a person's moral suitability
for high public office. William Safire's *New Political Dictionary* defines the
character issue as "the moral uprightness of a candidate; or, a euphemism
for an attack on a candidate for philandering." He adds that the term is
"almost always used in a verbal attack" that "insinuates a negative evaluation of a candidate's personal background."[1] While the character issue
often applies to a person's personal behavior, particularly sexual, it is also
applied to an official's public behavior, particularly with respect to truthfulness and consistency. But the issue of character is much broader than
these negative aspects of campaign invective.

This book takes the character issue seriously. Too often in campaign
rhetoric the phrase is used as a political weapon to impugn the integrity
of an opponent. Op-ed pieces also use the phrase to connote negative
traits. In the popular press, character is seldom used in a rigorous manner with specific meaning, though it often implies sex and lies. This book
takes the idea of character seriously by examining several traits that are
considered essential to the integrity of a person's character: truthfulness,
sexual fidelity, consistency, and promise keeping. Since these traits are
widely used in judging presidential character, I take them up in order to
put some content into them by being specific about how recent presidential behavior measures up in these categories.

The Importance of Character

Presidential character is manifestly important. The values, principles, and habits of behavior that mark an individual strongly influence that person's behavior, and the stakes are very high in the U.S. presidency. President Reagan's speechwriter, Peggy Noonan, states it cogently, if excessively: "In a president, character is everything. A president doesn't have to be brilliant; Harry Truman wasn't brilliant, and he helped save Western Europe from Stalin. He doesn't have to be clever; you can hire clever. . . . But you can't buy courage and decency, you can't rent a strong moral sense. A president must bring those things with him."[2]

Commonsense and popular-usage definitions of character include trustworthiness, fidelity, respect for others, willingness to accept responsibility, self-restraint, and compassion. The problem with applying the commonsense approach to presidents is that it is difficult to set aside one's own partisan preferences and apply the same criteria evenhandedly to presidents of both parties.

One problem is that the desirability of many character traits depends upon the historical circumstance. We admire loyalty, but should presidents remain loyal to old friends who, through their bad behavior, may jeopardize their presidencies, as in the Harding and Truman administrations? We admire honesty, but should Franklin Roosevelt have been completely honest in his public evaluation of the U.S. economy in the depths of the Depression, or was it better to encourage optimism in the face of such adversity? Should Eisenhower have been publicly honest about his private doubts about the wisdom of the Supreme Court decision in *Brown v. Board of Education?* We admire consistency and conviction, but Lyndon Johnson did not get much political credit for sticking with an increasingly unpopular war in Vietnam. Should Richard Nixon have shunned a historic opportunity to open relations with China in order to be consistent with his earlier political principles?[3]

Presidents must make tough decisions when the stakes are high, and many lives may be at risk. Their reactions in such situations are based not merely on the expert advice they get but also on their inner strengths and weaknesses. The values and principles that they have internalized, their instincts and character, matter, as the following examples illustrate:

- Franklin Roosevelt's optimism helped the United States weather the Great Depression, and his resolve helped lead the Allies to victory in World War II.
- Harry Truman had to decide how to use the newly invented atomic bomb in ending World War II.
- Dwight Eisenhower resisted strong political pressures to provoke military confrontations in Korea, China, Vietnam, and the Soviet Union.
- When John Kennedy confronted Nikita Khrushchev in the Cuban missile crisis, he combined toughness with restraint and allowed Khrushchev to back down without losing face and possibly lashing back with a nuclear strike.
- When Lyndon Johnson decided to put all of his political capital behind the 1964 Civil Rights Act, he made a decision that would hurt the Democrats in the South but would move the United States closer to justice.
- Richard Nixon disappointed many of his conservative supporters when he made his historic trip to China.
- Gerald Ford risked his reelection prospects when he decided that pardoning Richard Nixon was in the best interests of the country.
- By compromising with the Senate, Jimmy Carter was able to fight the Panama Canal Treaty through to ratification.
- When Ronald Reagan faced the Soviet Union he was firm in his stance against Communism, but he was open to cooperation with Gorbachev in ending the Cold War.
- George Bush Sr. skillfully put together the coalition that won the Persian Gulf War, tenaciously conducted the war, and used restraint at the end, when U.S. forces could have killed many thousands of Iraqi soldiers who were unable to defend themselves.
- Bill Clinton confronted unanimous Republican resistance and disappointed many of his own campaigners in pushing through his 1993 deficit-reduction package.
- In the aftermath of the terrorist attacks of 9/11 George W. Bush Jr. symbolized the nation's determination to defeat terrorism and led the United States to end the reign of the Taliban regime in Afghanistan. In 2003 he used his power and popularity to send U.S. forces to defeat Saddam Hussein and occupy Iraq.

One might disagree with the wisdom of the judgment of these presidents in the preceding situations, but it is hard to deny that the character of the different presidents affected the outcomes of these highly contentious and historic turning points. Their decisions could not be fully predicted from campaign promises or good intentions, and the outcomes were not determined merely by historical forces and circumstances. Character counts. Character also counted when Richard Nixon decided to systematically cover up the Watergate "horrors" and when Bill Clinton decided to deny that he had had an affair with Monica Lewinsky.

There is a widespread consensus in American politics that presidential character is just as important as intellect, organizational abilities, television presence, or effectiveness in public speaking. Public-opinion polls show widespread agreement on the importance of character in the life of the polity. But just as striking is the lack of clear content to the term. From eighty-one to ninety-five percent of respondents agree that the following are important attributes of good character: obeying those in positions of authority, following your own conscience, sacrificing your own interests for the good of others, protecting your own interests, sticking to your own principles no matter what, and enjoying yourself.[4] It is immediately evident that these aspects of character are often mutually exclusive.

From a historical perspective, "Fame is a vapor, popularity an accident, riches take wing, and only character endures," in Horace Greeley's words.[5] From the perspective of American politics Fred Greenstein argues, "the personalities of presidents are as integral a part of the American political system as the constitutionally mandated instruments of government. . . . [O]ne need only think of the natural counterfactuals that are provided by the possible substitution of presidents with their vice presidents."[6] The American political system, perhaps more than a parliamentary system, is dependent upon the fundamental makeup of the individuals who are chosen to be its chief executive.

From the perspective of citizen voters, character is crucial because no one can predict the situations that will confront a president once in office. The issues that were pressing in a campaign may no longer be important, and the promises made in a campaign may not be appropriate for new circumstances. New and unforeseen crises may face the country. No one predicted, for instance, the terrorist attacks on the United States in 2001. Thus it is more important to select an individual who will apply a sound set of principles and values in unexpected circumstances, someone who citizens can be confident will make the right decision. Robert Teeter, the first President Bush's pollster said, "Voters know that the issues a president will have to face will change in time. But his character will always be there."[7]

Character is particularly important in the presidency because the issues reaching the president are often of great consequence and hotly contested. Compelling arguments buttress all sides of the issues; if the issues were simple, they would have been decided at lower levels. According to Alexander and Juliette George, "The need to act on important matters that are characterized by uncertainty and value complexity can be the source of considerable stress for a president."[8] Thus the deeper roots of presidential behavior, that is, character, come into play at the most crucial times in a presidency.

Public versus Private Morality

In judging presidents we must consider the possible differences between private and public morality. In some cases public leaders may not be bound by the same ethical strictures as those that constrain people acting in private life. Machiavelli argued that leaders are duty bound to violate the mores of private relationships if doing so will help them serve the stability of the state.[9] This book posits that national leaders are not bound by the normal bonds of private morality when, in certain circumstances, they take actions that are necessary for the protection of the national security. For example, lying about the location of U.S. troops or the timing of military operations would be legitimate if it were necessary to protect the safety of our military forces (presuming that the military action has been taken in accord with accepted constitutional processes).[10] Of course, a private citizen could also justifiably lie in such circumstances.

On the other hand, one can argue that public leaders have *additional* duties to act ethically because of their public office. The consequences for individuals of acting unethically (in addition to the harm they may cause others) are the tarnishing of their reputation and the bad example they might set for those who are aware of their bad behavior. But the consequences for public figures, and especially presidents, for acting unethically are multiplied manyfold. Richard Posner argues that presidents have dual responsibilities: *executive* moral duties and *exemplary* moral duties.[11] Executive moral duties result from their constitutional duties as president and include the diligent and prudent exercise of their obligations as head of the executive branch of government. In addition to these, presidents also have exemplary moral duties that relate to the public nature of their behavior. That is, presidents—whether they like it or not—are often seen as role models for Americans in general and children in particular. The seeking of public office ought to include the understanding that elective office imposes moral obligations beyond those of private behavior and the willingness to accept the additional moral duties of upright behavior.

The additional duties of the role of moral exemplar are relevant to the dimensions of character this book takes up: lies, extramarital sex, and promise keeping. A certain level of honesty is a necessary premise in human societies; without a general expectation of truth telling, social cooperation, not to mention healthy economic activity, would be virtually impossible. This is true despite the fact that many lies are told and that some of them may be justified in everyday human interactions. Truth telling is important for people in order for them to protect their reputations and for others to be able to respect and trust them. It is also important to set good examples for others, including children and young people, whose behavior and values may be influenced by good or poor role models.

The same importance of truth telling in individuals is magnified in the obligation of public officials, and thus presidents, to tell the truth. The consequences of bad example by presidents are far broader than those by other people both because of the wider exposure of the behavior and also because of the role of the president as moral exemplar. This issue was widely discussed during the impeachment of President Clinton for lying under oath.

Lying takes on broader significance when it is linked to the democratic aspects of presidential leadership. In a democracy the premise is that the government ought to do what the people want it to do (of course, within constitutional limits to majority rule necessary in any liberal democracy such as the United States). But that premise is seriously undermined if public officials lie to the public by misleading them about the actions of the government and its officials. Thus in the range of lies this book examines later, lies of policy deception are considered to be the worst kind of presidential lie.

With respect to extramarital sex, presidents have the same obligations as private individuals not to cause pain in their families, but they also have duties because of their public office. Personal sexual morality is often based on religious and ethical codes that are important to social stability within societies. Sexual practices vary widely across human cultures, but the bottom line of sexual morality is the duty to act so as not to hurt others (physically or emotionally). Whether one is hurt emotionally, of course, depends importantly on the mores of one's society. Thus if polygamy or polyandry is acceptable in a society, its practice may not be considered immoral or cause emotional harm to one's spouse(s). In the United States marriage is considered to entail a serious commitment to be sexually faithful to one's spouse, despite the failure of many to live up to this ideal. Thus presidents as well as other people are bound to take their marital vows seriously.

But presidents are bound beyond their interpersonal moral obligations to respect the conventional morality of society with respect to extramarital sex. These obligations apply to a president, even if one waives interpersonal obligations. For instance, one might argue that relations between spouses cannot be fully known and therefore we ought not to judge others' private sexual practices. Even if we stipulate that sexual behavior ought to be private and the privacy of presidents ought to be respected, presidents are still bound to respect conventional sexual morality. The premise of this argument is that the conventions of sexual morality are so strongly held in the United States that flouting them can have serious consequences for the president's ability to fulfill the duties of the office. The virtue of prudence brings one to the conclusion that presidents ought to avoid scandal for public purposes as well as for their personal best interests.[12]

One consequence of the widely accepted proscriptions on adultery is that politicians who violate them are vulnerable to political attack that may jeopardize their political future. Thus engaging in extramarital sex may make a president subject to blackmail for money or raise national-security risks. This argument has been made with respect to John Kennedy's relationship with Judith Campbell Exner at the same time that she had relationships with organized crime figures. In addition, reckless sexual behavior (if it is exposed) risks public scandal and the distraction of the president from constitutional duties. This became painfully evident in the uproar over President Clinton's relationship with Monica Lewinsky. Finally, the flouting of conventional morality, regardless of its personal morality (e.g., permission from a spouse), will likely result in public scandal that will undermine the ability of an administration to pursue the policies it was elected to pursue. Thus the lack of sexual restraint in a president may indicate a lack of commitment to t of public office in terms of both policy goals and moral example

The irony of the argument that the president has duties as a moral exemplar is that it applies only to behavior that is publicly known or revealed. In this argument, what the people do not know will not hurt them.[14] John Kennedy was able to inspire a generation of young people to enter public life for idealistic reasons, despite his irresponsible sexual behavior. If this behavior had been revealed while he was president, it is not likely that he would have been as admired as much as he was while he was president.

The question of public versus private morality raises the issue of moral seamlessness. That is, can a person be an immoral individual and still be a good political leader? The overall argument of this book is that people are multidimensional and that it is possible for presidents to behave poorly in some aspects of their moral obligations and very well in other aspects of their duties. Thus they can be good people and ineffective political leaders or very effective political leaders while having personal moral deficiencies. Presidents, as individuals, have moral obligations as all of us do. But as presidents they have additional duties. Some presidents, such as Kennedy, Johnson, and Clinton, have been effective leaders in some aspects of their official duties and remiss in the area of sexual probity.

The relationship of private to public obligations in promise keeping runs closely parallel to the obligations to tell the truth. They are not the same, because failing to keep a promise is a lie only if the promise maker does not intend to keep the promise at the time it is made. But if one makes a promise, one is obligated to take it seriously because of reasons similar to those about lying. At a personal level, the failure to keep promises undermines one's own credibility and social trust more generally and may cause harm to individuals who expect the promise to be kept. The failure of a president to keep a public promise has a similar but much broader effect; the undermining of trust is more insidious because the president's role as moral exemplar may encourage or seem to excuse imitative behavior. And many more people may have taken actions based on a president's public promise.

The broader obligation of promise keeping in politicians has to do with the nature of democracy and accountability. If politicians do not keep their promises after they are elected, how can citizens know for whom to vote? Thus blatant promise breaking undermines faith in politicians generally and may lead to cynicism in the public about government and undermine the premises that hold a polity together. This obligation to keep promises is not absolute, and, in a system of limited powers, it is understood that politicians are obligated only to make a serious effort to keep their promises and that other forces in the political system may keep them from fully accomplishing all that they had hoped to accomplish. And a certain amount of exaggeration in campaign promises is part of the rhetoric of political campaigns and not always taken literally. In addition, conditions may change, and an elected official may have an obligation not to keep a promise if fulfilling it would lead to bad consequences for the country as a whole. A promise to balance the budget (e.g., Reagan) or to cut taxes (e.g., Clinton) or not to raise taxes (e.g., Bush) might be reevaluated in light of changing economic circumstances.

Thus strong parallels exist between private and public morality. As individuals, public officials have the same moral obligations as do other individuals although, in some limited circumstances, public officials may justifiably violate the strictures of private morality. More commonly, however, public office expands the obligations of private morality because the consequences of public immorality are broader.

Commonsense and Popular Definitions of Character

The ordinary usage and commonsense way of talking about a person's character encompass a number of traits that include trustworthiness, respect for others, the willingness to accept responsibility, self-restraint, and compassion. Though these traits make sense when applied to people in everyday life, their application to presidents is more problematical. First, we expect more from presidents than that they be good people. We expect that presidents will exercise their considerable political power in ways that will produce the political outcomes that lead the country forward. This necessarily entails putting together political coalitions of people who disagree with each other, sometimes with some vehemence.

Presidents must be shrewd users of power in order to be effective leaders. But we also expect them to be statesmen, above petty politics, and to represent what is best in the nation. Whereas parliamentary systems often separate the roles of political leader from the symbolic chief-of-state functions, the U.S. system combines the two and imposes contradictory expectations on our presidents. We expect them to be effective users of partisan power as well as nonpartisan symbols of national pride and unity.

Another reason presidents may have difficulty measuring up to commonsense measures of character is that they are the focal point of the most intense political battles that our system creates. That is, they must make decisions and take sides on intractable issues that provoke intense disagreement in the political system. Very few easy issues reach the president's desk; the easy issues are settled at lower levels in the system.

The third reason that presidents have difficulty living up to the high expectations of conventional judgments about character is that the types of people who are able to win the presidency in the United States are ambitious politicians who have had to fight their way up a very unforgiving ladder of political power. Any mistake along the way can come back to haunt a candidate because an opponent can twist even good decisions in order to smear a rival. Thus those seeking the presidency must walk a tightrope.

In order to create a winning electoral coalition, candidates often present their stands on political issues in different ways to different groups. They must often reinterpret what they have said in the past to present it in the most acceptable light under new circumstances or when talking to a new audience. They are tempted to tell their audiences what they want to hear. We can interpret this as merely packaging their position so as to make it the least offensive to different groups. Or we can interpret it as "talking out of both sides of one's mouth." Or we can interpret the practice as lying. The following traits are often considered to be aspects of good character:

Trustworthiness in common usage refers to honesty, integrity, reliability (promise keeping), and loyalty.[15] Honesty, at the most basic level, means not telling lies—that is, not telling a deliberate untruth. One of the most devastating criticisms one can make of a politician (or any person) is that the person is a liar. But an absolute prohibition against any lie is unusual in moral philosophy; both St. Augustine and Immanuel Kant held an absolutist position on lying, but they are in the minority. Most moral systems would allow lying to protect someone against murderers, robbers, and so on. And at the quotidian level of polite society, lying in harmless ways is often acceptable and expected (e.g., "I just love the plaid tie you gave me for my birthday." "Your new hairdo is just fabulous."). So a moral judgment about lying may be relative to the situation, but that does not mean that all lies are acceptable. Lying about significant things is wrong (except under exceptional circumstances), both for individuals and for politicians. It may be even more important in politicians because they wield power that the citizens of the polity have delegated to them.

Other dimensions of honesty include **sincerity and candor.** Sincerity implies that, even if one is telling the literal truth, one will not mislead others, for instance, by telling the truth (or a partial truth) in order to deceive or intending special meanings of words that mislead others. On important matters sincerity is expected in everyday interactions among people. For politicians, sincerity is more difficult because of the contentious nature of the issues they regularly have to deal with and the ability of their electoral opponents to use their words against them in a campaign. Thus politicians are tempted to use partial truths to avoid discussing issues that might harm their electoral opportunities. For example, politicians often do not answer questions about drug use earlier in life completely and sincerely. Candor—that is, being frank, honest, and forthcoming about all significant aspects of a situation—is even harder for politicians than for most people. One does not win votes by admitting that a policy aspiration has little chance of getting through a legislature, as attractive as the idea might be. Thus politicians, particularly during campaigns, are often not fully candid.

Integrity implies a wholeness or consistency between one's outward and inner life and a consistent presentation of one's self from group to group. It also implies the avoidance of decisions based on expedience, that is, just for temporary personal or political benefit. Another dimension of integrity is "playing by the rules," that is, not excusing oneself from behavior that one expects from others. President Clinton's advice to the Russians in international affairs illustrates this: "You have to play by the rules that everyone else has to play by. That's what this crisis is all about."[16] The irony of Clinton's comment is that while he publicly chided others for not playing by the generally accepted rules, in his personal life he himself was ignoring the rules and acting as if they did not apply to him.

Again, politicians have a more difficult time maintaining their public integrity than ordinary citizens whose lives are not under a public microscope. The give-and-take of politics and the shifting nature of political coalitions make integrity and consistency difficult for politicians to maintain.

Reliability is also an important aspect of good character. Does one keep one's word? If one makes a promise, can one be counted upon to keep it? This implies that if one makes a commitment, one will make every reasonable effort to keep it. It also implies that one will only make promises carefully, that is, only if one has the expectation of being able to deliver on a promise. Promises are the stock-in-trade for candidates for office: "If I am elected, I promise to restore honor to the government and achieve these policy goals." In the heat of campaigns, politicians often get carried away, exaggerate, and promise more than they can deliver. They often feel that doing so is necessary in order to get elected.

The moral implications of these political campaign promises are somewhat mitigated by the fact that voters often do not take them literally. They realize that these are ideal goals, that circumstances change, and that no one politician controls the whole political system and thus no one can be expected to deliver on all promises. But this skepticism tempts politicians to make promises that imply more than the usual casual commitment of campaign promises. Thus they might uses phrases that indicate a greater seriousness than usual, such as "read my lips."

Loyalty is another dimension of character that is important to ordinary citizens as well as to politicians. One expects that a person will not lightly abandon a friend or ally merely because circumstances make it difficult to remain loyal. Since politics is such a precarious profession, loyalty is deeply valued. But loyalty in an individual to the point of covering up a crime of a friend is not acceptable. The danger for presidents is less the maintenance of loyalty to one's allies than the maintenance of loyalty beyond the appropriate point. Presidents appoint their friends and cronies to positions of power and responsibility, and this is seen as a mark of their loyalty to those who supported them in their pursuit of the presidency.

But presidents are often unwilling to face the true suitability of people for high office. So it is incumbent upon presidents to look very carefully at those in whom they place large public trust. In addition, it is crucial for presidents to fire those who are incompetent or who have violated their public trust. Thus presidents are sometimes obliged to be ruthless and fire those who are, for whatever reason (incompetence, venality, or mere mediocrity), incapable of acting in the public interest. The consequences of incompetence in high office are greater than in the ordinary run of affairs, and presidents are elected to make these tough personnel decisions. So the need to set aside personal loyalty and make tough personnel decisions is an important obligation for presidents. Presidents do not have to fire people in a harsh manner, but sometimes they must be fired.

Another important dimension of good character is **responsibility**, that is, the willingness to be accountable for one's actions, to strive to do one's job well, and to exercise the restraint necessary for self-control. One admires this in ordinary citizens and politicians. As Bill Clinton declared: "I hate it when people blame someone else and don't take responsibility."[17] Of course, a major criticism of Clinton by Republicans and Democrats alike was that he failed to take responsibility for his own actions and excused himself by blaming others for his problems.

But politicians are often tempted to blame public-policy problems on others, especially on predecessors from the other party (e.g., "the terrible economic situation we inherited from Carter" or "the terrible deficits we inherited from Reagan"). It is sometimes even in a politician's self-interest to be seen to accept responsibility for failures, such as when John Kennedy took responsibility for the failure of the Bay of Pigs invasion and his public approval ratings went up.

Conducting oneself with **self-restraint** is an important personal and public virtue. In Hillary Clinton's words (with respect to gun-control legislation), "Part of growing up is learning how to control one's impulses."[18] Her husband found out that violating this stricture of character could have serious consequences in the aftermath of his affair with Monica Lewinsky. The lack of self-restraint is also evident in the self-aggrandizing behavior of Lyndon Johnson at times when he was in office or the profligacy of John Kennedy in his many affairs while he was in office.

Compassion for others is an important element of character, for if one cannot be sympathetic toward others, one's actions will be based on criteria that do not take into account a full respect for human beings and their circumstances. This is primarily a personal dimension of character, but it can enter the public realm when a president is mean toward others. Most presidents are shrewd enough to avoid appearing callous even though their public behavior may contrast with the ways they treat their family and staffers in private. But presidents ought to have sufficient compassion to take into consideration the impact of their policies on others, especially the less fortunate.

One common aspect of character is vision, which is related to **consistency,** or fixedness of purpose. Americans say that they admire this in political leaders, who too often seem to vacillate with the winds of public opinion. One of the most devastating charges that can be brought against politicians is that they have flip-flopped on an important issue, and politicians will go to great lengths to avoid the charge. Politicians are so afraid of being perceived as inconsistent that they will go through many contortions to show how their present statements are consistent with past positions they have taken. Political opponents will quickly exploit any deviation from a past position.

Despite Emerson's admonition that "a foolish consistency is the hobgoblin of little minds," politicians would much rather be seen to be consistent than changing.[19] Changing one's position on a policy issue might very well be seen as intellectual growth or judicious change in response to new evidence. But the temptation in politics to change policy positions for expedient reasons is so great that the presumption is that any change is made for opportunistic rather than principled reasons.

Political **prudence** calls attention to important considerations leaders ought to take into account when exercising power. Prudence includes using disciplined reason and attention to experience when making decisions. It includes a sense of proportion in judging the relationship of means to ends. It means considering the long-term consequences to the polity as a whole as well as the short-term benefits to any faction or political party. Prudent political leaders will not take inappropriate risks or use inappropriate means to accomplish their political goals.[20]

Given the lack of consensus on the nature of presidential character it is tempting to say that character comprises those facets of individual personality, attitude, and behavior to which people attribute presidential success and failure. Politicians often use character or the character issue merely as a negative campaign charge against their opponents. Although there is no complete consensus on what character is, there is a consensus that the character of a president has an important effect on the nature of an administration.

The Normative Approach of This Book

This book is about the perspective that we should bring to judging presidents, and it seeks to arrive at judgments about presidential character based on their behavior. Psychological analyses of character tend to see behavior as conditioned by psychological traits firmly established in people early in their lives and reinforced as they mature. The hope is to be able to generalize and to predict behavior based on the character of the individual.[21] This book, in contrast, does not try to predict behavior but arrives at conclusions about character by examining past presidential behavior.

Biographical studies of character by historians and biographers of presidents tend to see character as a result of the many influences, experiences, and other factors that make these people who they are. Thus the examination of early experiences, challenges confronted, and emotional relationships are part of the complex web that makes up a person's unique character. The point is not to see the individual as a certain type of person, but rather to understand the multiplicity of factors that make up the unique individual within that person's historical context.[22]

The approach of this book is not to develop a scholarly definition of presidential character. As the previous discussion in this chapter shows, reaching a consensus on any one approach to character is unrealistic. This book combines some notions from the commonsense approach with the biographical approach of presidential historians and develops a comparative-behavior approach. This approach to character derives from presidential behavior rather than attributing character to psychological predispositions, at least for the purpose of judging presidents.

There is an explicit moral tone to the common-usage approach to character that makes moral judgments about people based on their behavior. This book adopts a similar moral tone, but the judgments are limited. That is, limited aspects of the behavior of presidents are judged in moral terms, but the judgment is not extended to the whole of a president's character. The character of presidents as whole individuals is not rated as good or bad. But certain behaviors of presidents (such as lying or sexual infidelity) are evaluated, criticized, and compared to similar behavior in other presidents. The implication is that presidents are multidimensional and may be deficient in one aspect of their character and admirable in others.

In any general definition of good character the traits of truth telling, sexual fidelity, and promise keeping are central. This book takes up each of these traits and compares the behavior of presidents from Roosevelt through Clinton with respect to these behavioral elements of character. I conclude that presidential character is multidimensional rather than seamless. That is, presidents can do well on one criterion and poorly on another (e.g., Richard Nixon was probably a faithful husband, yet he was capable of serious lies). But more important, we should judge presidents comparatively only by examining the context of their behavior (e.g., Franklin Roosevelt's two love affairs were different from John Kennedy's reckless promiscuity). I conclude that presidents are complex people and that we ought to evaluate them by taking into account their full records as president. On the other hand, a balanced approach to evaluating presidents should not become an excuse for unacceptable behavior.

CHAPTER 2

The Nature of Presidential Lies

—⅏—

*It is only the cynic who claims "to speak the truth" at all times and in all
places to all men in the same way. . . . He dons the halo of the fanatical
devotee of truth who can make no allowance for human weaknesses.*
—DIETRICH BONHOEFFER,
"What is Meant by 'Telling the Truth?'"

Virtually everybody lies, at least in the conduct of everyday life.[1] We say
the equivalent of "I'm pleased to meet you" to people we consider our
adversaries or enemies. When asked by a casual acquaintance, "how are
you?" we say "fine," even though we may feel rotten for emotional or
physical reasons. When a friend has been sick, we may say "you look
great," with the mental reservation "compared to what I had expected."
We also pay compliments of sincere flattery, such as "your new hairdo
looks nice," even if we don't think so. "The reason that we have etiquette
books is that not only does the truth not set you free, it gets you in
trouble."[2] These minor lies smooth human relations in important ways.[3]
But many people engage in lying for more serious and sometimes
justifiable purposes.

Just as most people lie, so do most presidents. But presidents are in a
special position because of the power they wield in the name of the electorate and because of the far-reaching consequences of their actions. They
have the power to make life-and-death decisions that affect millions of
people throughout the world. Besides the duties of office, they also have a
responsibility to fulfill the high expectations the American people have of
them; that is, many people see them as role models as well as decision
makers. Because of the great power vested in them and the leadership
responsibility entrusted to them, we have the right to expect a high level
of ethical behavior by the presidents we elect. Telling the truth, particularly with respect to public policy, is an important ethical imperative for
presidents. That presidents do not always tell the truth is evident, but that
does not mean that all untruths are equally wrong.

The absolutist view against lying was taken by Saint Augustine, who argued that "every lie must be called a sin. . . . Nor are we to suppose that there is any lie that is not a sin, because it is sometimes possible, by telling a lie, to do service to another."[4] He held that regardless of the circumstances or the consequences, lying is strictly prohibited: "[N]o perfect and spiritual man is free to tell a lie to save his transitory life either for himself or for another, since its loss does not kill the soul."[5] Similarly, Immanuel Kant ruled out lies for any reason: "Truthfulness in statements which cannot be avoided is the formal duty of an individual to everyone, however great may be the disadvantage accruing to himself or to another."[6] Anne Frank would not have wanted to be hiding in the home of a philosophical Kantian when the Nazis came knocking at the door.

William J. Bennett presents a contemporary form of the absolutist position in *The Death of Outrage*, in which he argues: "In general, if the president's word cannot be trusted—an issue of character—voters cannot take seriously his election platform or his campaign promises—an issue of public duty. Words are deconstructed, promises emptied of meaning. Politics is reduced to a mere game. It is all very straightforward: if a man's word means nothing, it means nothing. It is folly to believe otherwise."[7]

The problem, of course, is that it is not a straightforward task to determine the point at which a president's word "means nothing." The argument of this book is that all lies are not equivalent and that their seriousness depends on the circumstances, motives, and consequences of the lies.

In contrast to the absolutists, most people take a utilitarian perspective and justify lying in certain circumstances. This perspective sees truth telling as an instrumental rather than an ultimate value and admits of the possibility of the justified lie. We might even derive a utilitarian perspective on the truth from Kant's categorical imperative: "Act only on that maxim whereby thou canst at the same time will that it should become a universal law."[8] For example, one might wish that any person ought to lie in order to save an innocent life from a murderer. The social consequences of telling the truth are certainly important. We must have the expectation that in general most people will tell the truth most of the time or society would not function and advanced economies could not be developed. On the other hand, we might agree that in certain circumstances telling a lie is justified, even though we might not all agree on what those circumstances ought to be.

In a democracy or a republic based on the consent of the governed, citizens need accurate information in order to make informed decisions about elections and public policy. Thus it is wrong for public officials to lie about public issues. But the well-being of the polity might, in special circumstances, outweigh the general obligation of public officials to tell the truth. Such situations should be those in which reasonable citizens would agree that presidents of either party could justifiably lie to them. Lies might be justified to protect lives or the effectiveness of national-security operations that the government is undertaking in support of a legitimate policy (e.g., a hostage-rescue attempt or espionage). This would include covert actions taken in support of legitimate (constitutionally acceptable) policies, but it would exclude covert policies (e.g., when the government says it is pursuing policy X, but it is in fact pursuing policy Y). For instance, lying about specific actions (such as selling arms) to aid Afghanistan in its resistance to Soviet occupation in the 1970s might be justified because the actions were part of acknowledged U.S. policy.

Presidents have told public lies in a variety of contexts, and not all lies are equivalent. What follows is a rough taxonomy of presidential lies, in order from the most justifiable ones to protect national security to the most harmful lies of policy deception. The examples associated with each category are documented and analyzed in some detail. In addition, hypothetical lies are posited to make some important points. The analysis is narrowed to statements made by modern presidents (or at their personal direction) intended (arguably) to deceive the public. The analysis does not deal with all lies by presidents or with other misleading actions (e.g., truths intended to deceive) nor does it deal with all possible justifications for presidential lying.

The premise is that lies must be evaluated according to the intent of the teller and the seriousness of the lies told. The argument that there are different types of lies is not an attempt to reinforce the cynical view that "they all do it." The purpose, rather, is to focus the range of criteria that we as citizens can use to evaluate presidential lies. The following list of lies is separated into categories of relative seriousness. The categories and the placement of lies within them are not intended to be definitive. The point in this approach is to argue that not all lies are equivalent and that some are more justified than others. The reader might disagree with any specific example, yet accept the general proposition that not all lies are equivalent.

Categories of lies—from the most to the least justifiable—with examples

1. Lies to protect national security
    • Nixon's lies about Cuba in his 1960 debate with Kennedy
2. Minor lies
    • Lyndon Johnson's claim that his great-grandfather died at the Alamo
    • Kennedy's claims about speed-reading
3. Lies to prevent embarrassment and preserve political viability
    • Kennedy's denial that he had Addison's disease
    • George Bush Sr.'s statement that Clarence Thomas was the most qualified Supreme Court candidate
4. Lies to cover up important facts
    • President Roosevelt and the *Greer* incident
    • Eisenhower administration lies about the U-2
    • Nixon's lies to cover up Watergate activities
    • George Bush's claim of being "out of the loop" concerning sending arms to Iran
    • Bill Clinton's denial of his affair with Monica Lewinsky
5. Lies of policy deception
    • Lyndon Johnson's lies about U.S. military involvement in Vietnam
    • Richard Nixon's secret bombing of Cambodia
    • Ronald Reagan's untrue statements about Iran-Contra

This chapter examines categories one, two, and three; Chapter 3 takes up categories four and five.

The most convincing justification for lying is to prevent harm from happening to another, such as lying to a murderer about the whereabouts of the person he intends to kill or to a robber about the location of valuables he intends to steal. Presidential lies to protect national-security secrets and the lives of soldiers or spies could be justified by this reasoning. If one accepts the legitimacy of a military establishment and the need to protect one's country in a hostile world, one must accept the occasional need for presidents to lie. Of course, the compelling nature of this justification often tempts presidents to lie about things not essential to protect national security.

We must also admit that politicians in a democracy are in particularly difficult positions with respect to complete truth telling. In order to knit together coalitions of support they must often present the same policy position to suit the goals of different groups. This shading of one's position can easily slide into misrepresentation or lying. Politicians are also at a disadvantage because their opponents will use any fact about them to their greatest disadvantage. Thus behavior that would be unremarkable in a private citizen might be used to attack a person running for office. So a U.S. politician might be tempted to deny, for instance, that one was gay, that one had had an abortion, that one had been treated by a psychiatrist, or that one had used illegal drugs in the past. Even though these would be lies, we can understand how a politician might be tempted to conclude that a lie would be justified when running for office.

The following sections first take up legitimate lies, particularly for national-security purposes. After that, "minor" lies are examined. These can be disturbing because they may be symptoms of more serious problems. But they are not important enough to get upset about in themselves. Finally, lies that are understandable, even if wrong, are analyzed.

Justifiable Presidential Lies

> *You know I am a juggler, and I never let my right hand know what my left hand does. . . . I may have one policy for Europe and one diametrically opposite for North and South America. I may be entirely inconsistent, and furthermore I am perfectly willing to mislead and tell untruths if it will help win the war.*
>
> *—Franklin D. Roosevelt, May 15, 1942*

RICHARD NIXON AND CUBA

During the 1960 campaign for the presidency, U.S. policy toward Cuba was an important issue. Fidel Castro had led a revolution that had overthrown the corrupt Batista regime in 1959 and had allied Cuba with the Soviet Union and other Communist powers. The Eisenhower administration had been supporting and training anti-Castro exiles for a possible future invasion of the island to overthrow Castro. (The invasion did take place in the early months of the Kennedy administration at the Bay of Pigs and was widely seen as a failure.) Shortly before the final presidential series of debates between Kennedy and Nixon, Kennedy came out publicly in favor of active U.S. intervention in Cuba and support of the Cuban anti-Castro forces saying, "Thus far, these fighters for freedom have had virtually no support from our government."[9]

This put Nixon in a difficult situation. He knew that the government was actively involved in support of the Cuban exiles, but the operation was covert and could not be publicly acknowledged for fear of disclosing its existence and putting Castro on guard. So he could not come out and say that he agreed with Kennedy and that such operations were already under way. He had to preserve the secrecy of the operation, but how could he do this and accurately represent his own position and that of the Eisenhower administration? The situation was made more galling to Nixon because he was convinced that Kennedy had in fact been briefed on the Cuban operation and was unfairly raising the issue for campaign purposes.

Nixon concluded that the only responsible action was for him to attack Kennedy's proposal as being reckless and irresponsible: "I think that Senator Kennedy's policies and recommendations for the handling of the Castro regime are probably the most dangerously irresponsible recommendations that he's made during the course of this campaign. . . . [I]f we were to follow that recommendation . . . we would lose all of our friends in Latin American, we would probably be condemned in the United Nations, and we would not accomplish our objective. . . . [I]t would be an open invitation for Mr. Khrushchev . . . to come into Latin America and to engage us in what would be a civil war and possibly even worse than that."[10] Ironically, and to Nixon's dismay, the *New York Times* commented favorably on Nixon's forbearance. In addition, Nixon accurately predicted the eventual outcome of the Bay of Pigs invasion: It did not achieve its objective, and it encouraged Khrushchev to place midrange nuclear missiles in Cuba a year and a half later, leading to the 1962 Cuban missile crisis.

In his first memoirs, *Six Crises*, Nixon recalled his moral position: "I was in the ironic position of appearing to be 'softer' on Castro than Kennedy—which was exactly the opposite of the truth, if only the whole record could be disclosed."[11] Thus Nixon in this situation was telling a blatant lie, saying exactly the opposite of what he believed and covering up the actual actions of the Eisenhower administration. But from his perspective, his statement has to be seen as a legitimate, justified, and even necessary lie. The United States was undertaking a covert operation against what was seen as a Communist enemy, and disclosure of the operation could have led to its failure.

Setting aside what we now know about the Cold War and the future consequences of U.S. actions toward Cuba, we have to admit that Nixon's actions were ethical, even courageous, since he may have jeopardized his chance of being elected. As to whether Kennedy was acting ethically in raising the issue in the way that he did, the White House denied that

Kennedy had been briefed specifically about the Cuban plans, and John Foster Dulles even admitted that the controversy was due to an "honest misunderstanding."[12] But circumstantial evidence seemed to indicate that Kennedy could well have known in general about the Eisenhower administration's planning activity. Had Kennedy known of the plans, it would have made his criticism of the Eisenhower administration ethically suspect.

NIXON AND KOREA

Another incident from the Nixon administration illustrates the problems that may arise if the president is too forthcoming and truthful in dealing with national-security matters. On April 14, 1969, a North Korean jet fighter destroyed a U.S. Navy aircraft (an EC-121) that was unarmed and carrying espionage electronics. Thirty-one men went down with the plane. The plane was ninety nautical miles off the coast of Korea and clearly over international waters. In the midst of deciding how to respond to the incident Nixon held a news conference in which he announced that the reconnaissance flights would be continued under armed protection.[13]

But in explaining that the plane was over international waters, Nixon emphasized how he could be so certain. "There was no uncertainty whatever as to where this plane was, because we know what their radar showed. We, incidentally, know what the Russian radar showed. And all three radars [Russian, United States, and North Korean] showed exactly the same thing."[14] The problem was that the Soviets and North Koreans did not realize that the United States was able to read their encrypted signals, and Nixon's disclosure of our intelligence capabilities constituted a major (though probably inadvertent) breach of security. As a National Security Agency (NSA; the agency that handles electronic intelligence and encryption) official explained: "The Soviet Union and other countries changed every frequency, every crypt system, every net structure—all at once. It took months to work it out."[15] The North Koreans, the Soviets, and the Chinese had been using relatively simple encryption codes and quickly changed to more sophisticated ones.

This incident did not entail a lie by the president, but it illustrates the danger of too much or inadvertent truth telling with respect to national security. If President Nixon had been asked whether the United States had the capacity to break Soviet encryption codes, a direct lie would have been appropriate and justifiable.

KENNEDY AND CARTER HYPOTHETICALS

Two hypothetical examples can illustrate the justification and necessity for presidents to lie in the interests of national security. During the Cuban missile crisis in 1962 President Kennedy had to return to Washington, and in order to hide the real reason for his otherwise unexplained change in schedule the press was told that he had a cold. If Kennedy had been asked by a reporter whether a national-security crisis was going on, he would have been fully justified in telling a lie. To acknowledge publicly and thus let the Soviets know that the United States was aware of the missiles in Cuba would have severely constrained Kennedy's ability to carefully plan a response to the Russian actions.

During the Carter administration U.S. hostages were being held in Tehran, and in April of 1980 U.S. military forces were planning and training for a mission to rescue the hostages. (The rescue attempt was aborted when eight servicemen died as a result of an accident at "Desert One," a staging area in the desert.) If President Carter had been asked during this time whether the United States was planning or undertaking such a rescue attempt, certainly he would have been fully justified in lying about it. Hamilton Jordan, Carter's top White House adviser, directly lied about the preparations to those attending the senior staff meeting on April 22 in order to preserve secrecy.[16]

But this hypothetical example leads one to question Jimmy Carter's statement as a presidential candidate that "I will never lie to you."[17] If Carter was being honest, he meant that he would have intended to answer a question about a hostage-rescue attempt truthfully, thus endangering the lives of both the hostages and rescuers. If he was not being honest in his promise not to lie, was he being naive? Was he incapable of imagining a situation in which he would be obliged to lie? Perhaps he was disingenuously setting up an expectation of his truthfulness that would help him tell a lie more effectively in case he had to do so. Or perhaps he was merely being opportunistic in making a campaign statement to contrast himself to the Nixon administration and appeal to Americans' hopes for honesty in government.

In 1975, during Carter's campaign, he was warned against such a blanket statement by his mother and Charles Kirbo, an adviser. But Carter realized the potency of his pledge with voters. It conveyed the message that he would do what was right rather than what was politically expedient. Ironically, his rash promise was itself made from political expedience.[18]

His promise never to lie made it difficult for him in the presidential campaign since the press would be looking very carefully at his statements. Shifts in position were less likely to be seen as the usual necessity of crafting positions for different groups and more as potential lies. For instance, Carter had been quite critical of the national government throughout his campaign. He said that "Our government in Washington now is a horrible bureaucratic mess."[19] In a radio ad in Pennsylvania he said, "We know from bitter experience that we're not going to get the changes we need simply by shifting around the same group of Washington insiders. They sit up in Congress every year making the same political speeches and the same unkept promises." Yet two weeks later he asserted in a press conference, "I've never made an anti-Washington statement."[20] In his previous political career and campaigns Carter had made a number of statements about his past that were arguably not entirely accurate.[21]

Despite the Carter example from the 1976 campaign, Senator John McCain declared during the 2000 Republican primary campaign, "As President of the United States I will always tell you the truth, no matter what."[22] McCain later called attention to his idealistic statement by saying that he had lied about his true feelings when he said that it was up to the people of South Carolina to decide whether flying the Confederate flag above their capitol was appropriate. "I feared that if I answered honestly, I could not win the South Carolina primary. So I chose to compromise my principles. I broke my promise to always tell the truth."[23] McCain thus admitted that his previous position that the flag issue was up to those in the state was opportunistic. But his later self-criticism could also be seen as an opportunistic attempt to reposition himself on the contentious issue by engaging in his self-criticism. That is, he may have been opportunistic in admitting to his previous opportunism.

Minor Lies by Presidents

When in doubt, tell the truth. It will confound your enemies and astound your friends.

—Mark Twain

Presidents have told a number of lies that are trivial in nature but are nevertheless clearly lies.[24] Sometimes the intention is unclear, and sometimes the lies are gratuitous and thus disturbing. Why would a president or candidate lie if it were not necessary?

In examining minor lies it might be useful to consider the archetypical American story of presidential truth telling that has worked itself into the American subconscious: George Washington and the cherry tree. According to Mason Locke Weems, a parson, in his 1800 biography, *The Life of George Washington*, as a child Washington was questioned by his father about the felling of a cherry tree and confessed, "I can't tell a lie, Pa. You know I can't tell a lie. I did cut it with my hatchet."[25] Weems then quotes Washington's father's reaction, "Run to my arms, you dearest boy. . . . [G]lad am I, George, that you killed my tree; for you have paid me for it a thousandfold. Such an act of heroism in my son is more worth than a thousand trees, though blossomed with silver, and their fruits of purest gold."[26]

According to contemporary scholarship, the incident did not take place.[27] Stories like this are often considered apocryphal, that is, not true, but told to make a certain point. This raises an interesting conundrum: Is it helpful (or morally right) to tell a lie in order to make the point that truth telling is important? What message would this convey? Was George Washington a man of such integrity that, if faced with such a situation as a boy, he would have told the truth? The intended message seems to be that even though this story is false, the larger truth is that Washington was an honest man, and you should be honest also.[28]

But this story, though seemingly harmless, may in fact lead to cynicism. The danger of reporting unrealistic accounts of presidential probity for the edification of the youth of the nation is that if they later find that the stories are not true, they may become disillusioned and overreact by becoming cynical and doubting all accounts of admirable presidential traits. Such stories about actual historical figures are not the same as stories told to children about Santa Claus, the Easter bunny, or the tooth fairy. Make-believe stories such as the latter are told to very young children who understand their fanciful nature by the time they are about eight years old.

Scholar Robert Dallek recalled an observation by one old pol that reflected a skepticism about Lyndon Johnson's veracity that went beyond his "credibility gap" regarding Vietnam. "When he's pulling on his ear lobes and stroking his chin he's telling the truth. When he's moving his lips, he's lying."[29] Johnson was fond of telling audiences that his great-

great-grandfather died at the Alamo. One of those instances was in Seoul, South Korea, on November 1, 1966, when he was addressing U.S. military forces.[30] When historian Doris Kearns was working on her biography of Johnson, she asked him about the story. Johnson complained that journalists were too picky and said, "The fact is that my great-great-grandfather died at the Battle of San Jacinto, not the Alamo. When I said the Alamo, it was just a slip of the tongue. Anyway, the point is that the Battle of San Jacinto was far more important to Texas history than the Alamo."[31] But when Kearns undertook the research she found no evidence for that story either. Johnson's ancestor had not even been at the battle of San Jacinto but was a real-estate trader who died in bed at home. Johnson probably felt that the fabrication was helpful to connect himself to his audiences, especially in Texas or with military audiences. His willingness to make up such stories might have indicated that he was willing to lie about much more important things during his presidency.

JFK AND SPEED-READING

John Kennedy exaggerated his ability to read quickly. Journalist Hugh Sidey had heard that Kennedy had taken a course in speed-reading. When he contacted the institute in which Kennedy had enrolled (but not completed the course), he was told that Kennedy could probably read at the rate of 700 or 800 words per minute, twice the average rate. When interviewing Kennedy about his reading skills, Kennedy told Sidey that John Kenneth Galbraith had timed him while he read a twenty-six-page memorandum and that he had done it in ten minutes. But the calculations showed a rate of 1,000 words per minute, not quick enough for the image Kennedy wanted to project. Sidey said, "How about 1,200?" And Kennedy said, "Okay." The 1,200 words per minute was reported in *Time* magazine and repeated in many other news stories.[32] Kennedy also lied when his official biography implied that he had graduated from the London School of Economics. In fact, he had enrolled at the LSE in 1935 but did not attend because of poor health.[33] Although this type of bragging and misrepresentation is minor, it is also disturbing in its implications about Kennedy's need to be seen as superior to others, despite his many genuine accomplishments.

RONALD REAGAN'S UNTRUE STORIES

Another type of nontruth spoken by a president occurred when President Reagan told Israeli Prime Minister Yitzhak Shamir on November 29,

1983, that he had photographed Nazi death camps at the end of World War II. Later, according to the Israeli cabinet secretary, Dan Meridor, Shamir repeated the story to the Israeli cabinet.[34] Reagan told the same story to Nazi-hunter Simon Wiesenthal and Rabbi Marvin Hier. But Reagan had been in California during World War II and not in Germany, and he had not photographed the Nazi death camps. In his work for the military, though, he had seen films of the death camps taken by U.S. soldiers and had saved copies. He said that he had later shown the films to friends who did not believe the tales of horror. The White House and President Reagan denied that Reagan had ever claimed to be in Europe during World War II.

How can we understand Reagan's misstatements in this case? It is possible that Reagan wanted to impress upon his Jewish visitor that he was sympathetic to the Israeli cause and exaggerated his connection with the films of the Nazi atrocities. Or, as Reagan biographer Lou Cannon speculates, he might have become emotionally engrossed in telling the story and adopted the point of view of the photographer rather than his accurate role of receiving the films in the United States. Michael Deaver excuses Reagan's version of the story by saying that "Reagan is a romantic, not an imposter. When he talked about seeing the bodies of Holocaust victims piled like firewood, he may or may not have explained he had been viewing the footage shipped home by the Signal Corps. (He saw this nightmare on film, not in person. That did not mean he saw it less.)"[35] But it is one thing for Reagan to say that the Holocaust had a great emotional impact on him and quite another to claim to have been there.

In his campaign for the presidency in 1980 Reagan told the story of a B-17 pilot whose plane was damaged by enemy fire and was going down. When the pilot gave the order for the crew to bail out, they did, but one crew member could not extricate himself from the crippled plane. According to Reagan, the pilot stayed with the plane and told his comrade, "we'll ride it down together." Reagan concluded his story: "Congressional Medal of Honor posthumously awarded."[36] The problem is that there is no record of any such incident or awarding of the Congressional Medal of Honor. But the story tracks closely with the 1944 movie *A Wing and a Prayer*, in which the star says to the crewman, "we'll ride it down together." This story was not presented by Reagan as a parable or in the style of "there once was a heroic man who...." That is, it was presented as a factual account of something that actually happened. Such stories lose much of their effectiveness as inspirational tales if it is admitted that they are not literally true. Ironically, the factual citations for actual Medal of Honor winners contain accounts of heroism just as impressive as those in Reagan's story.[37] Reagan could easily have found a true tale of heroism to tell.

At a White House luncheon for members of the Baseball Hall of Fame, Reagan told a story about when he had been a radio broadcaster in 1933 and had been announcing a Cubs game from a studio to which the events of the game were being relayed. When the wire relaying the progress of the game went dead, instead of admitting this to his audience, Reagan made up plays to keep his audience entertained until the line was restored.[38]

Walter Cronkite calls into question Reagan's story about his fictional baseball episode. Cronkite said that he was at the White House and told Reagan a similar story about a football game he had announced when he was young, making up plays when the wire went dead. Reagan told his baseball story after hearing Cronkite's rendition. Cronkite implies that Reagan may have made up his story after hearing Cronkite's. "I won't say that the President of the United States stole my story, but . . ." (end of paragraph).[39] Was Reagan fabricating when he told the story about his on-air baseball fabrication?

According to Cannon, Reagan also frequently told a story about his football-playing days at Dixon High School in which Reagan's honesty cost Dixon the game. The game was against Mendota, and Reagan recounted how he had committed an infraction of the rules that the referee did not see. When the referee asked Reagan whether he had broken the rules, Reagan recalled, "But truth-telling had been whaled into me. . . . I told the truth, the penalty was ruled, and Dixon lost the game." The only time that Dixon lost to Mendota when Reagan was on the varsity team was in 1927, and Mendota won 24 to zero.[40] In this case was Reagan embellishing a story in order to illustrate the importance of telling the truth? Telling an untruth to make the point that telling the truth is important is reminiscent of the Washington and the cherry tree story, but in this case the irony is double since Reagan was citing an example of his own veracity to make the point when in fact his story was not true. That is, Reagan was presenting an example of his own exceptional honesty to illustrate his strong character ("truth-telling had been whaled into me"), but Reagan was not telling the truth about the incident.

There are also stories of Reagan fastening onto bits of inaccurate information that fit with his political predispositions and repeating them as established fact, as when he claimed that most air pollution was caused by trees or that the Russian language had no word for freedom. Perhaps more disturbing in the commander in chief was Reagan's claim that sub-marine-launched nuclear missiles were not so dangerous because they "can be intercepted. They can be recalled."[41]

How should we evaluate untrue statements of these types by President Reagan? He might justify telling stories that did not happen by arguing that he was trying to illustrate a larger truth, such as the selflessness of the plane pilot. Even though we might see this as a relatively harmless lie, what about anecdotes that perpetuate stereotypes such as stories about "welfare queens"? Reagan continued to tell his story of the welfare queen after it had been shown to be grossly exaggerated.[42] It is also possible that President Reagan over the years convinced himself of the accuracy of the untrue stories that he told. Self-deception may have been the case when, after his operation for colon cancer, President Reagan said, "I didn't have cancer. I had something inside of me that had cancer in it and it was removed."[43]

Reagan's dubious stories were troubling. They sometimes seemed to indicate that he was either out of touch with reality or was willing to embellish reality in order to make a political point in his favor.[44] In some of these cases it is hard to accuse Reagan of an outright lie. But we might conclude that he was not sufficiently responsible in ensuring the truth of the statements that fit nicely with his political interests. The statement about Trident nuclear missiles was not a deliberate lie, but it is disturbing that one of the only human beings capable of authorizing the use of nuclear weapons had such illusions about the nature of the weapons he was charged with controlling.

IS CHEATING AT GOLF LYING?

Bill Clinton was often criticized for taking liberties on the golf links, and his shading of the rules was often seen as part of his character problem with truthfulness. He was known for taking "mulligans," a term for tak-ing a second shot off the tee if the first one does not land in a good posi-tion. Since the mulligan is not counted against one's score, the final score makes the golfer look better than a full count would. Mulligans are never allowed in match or tournament play and are usually allowed only in games among friends. In addition to mulligans, Clinton often took "prac-tice" shots during games, which is explicitly forbidden by the rules. Jour-nalist Don Van Natta reports that, in a game with him, Clinton scored himself 82 for an eighteen-hole round on which he actually took more than 200 total shots.[45]

In addition, Van Natta reports that Clinton did not bother actually to putt the ball on at least half of the holes they played, instead taking "gimmes" for putts as long as fifty feet. A gimme is another courtesy among friends (not in tournaments) of conceding an easy putt (usually less than three feet) and not insisting that the golfer acutally putt the ball into the hole. Once when he was playing with former President Ford and professional golfer Jack Nicklaus, Clinton told reporters that he had shot eighty (a respectable score for eighteen holes). But Nicklaus whispered to Ford, "Eighty with fifty floating mulligans."[46]

Whether not playing by the rules constitutes cheating or lying depends on the seriousness with which one is playing the game. If the president is out on the golf course merely to relax and get some exercise, it may not make any difference how many shots he takes. If, however, the president claims to have shot a certain score, the rules do make a difference. Claiming to have shot a certain score after taking more than a few mulligans, practice shots, and gimmes is not honest since golf scores are based on the presumption that one has played according to the rules of the game.

So Clinton's bragging about his golf score was taken as symptomatic of his tendency to stretch the truth; the indicator was important because it fit into a broader pattern of his behavior. It is interesting that similar behavior is not taken as representing a character flaw if there is not a broader pattern of behavior. Such is the case with Dwight Eisenhower. According to Stephen Ambrose, speaking about Eisenhower's character, Ike "was certainly no saint on the golf course." He explained that Ike would sometimes pick up an eight-foot putt and say, "That's a gimme." Ambrose was also told by people who had played golf with Ike that "if he got it in the rough, he would look around, and then kick the ball out."[47] But people saw Eisenhower's character as honest and upright, so such behavior was little noticed. Thus it is interesting how the perception of certain behavior is filtered through the expectations we have of the person. In Eisenhower this minor cheating at golf is seen as an exception; in Clinton his minor cheating is seen as symptomatic of his character.

Lies to Prevent Embarrassment and Preserve Political Viability

> *You don't know how to lie. If you can't lie, you'll never go anywhere.*
> —*Richard Nixon to a political associate*

Although one might argue that the lies from the previous section were not minor in their implications, the following lies seem to be more serious in their nature, though they are not of the gravity of the lies examined in the next chapter.

KENNEDY DENIES HIS ADDISON'S DISEASE

Presidential health is always a sensitive subject, and administrations will go to great lengths to minimize any question about the president's full capacity to do the job. Rumors that John Kennedy had Addison's disease, a disease of the adrenal gland that was often fatal, swirled around the 1960 campaign. On January 19, 1961, when a reporter asked Kennedy if he had had Addison's disease, he said, "I never had Addison's disease . . . and my health is excellent."[48] But the fact was that Kennedy did have Addison's disease and serious medical problems all of his life.

Indeed, Kennedy had been given the last rites (extreme unction) of the Catholic Church four times as an adult. Kennedy was often in great pain because of his back and other medical problems, but he went to great lengths to project an image of physical vigor.[49]

According to historian Robert Dallek, in the first six months he was in office, "Kennedy suffered stomach, colon, and prostate problems, high fevers, occasional dehydration, abscesses, sleeplessness, and high cholesterol, in addition to his ongoing back and adrenal ailments."[50] To deal with these maladies, Kennedy took corticosteroids, procaine shots, Lomotil, paregoric, phenobarbital, testosterone, Trasentine, penicillin, other antibiotics, and Tuinal.[51] Kennedy and his family hid his medical problems from the public before and during his presidency, and as Dallek points out, it is highly unlikely that he would have been nominated or elected if the extent of his medical problems had been known. Although Kennedy's deception reflected negatively on his character, Dallek argues that Kennedy's medical troubles also revealed a more admirable dimension of his character, "as the quiet stoicism of a man struggling to endure extraordinary pain and distress and performing his presidential (and prepresidential) duties largely undeterred by his physical suffering."[52]

HYPOTHETICAL: THOMAS EAGLETON
AND ELECTRIC SHOCK TREATMENT

In 1972 George McGovern chose Senator Thomas Eagleton as his vice-presidential running mate. But on July 25 Eagleton held a press conference to disclose that between 1960 and 1966 he had on three occasions admitted himself to hospitals for treatment of depression. On two of those occasions he had been treated with electroshock therapy. Although McGovern said that he was "absolutely" behind Eagleton staying on the ticket and that he backed him "1000 percent," pressure mounted for his withdrawal. Within several days he was off the ticket.[53]

Given the political culture in the United States and the stigma placed on people who seek professional help for depression or any other form of mental problem, it was predictable that Eagleton would be forced from the ticket. But hypothetically, if Eagleton could have denied his hospital-ization without being caught, would it have been ethical for him to lie about it? He certainly thought that his previous depression and treat-ment would not affect his performance in office, but his political oppo-nents would certainly have made much of it through innuendo if not forthright argument. The lie would not have been right, but it would have been understandable.[54]

Similarly, if a candidate for political office were a homosexual, the stigma in U.S. political culture is so great that a lie would be understandable, even if not right. This was true in the late 1990s, as it was in the 1980s, when conservative Republican Congressman Robert Bauman was forced from Congress because it was discovered that he was gay.[55] Even though there are several openly gay and successful politicians in national politics, such as Barney Frank of Massachusetts, this reality of political life in America has not yet changed.

PRESIDENT BUSH AND THE CLARENCE THOMAS NOMINATION

In 1991 George Bush was in trouble with the conservative wing of the Republican Party. They were outraged that he had broken his promise of "no new taxes" in his compromise with Congress to reduce the deficit. They were also suspicious of his first appointment to the Supreme Court, David Souter. At the ceremony for Souter in the White House, chief of staff John Sununu had promised conservative Republicans that the next nominee would be one of them. When Justice Thurgood Marshall unex-pectedly resigned on June 27, 1991, it came time to deliver on the promise, and Bush nominated the conservative African American lawyer Clarence Thomas.[56]

President Bush invited Thomas up to Kennebunkport, Maine, before the Fourth-of-July weekend in 1991 and held a press conference to pub-licly introduce him. After some remarks by Thomas, President Bush said that Thomas was "the best qualified" person for the position. In addition, Bush said that "the fact that he is black and a minority had nothing to do with this." Critics argued that both of these statements by President Bush were stretching the truth, and civil rights' activist Roger Wilkins argued that they were cynical lies on the part of President Bush.[57]

Although Thomas began life in a poor household and very impressively worked his way up the educational and professional ladders and was on the District of Columbia Circuit Court of Appeals, his credentials were not impressive compared to those of past Supreme Court nominees. Thomas had only briefly practiced law a decade before and had been on the bench for less than two years. Thomas had never litigated a case before a jury, and while on the bench he had not issued a substantive constitutional opinion. It was apparent to all that Bush had nominated him primarily because he was a very conservative African American. He was to replace the revered Thurgood Marshall on the Court, and his race would inhibit liberals from mounting an effective attack on his candidacy.

The reason for Bush's statements, which virtually no one believed, was to maintain the political viability of the nomination and to reduce embarrassment to Clarence Thomas. If political opponents wanted to criticize Bush, it should have been for the nomination itself and based on Thomas's qualifications. Bush's critics claimed that Thomas was not as qualified as most Supreme Court nominees. The lies to defend the nomination, however, were incidental to it and meant to avoid embarrassment. They were also transparent to all informed political observers. It might be argued that transparent lies (insofar as they are transparent) increase cynicism in the public. Or it might be argued that since everyone sees through them, they are discounted as mere rhetoric and thus not harmful.

HYPOTHETICAL:

GERALD FORD AND TRANSITION PLANNING

In the summer of 1974 revelations about Watergate continued to come to light. Although it was not certain that the House would vote for impeachment or that the Senate would convict President Nixon, Phillip Buchen, one of Vice President Ford's advisors, felt that it was necessary to plan for a possible transition, so he put together a small planning group. He also felt that the planning should be hidden from the vice president. The planning itself was not wrong, but if discovered, it would have been seen by

Nixon as a betrayal, and the public would view it as a signal that Nixon was on the verge of resignation. Ford denied that his staff had been doing any transition planning, and he probably did not know about it.[58]

The hypothetical assumption is that Phillip Buchen confidentially told Ford and that Ford thought it prudent to do contingency planning and allowed them to continue. If a reporter had then asked him whether his advisers were planning for a possible transition, what should he have said? The likelihood is that he would have told a lie and felt justified in doing so. His argument would have been that admitting to the planning would have led to the incorrect conclusion by Nixon that Ford was being disloyal (rather than merely prudent) and that Nixon might have overreacted to the knowledge. Admitting his planning publicly might also have led Americans to think that Nixon's situation was so bad that his resignation was imminent. Thus Ford could have lied legitimately and justified it on prudential political grounds.

GERALD FORD LIES ABOUT HIS MEETING
WITH ALEXANDER HAIG

Vice President Ford did, however, lie to reporters about the nature of his meeting with Alexander Haig. On August 1, 1974, Haig met with Ford and presented a list of several options concerning President Nixon's possible resignation; one of the options included a Ford pardon for Nixon after his resignation. Ford listened to Haig but later told him that there was no agreement or deal between them. The situation was very delicate because if there were any hint of a deal to pardon President Nixon in exchange for his resignation, Ford could have been accused of accepting a bribe to take an official action for the benefit of being elevated to the presidency.

On August 3 Ford was asked at press conferences about his meeting with Haig. Ford admitted that he had met with Haig but lied about the purpose of their meeting. He said that the purpose was to discuss "what could be done, if anything, to convince the members of the House that the president was innocent as both of us feel." He later said, "It was an ordinary meeting of the kind that we frequently have and has no extraordinary implications."[59] These were clearly lies, but they were possibly justified by the volatile nature of the political situation and President Nixon's state of mind at that time. On the other hand, Ford may have lied in order to avoid the appearance of an illegal quid pro quo with regard to Nixon's resignation. Possibly both motives were involved.

Conclusion

What is disturbing about minor lies is that they are often gratuitous; that is, there is no significant political gain to be had in telling them. But if the advantage to be gained is trivial, why tell them? Even though the trivial lies discussed in this chapter were not momentous, they are still unsettling. In the cases of Lyndon Johnson and Ronald Reagan, early untrue stories foreshadowed future deception of the American public about important issues of national policy. Yet we can understand the tendency for politicians to tell stories that might not be literally true. As Elliot Richardson observed, "It would be hard to say where in the world of politics lies leave off and some combination of simplemindedness, wishful thinking, and eagerness to please takes over."[60] Many politicians want to entertain their audiences, and exaggerating stories is a way to make them more dramatic. Putting oneself at the center of a story is more engaging than telling a story about another. If the audience clearly understands that a story is merely an illustration, of course, there is no problem of deception. But telling illustrative stories is not nearly as riveting as telling one that is true: thus the temptation to present illustrative stories as true.

Occasionally, however, telling minor lies can have serious consequences for politicians. In the 2000 campaign for the presidency Al Gore told several dubious stories that may have affected the outcome of the race. In order to make a point about the price of medicines, he said that one medicine cost more for his mother to buy than the same medicine purchased for his dog. Although his point about the price of medicines may have been true, he personalized the story in an inaccurate way; his mother and his dog were not in fact using the same medicines. He also said that he went to Texas with the Federal Emergency Management Agency (FEMA) director to examine the damage in an area devastated by wildfires. He did visit the area, but not with the FEMA director.

Gore was attacked by political opponents for these and several other inaccurate or exaggerated stories he told during the campaign. The concern was, as his primary election opponent, Bill Bradley, put it: "Why should we believe that you will tell the truth as president if you don't tell the truth as a candidate?"[61] The consequence for Gore was that toward the end of the campaign, the Republicans made a big deal about his tendency to exaggerate and tried to tie his untruths to the character problems of President Clinton.[62] You do not have to stretch things too far to speculate that Gore's repeated misstatements of fact and the Republicans' calling attention to them in the campaign may have swayed the votes of several hundred voters in Florida in the 2000 election—enough to cost him the presidency. George Bush also made a number of statements of dubious accuracy, but the Democrats were not able to effectively capitalize on them.[63]

Telling lies to prevent embarrassment is understandable in everyday life as well as in politics. We often forgive such lies with the realization that we ourselves might be tempted to tell them in similar circumstances. But lies to prevent embarrassment can also constitute serious lies, as when President Clinton lied about his relationship with Monica Lewinsky. The next chapter takes up more serious and consequential lies by presidents.

CHAPTER 3

Serious Presidential Lies

—⚬—

Men are so simple and so ready to obey present necessities, that one who deceives will always find those who allow themselves to be deceived.
—NICCOLO MACHIAVELLI

In addition to justifiable lies, the lies analyzed in the previous chapter range from relatively innocuous exaggerations about the personal background of presidential candidates to lies meant to maintain political viability. This chapter turns to presidential lies that are more serious and have more far-reaching consequences than those in Chapter 2. First considered are "cover-up" lies—lies that deny past behavior. The final type of lie to be analyzed is the "policy deception" lie, in which the president says the government is doing one thing when in fact it is doing another.

Lies That Cover Up or Omit Important Facts

Nearly everyone will lie to you, given the right circumstances.
—*Bill Clinton, 1992*

This observation by President Clinton introduces a discussion of the first category of lies: those intended to cover up illegal or embarrassing facts about past behavior.[1] The teller might rationalize this type of lie with the argument that even though the past behavior was wrong or questionable, the publication of it now would lead to negative political consequences. These consequences would undermine the president's political power and ability to pursue a mandate received from the voters. This category includes FDR's misleading statements about the *Greer* incident, the Eisenhower administration's U-2 lie, Nixon's lies to cover up Watergate, Bush's claims to have been "out of the loop" about Iran-Contra, and Clinton's denial of his affair with Monica Lewinsky.

FDR AND THE *GREER* INCIDENT

In the fall of 1941 Franklin Roosevelt believed that the United States had to help Britain against the Nazis and was under some pressure from Winston Churchill to provide more support. At the same time, Roosevelt had to deal with American public opinion, which was ambivalent toward war. Many Americans felt it was inevitable, but there were strong undercurrents of isolationism and fear of being dragged into a European war. The draft was extended by a very slim margin in Congress—a single vote in the House in the late summer of 1940.

On September 4, 1941, an American destroyer, the *U.S.S. Greer*, was transporting mail and supplies to a U.S. military outpost in Iceland when it was signaled by a British plane that a German submarine was in its course. The U.S. ship continued on its course and plotted the location of the submarine for the British plane, which dropped four depth charges that did not hit the boat. When the plane left the engagement because its fuel was low, the *Greer* continued to track the submarine for two hours. The sub then fired a torpedo at the *Greer*, which responded by dropping depth charges. Each of the boats then disengaged without damage.[2]

Roosevelt took the incident as an opportunity to move the United States toward more support of the British. The Germans had attacked several other American ships in the preceding months, and Roosevelt decided to take a more aggressive policy. But his announcement on September 11, 1941, to the American public presented a not-entirely-accurate account of the incident: "This was piracy—piracy legally and morally."[3] He declared, "I tell you the blunt fact that the German submarine fired first upon this American destroyer without warning, and with deliberate design to sink her. . . . These Nazi submarines and raiders are the rattlesnakes of the Atlantic." He then announced that "the time for active defense is now," which was interpreted as a "shoot-on-sight" policy for U.S. naval vessels encountering German ships.[4] "From now on, if German or Italian vessels of war enter our waters . . . they do so at their own peril."[5]

Roosevelt's public account of the incident was misleading because he implied that the attack was unprovoked and that the German submarine knew that it was firing at an American ship. In fact, the U-boat was pursued by the *Greer* and attacked by the plane's depth charges, which the U-boat commander may not have known came from the plane rather than the ship. It then fired at the U.S. ship, but there is no evidence that it knew that the ship was American, and the U-boat commander might easily have concluded that the ship was one of the destroyers that the U.S. had transferred to Britain previously.[6]

Thus Roosevelt used this incident in a misleading way to build U.S. support for England and to escalate hostile actions in the Atlantic. He did not, however, directly lie about what had happened though his selective use of the facts may have had the effect of misleading the public, which his political adversaries pointed out.[7]

EISENHOWER AND THE U-2 INCIDENT

In the spring of 1960 President Eisenhower had proposed to negotiate with the Russians a test-ban treaty that would end the testing of nuclear weapons, and Khrushchev had expressed interest in a treaty. In order to lessen the chances for a mishap that might undermine the summit conference, Eisenhower severely cut back the U-2 flights that were gathering valuable intelligence information. The CIA requested another flight at the end of April, and Eisenhower reluctantly agreed, provided that it was "carried out prior to May 1. No operation is to be carried out after May 1."[8] Because of a cloud cover over Russia, the flight was delayed until the weather cleared, and Gary Powers took off in a U-2 the morning of May 1. When the plane did not return for several days, it was presumed to be destroyed and the pilot dead because of self-destruct mechanisms built into the plane and the likelihood that the pilot could not have survived.[9] According to Eisenhower, the CIA had assured the White House that "in the event of a mishap the plane would virtually disintegrate" and that it was highly unlikely that a U-2 pilot would survive.[10]

The administration's decision to lie about the U-2 affair was important to Eisenhower. He had told advisers in February of 1960 that he would have "one tremendous asset" in negotiations about his hoped-for treaty with the Russians, and that was his reputation for honesty. "If one of these aircraft were lost when we were engaged in apparently sincere deliberations, it could be put on display in Moscow and ruin my effectiveness."[11] Eisenhower once told a friend that if a president has lost his credibility, "he has lost his greatest strength."[12]

On May 5 Khrushchev announced that the Soviet Union had shot down an American spy plane and denounced the United States for "aggressive provocation." Ike knew that the Soviets were aware of the U-2 overflights, but he presumed that Powers was dead and the plane destroyed. So he approved a statement by NASA that the plane was not a spy plane but instead a weather-research plane that had been over Turkey "to obtain data on clear air turbulence" and might have strayed into Soviet air space.[13] Then, after the administration had lied about the plane, Khrushchev announced on May 7 that he had the pilot, Gary Powers, "alive and kicking," and wreckage from the plane.[14] Faced with this incontrovertible evidence, Eisenhower compounded the lie by having the State Department say that the pilot could have lost consciousness from lack of oxygen and that the automatic pilot might have taken the plane "for a considerable distance and accidentally violating Soviet airspace."[15]

Finally Eisenhower had to admit publicly that the United States had been spying on the Soviet Union and that the administration had authorized the flights. Eisenhower felt personally mortified and told his secretary, Anne Whitman, on the morning of May 9, "I would like to resign."[16] Eisenhower did not want himself tied to the May 1 U-2 flight, and on May 9 authorized White House spokesman Lincoln White to say that the president had approved of general programs of surveillance but that "Specific missions . . . have not been subject to Presidential authorizations."[17] This was not true; the president had in fact played a major role in planning each of the overflights.[18] In Eisenhower's words, "Each series of intrusions was planned and executed with my knowledge and permission."[19]

Having resolved to try to salvage the summit conference, Eisenhower went to Paris to meet Khrushchev. Even though Eisenhower had privately argued that the U-2 flights were provocative, he refused to apologize to Khrushchev and defended the right of the United States to conduct the flights. Khrushchev felt that the overflights were a violation of the sovereignty of the Soviet Union and that the May 1 flight was especially provocative because it took place on the May Day holiday and would have demonstrated the Russians' inability to protect their own airspace. Without an Eisenhower apology, Khrushchev walked out of the summit. Thus Eisenhower's hopes for a test-ban treaty to crown his eight years in office were dashed, and he was severely disappointed.

Eisenhower was not able to prevent Congress from holding hearings on the U-2 incident, though he felt that intelligence secrets might be divulged. He told members of his cabinet, "The impression should not be given that the president has approved specific flights, precise missions, or the timing of specific flights."[20] During congressional hearings on the U-2 incident Secretary of State Christian Herter lied when asked by Senator Fulbright whether there was "ever a time" when President Eisenhower had approved individual U-2 flights. Herter replied, "It has never come up to the president."[21] Later, Douglas Dillon admitted "we were trying to hide the White House responsibility for this."[22]

The irony, as historian Stephen Ambrose has pointed out, was that the U-2 overflights were no secret to the Soviets, whose frustration had been growing for four years because of their inability to shoot down the planes, which were flying at an altitude of up to 70,000 feet, out of the range of their missiles or fighter planes, that is, until the Powers flight. Nor were the flights secret to U.S. allies in Britain, France, Norway, Turkey, or Taiwan. Those who did not know about the U-2 flights were members of Congress and the American people. Thus Eisenhower undermined his most important asset, his "reputation for honesty," and undermined the trust of the American people in their government because he thought that there was no evidence to prove the administration was lying.[23] The timing was particularly unfortunate for Eisenhower because 1960 was an election year.

Eisenhower's brother, Milton, suggested that he blame a subordinate for the U-2. But Eisenhower said that he refused to "be guilty of such hypocrisy"; it would indicate that he was not in control of his own government and undermine confidence in the U.S. government throughout the world.[24] This incident stands out and was very disillusioning to Americans because of Eisenhower's reputation for integrity. On the other hand, Eisenhower did engage in the strategic deception of presenting himself to the public as not involved in the partisan political aspects of his presidency. He emphasized his role as chief of state in order to take advantage of Americans' reverence for the presidency and disdain for politics.[25]

JFK LIES ABOUT CUBA AND VIETNAM

Late in 1961 the Kennedy administration, burned by the Bay of Pigs and believing that Castro was a thorn in their side, encouraged the CIA to continue planning for a possible assassination of the Cuban leader. There was considerable effort to keep presidential fingerprints off the policy, and National Security Action Memorandum 100 of October 5, 1961, merely confirmed oral instructions, without stating what they were about. Maxwell Taylor said that the preference was that "the President's interest in this matter not be mentioned."[26] But the next month Kennedy told a journalist, after the issue of assassination was discussed, "That's the kind of thing I'm never going to do." On November 16, Kennedy gave a speech at the University of Washington in Seattle and told his audience, "We cannot, as a free nation, compete with our adversaries in tactics of terror, assassination, false promises, counterfeit mobs and crises."[27] If one accepts the legitimacy of assassination attempts on foreign leaders, one might justify Kennedy's statement as protecting national security. But his statements clearly misled the public about an important U.S. foreign policy objective that there was no need to lie about. He could easily have avoided the issue of assassination.

In a news conference on January 15, 1962, a reporter asked Kennedy whether American troops were "now in combat in Vietnam." Kennedy replied, "No." But in fact American pilots were flying military missions for the South Vietnamese in helicopters that the United States was providing. Although American troops may not have been engaged as units in combat missions, individual soldiers were involved in South Vietnamese combat missions.[28] Kennedy's statement might have been, in some sense, technically correct, but it was not fully truthful.

NIXON AND WATERGATE

Although Richard Nixon told Republican delegates in 1968 that "Truth will become the hallmark of the Nixon administration," his more realistic judgment was reflected in a statement to a political associate earlier in his career: "You don't know how to lie. If you can't lie, you'll never go anywhere."[29] Nixon lied numerous times concerning his knowledge of the cover-up of the Watergate break-in in June of 1972. For instance, on May 21, 1973, he said in a public statement that he had "no part in, nor was I aware of, subsequent efforts that may have been made to cover up Watergate."[30] He repeated similar statements often during 1973 and 1974 as he tried to avoid public disclosure of the Watergate cover-up and other illegal activities the White House sponsored.

Perhaps the most important lie was recorded on the "smoking gun" tape from June 23, 1972, in which Nixon told Haldeman to have the CIA call the FBI and tell them to stop pursuing the trail of Watergate money because it would make public a CIA covert operation. Nixon told Haldeman to tell Richard Helms, "the president believes that it is going to open the whole Bay of Pigs thing up again. And . . . that they [the CIA] should call the FBI in and [unintelligible] don't go any further into this case period!"[31] This order to the CIA to lie to the FBI, when disclosed to the House Judiciary Committee, was the turning point in the impeachment proceedings against Nixon. The committee voted impeachment articles, and Nixon resigned before the full House could vote on them.

Nixon also lied in order to receive an income-tax deduction of more than $500,000 for the donation of his vice presidential papers to the National Archives. In December of 1969 the tax law was changed to eliminate tax deductions for private papers but with the provision that papers donated before July 25, 1969, were still deductible. Nixon had donated his papers in 1968, but they had been appraised at $80,000. In April, 1970, Nixon's lawyers prepared new tax documents establishing the value of the papers at $576,000, but in order to get the full value of the claimed deduction, they backdated the documents to March 27, 1969. Nixon signed the papers, thus testifying to the false date in order to escape paying full taxes on his income.[32] Nixon's income-tax evasion based on falsified documents was considered by the Judiciary Committee of the House of Representatives as an article of impeachment (Article V), but it was rejected 26 to 12 because it was considered to be a personal rather than a political crime.

GEORGE BUSH LIES ABOUT HIS KNOWLEDGE OF IRAN-CONTRA

During the 1988 presidential campaign George Bush was the sitting vice president and heir apparent for the Republican nomination. He was being challenged by Bob Dole in the primaries for the Republican nomination and in the general campaign by Democratic nominee Michael Dukakis. One of the issues that was raised was the level of his engagement in and knowledge of the Iran-Contra affair. Even though no one asserted that he had any prior knowledge of the diversion of funds to the Contras, the question of his involvement in the trade of arms for hostages was raised. If he knew about it and did not object, he was vulnerable to criticism for having participated in a questionably legal and probably unwise policy.[33]

With this potential vulnerability in the 1988 race for the presidency, George Bush made several statements about his being out of the loop during decision making on the arms-for-hostages deal with Iran. In his campaign autobiography, *Looking Forward*, he said:

> I was asked by reporters why I didn't know more. The answer was
> and is that the people running the operation had it compartmen-
> talized, like pieces of a puzzle. My first real chance to see the
> picture as a whole didn't come until December 1986 when Dave
> Durenberger, then chairman of the Senate Intelligence committee,
> briefed me on his committee's investigation of the affair. What

Dave had to say left me with the feeling, expressed to my chief of staff, Craig Fuller, that I'd been deliberately excluded from key meetings involving details of the Iran contra operations.[34]

During the airing of "This Week with David Brinkley" on November 9, 1986, Bush said that it was inconceivable even to consider selling arms to Iran for hostages.[35] In an interview with David Broder of the *Washington Post*, Bush said, "If I had sat there and heard George Shultz and Cap express it [opposition to the Iran arms sales] strongly, maybe I would have had a stronger view. But when you don't know something, it's hard to react. . . . We were not in the loop."[36]

The problem was that Bush had been at meetings when the Iran issues were discussed and had heard Shultz and Weinberger object to the project. Bush attended the August 6, 1985, meeting in which McFarlane reported that Iran wanted 100 tube-launched, optically tracked, wire-guided (TOW) missiles for four hostages and Shultz said that it was "a very bad idea."[37] He was also present on January 16, 1986, when the president was briefed on the plan to send 4,000 TOW missiles to Iran in exchange for hostages and signed a finding authorizing the plan, and at the meeting on January 17, when the president signed another finding.

Perhaps the key meeting was on January 7, 1986, at which Secretary of Defense Weinberger and Secretary of State Shultz objected to the arms-for-hostages policy. According to George Shultz in his memoirs, "I was astonished to read in the August 6, 1987, *Washington Post*" about Bush's statement that he was "not in the loop." "Cap [Weinberger] called me. He was astonished, too: 'That's terrible. He [Bush] was on the other side. It's on the record. Why did he say that?'"[38] In testimony to the congressional Iran-Contra committee Casper Weinberger said, "I made the same arguments [at the January 7 meeting] with increasing force, but apparently less persuasion, and George Shultz did the same thing."[39]

Shultz also accused the White House of attempting to lie about the decision making on the arms sales to Iran. On November 10, 1986, a press release was prepared, and Shultz was called to ensure that he would not object to it. The statement said that the president had met with his advisers about the hostages in Lebanon and that "there was unanimous support for the President's decisions." Shultz's reaction was "That's a lie. It's Watergate all over again. . . . They are distorting the record, and there's no end to it. They are lying to me and others in the cabinet right now."[40] Poindexter changed the wording slightly, but Shultz still felt it was misleading.

PRESIDENT CLINTON'S LIES ABOUT HIS
AFFAIR WITH MONICA LEWINSKY

Despite his many denials, President Clinton lied under oath about his relationship with Monica Lewinsky. He lied in intent and spirit as well as literally with respect to some of the particulars (e.g., who touched whom where). In a statement issued on his last day in office, he said, "I tried to walk a fine line between acting lawfully and testifying falsely, but I now recognize that I did not fully accomplish this goal and that certain of my responses to questions about Ms. Lewinsky were false."[41] So our analysis here will proceed on the broader issue of lying about sex and lying under oath. Of course, lying under oath puts Clinton's lies into a more serious category than ordinary lies to protect oneself. Thus Clinton's lies in this case are included in the category of covering up important facts (Type 4) and not merely lies to prevent embarrassment (Type 3).

One of the prominent arguments in defense of President Clinton during the Lewinsky affair was that "everyone lies about sex" and that lies about such private matters are less blameworthy than other lies. One justification for failure to tell the truth is the premise that one does not have to answer truthfully questions that people have no right to ask. According to philosopher H. Sidgwick, "it is obviously a most effective protection for legitimate secrets that it should be universally understood and expected that those who ask questions which they have no right to ask will have lies told to them."[42] This justification has the obvious disadvantage of the subjectivity of the liar deciding which questions are legitimate.

Two hypothetical situations might be useful to illustrate this argument. An eight-year-old boy, having just been informed about the facts of life by peers, comes home and asks his parents if they had sex last night. A discussion of sex at this time may be called for, but the appropriate answer to the specific question is "none of your business." But what about a newly married couple, one of whom asks the other spouse whether he or she had an affair with a mutual friend before they were married. The spouse did have such an affair but knows it will cause a problem if it is admitted now. A "no comment" or "none of your business" answer would be the equivalent of admitting that the affair took place. Is the spouse obligated to answer such a question truthfully? The answer is debatable, but a reasonable argument can be made that a lie would be justified in this case.

Part of the premise of this argument is that privacy is essential to liberty and that individuals have a right to protect that privacy. From this perspective, only serious circumstances can override a person's privacy.

Thus if one is asked about one's sexual practices, unless there is an over-riding justification for the question (e.g., a criminal inquiry), one could be justified in lying. President Clinton might have used such reasoning to justify to himself his lying about his sexual relationship with Lewinsky, despite the fact that he was involved in a judicial inquiry, first civil, then criminal.

He might also have felt that the process leading to his questioning was illegitimate. The Paula Jones lawsuit was filed at the last minute before the statute of limitations took effect, and it was financed by conservative enemies of Clinton. The lie that Clinton told was not about the Paula Jones affair but was about Lewinsky. The only reason that an affair with Lewinsky was relevant to the Jones case was that the law had recently been changed to allow questioning of a suspect in a sexual matter about previous sexual relationships in order to establish a pattern of behavior. Thus Clinton may have reasoned to himself that the Lewinsky affair was not relevant to the Jones case, that the Jones case was trumped up by his enemies, and that his private, consensual affair with Lewinsky was not illegal and thus none of their business. That Jones's suit for sexual harassment was subsequently dismissed would support this reasoning.

Of course, Clinton was also calculating the political repercussions of any admission of an extramarital affair while he was in the White House. On January 21, 1998, the story of the tapes and Lewinsky's conversations with Tripp became public, and the media began a feeding frenzy about all aspects of the scandal. Clinton adviser Dick Morris said that he told the president that his polls indicated that the public would not accept his lying about the matter under oath. President Clinton then made a strong statement, publicly denying that he had a sexual relationship with Lewinsky. "I want you to listen to me. I'm going to say this again. I did not have sexual relations with that woman, Miss Lewinsky. I never told anybody to lie—not a single time, never. These allegations are false. And I need to go back to work for the American people."[43] Later, of course, Clinton did admit to an "improper relationship" with Lewinsky.

The House impeachment managers made a powerful argument that the system of justice depends upon the assumption of truth telling under oath and that to lie under oath is therefore an offence serious beyond any specific telling of an untruth. In the impeachment proceedings, one side of the issue could be characterized by the absolutist position of Representative Tom Delay (R-Tex), who saw the impeachment controversy as "a debate about relativism versus absolute truth."[44] Those on the other side of the issue argued that circumstances do matter and that what one is lying about is relevant to the seriousness of the lie. A statement by Representative Henry Hyde (R-Ill) regarding the Iran-Contra affair illustrates this perspective: "It just seems to me too simplistic to condemn all lying. In the murkier grayness of the real world, choices must be made."[45] Ironically, Hyde was chair of the House Judiciary Committee that voted in favor of impeaching President Clinton for lying in 1998.

I conclude that Clinton's lie was wrong in several ways. Lying under oath undermines the assumptions upon which the judicial system is based and sends a message that the president thinks that he is not subject to the law. In addition, Clinton cynically used others in his lie by lying to his staff and cabinet with the expectation that they would innocently repeat his lies. This violation of the confidence of his friends led to their feelings of betrayal and to large legal fees for some. In addition, the president undermined his responsibility as a role model by his public lying.

Although we might argue that even presidents ought to have some privacy and we might deplore the tactics that Kenneth Starr used to obtain evidence of Clinton's sexual affair with Lewinsky, the president did in fact lie about it, and the lie was wrong. Whether the lies rose to the level of high crimes and misdemeanors, for which a president ought to be impeached and removed from office, are separate questions.[46]

Lies of Policy Deception

"I did that," says my memory. "I could not have done that," says my
pride, and remains inexorable. Eventually—the memory yields.
—Friedrich Nietzsche

At the most serious level are lies of policy deception, in which a president says the government is doing one thing when in fact it is doing another. The most basic premise of democratic government is that the government ought to do what the people want and that during elections the voters can choose the candidate they want to govern them. Misleading the public about the direction of government policy does not allow the electorate to make an informed choice and undermines the premise of democratic government. In the words of philosopher Sissela Bok, "Deception of this kind strikes at the very essence of democratic government. It allows those in power to override or nullify the right vested in the people to cast an informed vote in critical elections."[47] The policy deception lies include Lyndon Johnson's lies about U.S. military involvement in Vietnam, Richard Nixon's secret bombing of Cambodia, and Ronald Reagan's statements about Iran-Contra.

LBJ AND VIETNAM

It is now widely understood that Lyndon Johnson misled the American public and concealed his policy of escalation in Vietnam in 1964 and 1965. He had two main motivations for his deception. First, in the 1964 presidential election campaign Johnson presented himself as the "peace candidate" in order to contrast himself with Senator Barry Goldwater, who was a "hawk" on Vietnam and favored immediate and massive U.S. military action. The second reason was that Johnson was planning the spate of legislative proposals that would make up his "Great Society" program, which he felt would be his claim to historical stature and would rival Franklin Roosevelt's New Deal.

One of Johnson's most far-reaching deceptions was his orchestration of the Gulf of Tonkin Resolution in August, 1964. On February 1, 1964, Johnson had approved Operation Plan 34A, which the CIA had developed to harass North Vietnam with gunboat raids by South Vietnamese forces. Several days after one of the raids, on August 2, 1964, North Vietnamese torpedo boats attacked the U.S. destroyer *Maddox* sixteen miles from the North Vietnamese coast. U.S. forces returned the attack, sinking and damaging the North Vietnamese boats. Johnson did not immediately retaliate but ordered the *Maddox* to be reinforced by the destroyer *Turner Joy* and to operate in the area of the first attack. Another Operation Plan 34A raid was undertaken on the night of August 3 by the South Vietnamese.[48]

Then, on the stormy night of August 4, the *Maddox* reported that North Vietnamese gunboats were given orders to prepare for battle. Later, believing they were under attack by enemy torpedoes, the two U.S. destroyers began firing their weapons and taking evasive action. The activity was reported to the Pentagon and the White House as a second attack by the North Vietnamese. Johnson reacted immediately, ordering U.S. retaliatory air strikes on North Vietnam and plans for obtaining congressional approval for U.S. military action.

The problem was that on the afternoon of August 4 the commander of the *Maddox* expressed doubts about whether an attack had actually taken place. The *Maddox* reported that "a review of the action makes many reported contacts and torpedoes fired 'appear doubtful.' 'Freak weather effects' on the radar, and over-eager sonarmen may have accounted for many reports. 'No visual sightings' have been reported by the *Maddox*, and the commander suggests that a 'complete evaluation' be undertaken before any further action."[49] Alexander Haig, who was a deputy special assistant to Secretary McNamara at the time, concluded "that the North Vietnamese almost certainly did not attack the *Maddox* and *Turner Joy*, or any other United States naval vessel, on the day in question."[50]

But Johnson and McNamara continued to act as if the attack had in fact taken place and ordered U.S. air attacks against the North Vietnamese and pursued the approval of Congress. In a congressional hearing on August 6 Secretary of Defense McNamara was asked whether there were any connection between the Oplan 34A raids and the attack on the *Maddox*. McNamara stated: "Our Navy played absolutely no part in, was not associated with, was not aware of, any South Vietnamese actions, if there were any. . . . I say this flatly. This is a fact."[51] His statement was incorrect and misleading. The United States knew about and encouraged the 34A raids, and the Navy was aware of the raids. In his memoir, *In Retrospect*, McNamara claimed that he was unaware that the patrol commander had in fact known of the raids.[52]

In response to Johnson's request for support, Congress on August 7 passed the Gulf of Tonkin Resolution, which stated that "The Congress approves and supports the determination of the President, as Commander in Chief, to take all necessary measures to repel any armed attack against the forces of the United States and to prevent further aggression."[53] Johnson was to use this authorization of military action in Vietnam as a blank check for the remainder of his term to do what he thought best and to avoid asking Congress for a declaration of war. When asked about congressional criticism of his Vietnam policies, Johnson said, "Congress gave us this authority. In August 1964, to do whatever may be necessary. That's pretty far reaching. That's—the sky's the limit."[54]

The question arises as to whether President Johnson deliberately lied to the American people and members of Congress in characterizing the August 4 incident as a military attack against U.S. naval vessels. Initially Johnson can be seen as taking the best judgment of Secretary McNamara and Admiral Sharp that U.S. forces had in fact been attacked. But when subsequent reports indicated serious doubt about whether any attack had actually occurred, Johnson pushed ahead to further his initial reaction to order retaliatory raids, to address the American people, and to get Congress to pass a resolution of support for his reaction to the doubtful attack.

On August 6, 1964, Walt Rostow, Johnson's national-security advisor, said at a State Department luncheon that the supposed attack on August 4 probably did not take place.[55] Several days after the resolution passed, Johnson himself admitted to George Ball, "Hell, those dumb, stupid sailors were just shooting at flying fish!"[56] On September 18 Johnson said privately to McNamara, "When we got through with all the firing, we concluded maybe they hadn't fired at all."[57] In early 1965 Johnson said, "For all I know, our Navy was shooting at whales out there."[58] But Johnson publicly continued to present the second attack to Congress as completely true and confirmed.

In the fall of 1964 Johnson returned to downplaying any hint of an expanding U.S. involvement in Vietnam. Thus he told a campaign audience on September 25, 1964, "We don't want our American boys to do the fighting for Asian boys. We don't want to get involved in a nation with seven hundred million people and get tied down in a land war in Asia." Later, on October 21 in Akron, Ohio, he declared, "But we are not about to send American boys nine or ten thousand miles away from home to do what Asian boys ought to be doing for themselves."[59] In October he told a group of supporters in New Hampshire that he planned to "get them [the South Vietnamese] to save their own freedom with their own men."[60]

In December Johnson authorized planning for air strikes against the North, in part to convince the South Vietnamese that the United States would stick with them if they increased their own military efforts. But while he was planning his Great Society legislative program for the next year, he sought to conceal U.S. involvement in Vietnam from the public. The State Department was going to release a study showing an increase of North Vietnamese infiltration of the South, but Johnson told his advisers on December 1 that he would "shoot at sunrise" any official who made public the information in the report.[61] Johnson also sent a memo to Dean Rusk, McNamara, and McCone that his decision to approve the military plans for escalation should be kept secret. Johnson said that it was "a matter of the highest importance that the substance of the decision should not become public except as I specifically direct" and that knowledge of the plans be kept "as narrowly as possible to those who have an immediate working need to know."[62] In December, 1964, General Harold K. Johnson predicted that it would take 500,000 men and five years to achieve victory in Vietnam.[63] In late January of 1965 a study for the Joint Chiefs of Staff (JCS) estimated that 700,000 troops would be necessary.[64] Johnson kept this information secret because he did not want to acknowledge to Congress or the public his judgment that war in Vietnam was likely.

On January 21, 1965, Johnson's first full day as an elected president, he and McNamara met with a bipartisan group of members of Congress from both houses. He misled them by presenting the bombing of Laos and covert operations against North Vietnam as being successful and misrepresented his military advisers' judgment about the status of South Vietnamese military readiness.[65] He presented a much more optimistic picture than the judgment of military leaders warranted. Johnson told the congressional leaders that he had "decided that more U.S. forces are not needed in South Vietnam short of a decision to go to full-scale war ... war must be fought by the South Vietnamese. We cannot control everything that they do and we have to count on their fighting their war."[66] He did not tell them of the plans to begin bombing North Vietnam. On March 8, 1965, the first combat troops, 3,500 U.S. Marines, arrived at Danang in South Vietnam. On March 6 Johnson told McNamara that "the psychological impact of the Marines coming is going to be a *bad* one." He then asked McNamara whether they could be characterized as "security battalions similar to MP's that preserve security." McNamara said that they could not get away with that but that he would make the public statement late in the day so as to "minimize the announcement."[67]

These troops, although engaged in combat, were supposed to be assisting the South Vietnamese in defensive operations. But in April an increase of eighteen to twenty thousand in the U.S. Marine forces was authorized, and their mission was changed by National Security Action Memorandum (NSAM) 328, which authorized the offensive utilization of U.S. ground troops against the Viet Cong. NSAM 328 stated explicitly that the change in mission was to be kept secret: "(P)remature publicity [should] be avoided by all possible precautions. The actions themselves should be taken as rapidly as practicable, but in ways that should minimize any appearance of sudden changes in policy. . . . [C]hanges should be understood as being gradual and wholly consistent with existing policy."[68] Ambassador Maxwell Taylor sent a cable to Secretary of State Dean Rusk saying that "we believe that the most useful approach to press problems is to make no, repeat, no special public announcement to the effect that U.S. ground troops are now engaged in offensive combat operations."[69]

On April 7, 1965, Johnson gave a speech in which he said that he would "never be second in the search for a peaceful settlement in Viet-Nam" and proposed a huge public-works program similar to the Tennessee Valley Authority as aid to the North Vietnamese if they abandoned their plans to reunify their country. At the same time, of course, the mission of the U.S. Marines had changed to "offensive killing operations."[70] And McNamara had requested a JCS schedule for deploying two or three divisions to Vietnam "at the earliest practicable date."[71] On June 8 Johnson's press secretary George Reedy stated, "There has been no change in the mission of U.S. ground combat units in Viet Nam in recent days or weeks."[72]

By July 28, 1965, U.S. troop strength would be authorized to increase to 125,000 along a gradual escalation to a peak of 500,000 troops.[73] But in a July 27, 1965, meeting with members of Congress Johnson did not disclose the true number of additional troops that General Westmoreland had requested and said that there was an "immediate need" for 50,000 additional troops.[74] McNamara and Johnson also understated the needed additional financial support by $10 billion and argued that military mobilization was not necessary, and McNamara incorrectly said that U.S. troops were not involved in combat operations.[75] Johnson refused to ask Congress for the money that he knew would be necessary to support the war effort for fear that a request would undercut the possible passage of his full Great Society program. In the judgment of scholar H. R. McMaster:

> LBJ had misrepresented the mission of U.S. ground forces in Vietnam, distorted the views of the Chiefs to lend credibility to his decision against mobilization, grossly understated the numbers of troops General Westmoreland had requested, and lied to the Congress about the monetary cost of actions already approved and of those awaiting final decision.[76]

By the time Johnson left office in 1969, 30,000 U.S. troops had died as well as hundreds of thousands of Vietnamese. Thus Johnson had led the United States into a major land war in Asia in 1964 and 1965 while doing his best to conceal the increasing U.S. participation. Instead of choosing to present Congress and the public with the choice he had made and calling up reserve units, requesting adequate funds from Congress, and asking for a declaration of war from Congress, he chose to mislead the country as he quietly escalated the war. At first he was afraid of being honest before the 1964 elections; then he was afraid of losing public and congressional support for his Great Society Program. In the end he wanted to have it both ways: guns and butter, but he ended up destroying his presidency and putting the United States through a divisive war during which 58,000 U.S. soldiers lost their lives, in addition to several million Vietnamese.

NIXON AND THE SECRET BOMBING OF CAMBODIA

The secret bombing of Cambodia in 1969 involved elaborate deception and falsification of reports. President Nixon and Henry Kissinger were concerned with North Vietnamese supply routes and command capability (COSVN) in Cambodia, which was officially a neutral country, but the Cambodian government could not control North Vietnamese activities in the border regions of its country. Nixon decided to pursue a systematic bombing campaign to attack North Vietnamese strongholds and supply routes in Cambodia. But in order to do this secretly, a dual reporting system had to be developed. Nixon ordered that a cable be sent to our ambassador to South Vietnam, Elsworth Bunker, saying that all discussion of the possible bombing of North Vietnamese targets in Cambodia was suspended. At the same time he had a separate, backchannel message sent to the commander of American forces in Vietnam, General Creighton W. Abrams. Abrams was instructed to disregard the cable to Bunker and to plan for the Cambodian bombing campaign.[77]

The pilots of the B-52s were briefed on missions in South Vietnam, but a subset of the pilots were told that they would get special orders while they were in flight. Once on the mission, they would then be instructed to leave the other planes and deliver their bombs to specific coordinates in Cambodia. After dropping the bombs, they returned to their bases and reported as if they had been bombing in South Vietnam. These were the official reports in the Air Force and Defense Department records. The secret reports of the actual bombings went through backchannels to the White House. Not even the Secretary of the Air Force knew of the secret bombings.[78]

It was only in the Watergate hearings that the truth of the bombings became public, and one of the air force officers involved testified about the operation. The major outright lie in this incident was Nixon's cable (whether under his name or not) to Ambassador Bunker that planning for bombing Cambodia was being suspended. In addition, official reports of the bombing targets were falsified at the president's order. But the larger deception was that the United States was secretly bombing a neutral country without the knowledge of Congress, to which the Constitution gives the power to declare war.

The question arises as to the purpose of the secrecy. Originally Secretary of Defense Melvin Laird favored making the bombing public, but Nixon and Kissinger overruled him. After all, the North Vietnamese knew they were being bombed, the Cambodians knew bombs were dropping on their country, and the Communist allies of the North Vietnamese were informed of the bombing. The only implicated parties who did not know were the U.S. Congress and the American people. Nixon argued that diplomatically, if the bombing were acknowledged, the Cambodian government might have felt compelled to protest or the North Vietnamese might have protested. But the real reason was probably revealed by Nixon in his memoirs: "Another reason for secrecy was the problem of domestic antiwar protest. My administration was only two months old, and I wanted to provoke as little public outcry as possible at the outset."[79]

Nixon's deception about the secret bombing of Cambodia was wrong because it was a (legally and militarily) significant expansion of the war into a neutral country (even though the North Vietnamese were not respecting its neutrality). The war at that point was controversial, and its expansion would have increased political opposition to it and to President Nixon (as did the public invasion of Cambodia in May, 1970). Thus the lies and secrecy were intended to pursue a significant foreign policy change without the knowledge of Congress or the American people. The Judiciary Committee of the House of Representatives considered the secret bombing of Cambodia as an article of impeachment (Article IV), but it was rejected, 26 to 12.

PRESIDENT REAGAN AND IRAN-CONTRA

This section analyzes some of President Reagan's misstatements during the Iran-Contra affair from 1985 to 1987. The analysis includes (1) President Reagan's testimony to the Tower Commission about whether he had authorized the shipment of arms to Iran in exchange for hostages in 1985; (2) the question of whether the arms were intended to be exchanged for hostages; and (3) his denial of knowledge of the diversion of funds to the Contras and the question of whether he knew about continuing aid to the Contras during the period of the Boland amendment.

The Iran-Contra affair consisted of two parts: the sale of arms to Iran for the purpose of freeing U.S. hostages held in Lebanon, and the diversion of funds from the sale of those arms to support the Contras in Nicaragua when public law forbade aid to them. The sale of arms to Iran was first conducted through Israel in 1985 and later directly from the United

States. The secret sales were disclosed by the Lebanese newspaper *Al-Shiraa* on November 3, 1986, and became public. In December President Reagan issued an executive order (no. 12575) establishing a special review board, known as the Tower Commission, to investigate the matter. The commission interviewed President Reagan about various aspects of the Iran-Contra affair.

Misstatement 1. On January 26, 1987, President Reagan told the commission that he had approved in advance the shipment of TOW missiles from Israel to Iran in August, 1985, and also approved the replacement of those missiles by the United States to Israel. But in another meeting with the review board on February 11, 1987, he reversed himself. He said that he had gone over the issue with his chief of staff, Donald Regan, and that he had not approved the transfer before it was undertaken. Later, on February 20, 1987, in a letter he wrote to the commission, President Reagan stated: "The only honest answer is to state that try as I might, I cannot recall anything whatsoever about whether I approved an Israeli sale in advance. . . . [T]he simple truth is, 'I don't remember—period.'"[80]

The issue was important because the sales might have violated the Arms Export Control Act. In addition, Secretary of Defense Casper Weinberger and Secretary of State George Shultz objected to the United States trading arms in order to obtain the freedom of hostages held in Lebanon. They agreed with President Reagan's statement on June 18, 1985: "America will never make concessions to terrorists—to do so would only invite more terrorism. . . . Once we head down that path, there would be no end to it."[81]

When the Tower Commission was conducting its inquiry, making false statements could be punished under the criminal code (18 U.S.C., para. 1001), but independent counsel Walsh did not pursue the issue because "it was virtually impossible to prove beyond a reasonable doubt what the President remembered in January and February of 1987. Although it seems obvious that President Reagan made hopelessly conflicting statements to the Commission, it would be impossible to prove beyond a reasonable doubt that any misstatement was intentional or willful."[82]

Misstatement 2. Although the sale of arms to Iran was probably illegal under the Arms Export Control Act,[83] the largest political problem for President Reagan was that he did not want the American public to believe that he had traded arms for hostages. On November 13, 1986, after the arms deals had been revealed, President Reagan addressed the nation and said: "The charge has been made that the United States has shipped weapons to Iran—as ransom payment for the release of American Hostages in Lebanon.... Those charges are utterly false.... Our government has a firm policy not to capitulate to terrorist demands. That 'no-concessions' policy remains in force in spite of the wildly speculative and false stories about arms for hostages and alleged ransom payments. We did not—repeat—we did not trade weapons or anything else for hostages."[84]

John Poindexter testified before Congress that President Reagan signed a finding (an official statement that the president considers a covert action to be in the national-security interest of the United States) that, after the fact, authorized a secret arms-for-hostages deal with Iran. Reagan said that he could not remember signing the finding. Poindexter testified that on November 21, 1986, when the story about arms to Iran was breaking, he personally destroyed the finding. He said he "tore it up [and] put it in the burn basket behind my desk ... because I thought it was a significant political embarrassment and I wanted to protect him [Reagan]."[85] When questioning Poindexter under oath about the finding Senate counsel Arthur L. Liman asked: "Now Admiral, when you saw the finding, am I correct that the finding itself was essentially a straight arms-for-hostage finding?" Poindexter replied: "That is correct." Poindexter then confirmed that the president signed the finding: "He did sign it."[86]

But as more information about the arms-for-hostages deal with Iran came out in congressional hearings and testimony, President Reagan reconsidered his position. Just as President Eisenhower was forced to admit the U-2 overflight after Khrushchev had the evidence, and President Clinton was forced to admit that he had had sex with Monica Lewinsky when evidence proved that he had, President Reagan had to admit what the evidence showed. In a March 4, 1987, address to the nation he said, "I told the American people I did not trade arms for hostages. My heart and my best intentions still tell me that's true. But the facts and the evidence tell me it is not.... What began as a strategic opening to Iran deteriorated in its implementation into trading arms for hostages."[87]

With respect to lying or deception, it is difficult to evaluate these statements by President Reagan. Working papers had been developed to justify selling arms to moderates in Iran in order to effect a strategic rapprochement with Iran so that it would not fall into the Soviet orbit. That this was the primary motive behind the arms sales was undercut by President Reagan's personal obsession with freeing the hostages, by the overcharging for the arms by the United States, and by doubts about the influence of any moderates in Iran at that time.[88] It is possible that President Reagan did not want to reveal his actions that would be in contradiction to his own previous statements and thus politically damaging and that he did not want to be seen as selling weapons to a terrorist government that he had branded "Murder, Inc." At the same time, the secretary of state was urging European nations not to trade arms with Iran because it was a terrorist state. It is also possible that President Reagan had convinced himself that he would not do such a thing and thus he must not have done it.

Misstatement 3. The more disturbing part of the Iran-Contra scandal was Oliver North's diversion of funds from the Iran arms sales to support the Contras in Nicaragua. The Reagan White House had insisted that the Sandinista regime was a threat to U.S. security and that military aid to the Contra opposition was essential. But members of Congress, although not sympathetic to the Sandinistas, challenged the necessity of U.S. military involvement in Nicaragua. After a number of disagreements, Congress finally shut off funds for military aid to the Contras. On October 12, 1984, President Reagan signed a law that included the Boland amendment, which forbade the use of any funds to aid the Contras.

But Ronald Reagan was firmly committed to helping the Contras and told National Security Adviser Robert McFarlane to keep them together "body and soul."[89] There is no evidence that President Reagan had prior knowledge of the diversion of funds from Iran to the Contras, but it was clear to his national-security aides that he wanted the Contras taken care of. John Poindexter testified that Reagan was "steadfast in his support of the Contras. . . . I was absolutely convinced as to what the president's policy was with regard to support for the Contras. I was aware that the president was aware of third country support, that the president was aware of private support."[90]

Poindexter testified that he did not tell Reagan about the diversion of funds. "I made a very deliberate decision not to ask the president so that I could insulate him from the decision and provide some future deniability for the president if it ever leaked out."[91] Poindexter maintained that the president "would have approved the decision at the time if I had asked him."[92] Poindexter concluded: "On this whole issue, you know, the buck stops here with me."[93]

So Poindexter testified that he undertook under his own authority, without informing the president, the approval of the diversion of funds to the Contras: "I felt that I had the authority to approve it. . . . My role was to make sure that his policies were implemented. In this case the policy was very clear, and that was to support the contras. After working with the president for five and one half years, the last three of which were very close, probably closer than any other officer in the White House except the chief of staff, I was convinced that I understood the president's thinking on this, and that if I had taken it to him, that he would have approved it."[94]

These statements by Poindexter protected Reagan from being accused of prior knowledge of the diversion of funds. On August 12, 1987, Reagan declared, "in capital letters, I did not know about the diversion of funds,"[95] but it is also clear that Reagan clearly communicated to his staff his wishes about aid to the Contras.

On January 26, 1987, President Reagan told the Tower review board that he did not know that the National Security Council staff had been engaged in helping the Contras, aside from the diversion of funds.[96] But John Poindexter testified to Congress that the president had told him during the time that the Boland amendment was in effect, "I don't want to pull out our support for the Contras for any reason. Isn't there something I could do unilaterally?" Poindexter said that he had kept the president informed in "general terms" of Oliver North's efforts to help the Contras (through donation of funds from private supporters and other countries), though he did not inform him of the diversion of funds. Poindexter also said that he had specifically briefed the president about a clandestine airstrip that was built in Cost Rica by North's operation to support the Contras.[97] After the congressional hearing began, Reagan changed his story and said, on May 15, 1987, that he was "kept briefed" on private support to the Contras. "I was very definitely involved in the decisions about support to the freedom fighters. It was my idea to begin with."[98]

Thus President Reagan changed his story at least three times during the investigation: (1) about his advance approval of arms sales to Iran; (2) about whether the arms were intended to get the hostages freed; and (3) about whether he knew about U.S. aid (other than the diversion) to the Contras during the period the Boland amendment was in effect. If one wants to argue that Reagan told no lies during this period, one must argue that he was not in touch with what his administration was doing in his name in this important and controversial area of national-security policy. It seems that one must attribute either incompetence or conscious deception to President Reagan in these statements.

Conclusion

An important distinction must be made between telling an untruth and telling a lie. If one tells a lie, one must be aware of one's deception, or it is not a lie. For example, if one tells an untruth—for example, "The sun is shining"—and is unaware that a cloud bank has just rolled in and obscured the sun, we would not consider the statement a lie. This raises the issue of self-deception as a possible defense against the charge of lying. Is it possible that in some instances presidents actually believed the untruths they told and thus cannot be accused of lying?

Self-deception might occur as a way to reduce cognitive dissonance.[99] That is, it may be difficult to hold two conflicting ideas in one's mind at the same time. For example, "I am a good person, yet I am telling a lie."[100] In order to reduce the dissonance, individuals may come to believe their own lies. This would also have the effect of their being able to tell the lie with conviction. Two presidential lies examined here might fall into this category: Bill Clinton's denial of his sexual relationship with Monica Lewinsky and Ronald Reagan's denial that he had traded arms for hostages. Each president may have been subject to the psychological effect Nietzsche observed, quoted earlier in the chapter. Both Reagan and Clinton may have convinced themselves, at least temporarily, that they could not have done what they had, in the eyes of others, in fact done.

Clinton used the fig leaf of his own special definition of sexual relations (only sexual intercourse counts) to deny his sexual encounters with Lewinsky. Reagan used the fig leaf of seeking to influence the supposed moderates in Iran to rationalize his trading arms for hostages. Each of these presidents eventually was forced to give up his self-delusions and face the reality of his own actions after being confronted with overwhelming evidence. But even though self-deception may be seen to mitigate one's culpability in telling a specific untruth, it raises other disturbing questions about a president's judgment and connection with reality.

A question also arises about the similarities between FDR's use of the *Greer* incident in 1940 and LBJ's use of the Gulf of Tonkin incident in 1964, both of which preceded major wars. Each of the incidents was used in misleading ways to influence public and congressional opinion in the United States in favor of the presidents' war aims. What are the differences? One can argue that the two incidents differ in the following ways:

Accuracy: In the *Greer* incident FDR did not actually lie. LBJ admitted in private after the fact that the second Gulf of Tonkin attack probably did not take place, yet he did not publicly acknowledge this.

Motive: FDR used the *Greer* incident as part of a public strategy to change U.S. public opinion to accept the importance of supporting the British against Germany. LBJ used the Gulf of Tonkin incident to support his secret escalation of hostilities in Vietnam that he did not acknowledge publicly.

Consequences: The *Greer* incident itself was used only to change the rules of engagement in the Atlantic (though in a significant way, that is, to shoot on sight), and this change did not directly lead to war; the Pearl Harbor attack did. LBJ used the Gulf of Tonkin explicitly over several years as a justification of his continued escalation of the war in Vietnam.

Ultimate Outcome: In the end, the justness of the war is relevant. The end does not justify the means in all cases, but it is relevant. World War II saved much of the world from the Nazis and Japan. The Vietnam War was a disaster for the Vietnamese and Americans.

The question may also arise as to why LBJ's 1964 campaign promises to keep "American boys" out of war in Vietnam are included as part of his lies about the Vietnam War and why FDR's 1940 campaign promise to keep "your boys" out of war is considered in the chapter on campaign promises. Although FDR's promise is criticized in Chapter 5 as expedient and ill advised, much of the country had come to accept by then the probability of war with Germany, and in the 1940 election voters clearly preferred FDR to Wendel Wilkie as a war leader. In 1964 Johnson was contrasting himself with the more hawkish Barry Goldwater, yet he was secretly engaged in an escalation course that would present the country with a fait accompli in the summer of 1965. FDR used some questionable tactics to educate and lead the public in the direction he sought, but LBJ sought to mislead the country and Congress into thinking that U.S. actions in Vietnam were not major commitments likely to lead to war.

These last two chapters have addressed the issue of presidential lying, which undercuts the democratic link between citizens and their government. It also undermines trust in the government and all public officials. Obvious lying also sets a bad example and may lead others to justify their own lying. But this book argues that not all lies are equal; that is, some are worse than others. The argument that "they all do it," so there is no point in examining the issue, is insidious and undermines moral responsibility.

When presidents tell lies for reasons of state, they often justify their lies by arguing that their deception is intended for foreign governments. For the purposes of this book, deceiving foreign governments for national-security reasons is considered legitimate. The problem is that such lies may also deceive the American public. This deception raises important issues about democracy and sets the threshold for justifying lies much higher. This book contends that presidential deception of the American public is justified only in exceptional circumstances, such as when clear national-security interests are at stake. Otherwise, the presumption must be against lying.

I developed the taxonomy of lies to help us think about the substance and circumstances that might enable us to distinguish more from less dangerous lies. The point is not whether the cases cited fall into my categories, or even whether the categories are the right ones. My point is, rather, that presidential lies are common and that we, as citizens, have the responsibility to distinguish among different types of lies in order to decide which are acceptable and which are not.

We must also keep presidential lying in perspective. Lies are not the most important aspect of what presidents do, either in a negative or a positive sense. Lyndon Johnson's lies about Vietnam were not as damaging as the broader, flawed policies that got us into a land war in Asia. President Nixon's lies about Watergate were not as insidious as the broader aspects of his lack of scruples (e.g., using the IRS to harass his enemies, campaign "dirty tricks," creating the "plumbers," wiretaps on citizens without warrants, the Huston plan, etc.). President Reagan's lies or misstatements about Iran-Contra were not as bad as the deliberate breaking of the law by his administration.

But in criticizing these presidents we should not conclude that presidential character is only about character failings. Each of the presidents discussed in this book had admirable character qualities that enabled him to accomplish significant public purposes. From Eisenhower's peace-keeping record, to Kennedy's inspirational rhetoric, to Johnson's Great Society, to Nixon's diplomatic breakthroughs, to Carter's Panama Canal treaties, to Reagan's Cold War–ending diplomacy, to Bush's courage in Desert Storm, to Clinton's balanced budgets—each president has achievements that outweigh the lies he may have told.

CHAPTER 4

Sexual Probity and Presidential Character

—⚹—

*What counts with a candidate for president is his character, and nothing
shows it like his relationship with women. Here you have a man who is asking
you to trust him with your bank account, your children, your life and your
country for four years. If his own wife can't trust him, what does that say?*
—GEORGE REEDY

Even though the Clinton administration was accused of a number of
crimes and ethical lapses, the allegations of sexual impropriety attracted
the most attention and opprobrium. In public debate and campaigning,
the "character issue" became a shorthand reference to allegations of sexual
misconduct by Clinton. And amid other allegations, the charge that
Clinton had sex with a young White House intern was the most damaging, both because of the possibility that it had occurred and because of
allegations that the president had committed perjury in denying the sexual
relationship and obstructed justice by urging the woman to commit perjury by denying the relationship. Although there is no consensus on the
exact nature of presidential character, most observers believe that extramarital sexual behavior is relevant to it, though not necessarily its most
important aspect.

For some, the private sexual behavior of presidents should not be a
public issue since it usually does not have to do with the performance of
official duties or public policy. From this perspective there should be a
zone of privacy that journalists respect unless a clear connection exists
with the president's official duties. This view holds that regardless of the
personal morality of the behavior, it is not the public's business to be
concerned with the sexual conduct of presidents. The press largely respected this general norm into the 1970s.

On the other hand, the argument that sexual behavior is relevant to
presidential performance maintains that character is seamless. Sexual infidelity is seen as a breach of trust, and trust is seen as one of the most
important dimensions of the relationship between citizens and their gov-

ernment. If a president cannot be trusted to be faithful to his spouse and true to his marital vows, how can we have confidence that he will tell the truth to the American people?

One criticism of Bill Clinton in the 1992 campaign was "You can't be one kind of man and another kind of President."[1] William J. Bennett, editor of *The Book of Virtues*, argues that "The leader must be whole; he cannot have his public character be honest and his private character be deceitful." Bennett also argues that "adultery is a betrayal of a very high order, the betrayal of a person one has promised to honor. . . . It violates a solemn vow. When it is discovered, acute emotional damage almost always follows, often including the damage of divorce."[2] This line of argument leads to the conclusion that inappropriate sexual behavior is an important element of presidential character, that its uncovering is a legitimate focus of journalistic inquiry, and that the public ought to use the information in judging a president's fitness for office.

Even if we are inclined to reject the second argument—that taking adultery into account is essential to judging presidential character—the issue may be moot after President Clinton's impeachment. After the House of Representatives made public the report of independent counsel Kenneth Starr, the American public knew in lurid detail the physical aspects of the Clinton-Lewinsky sexual relationship. Public-opinion polls clearly showed widespread disapproval of President Clinton's character, in contrast to his performance as president, of which consistent majorities approved. Even though the formal articles of impeachment cited Clinton's lying and alleged obstruction of justice, the subtext of sexual irresponsibility was the source of much of the intensity of the hostility toward Clinton.[3]

The judgments about President Clinton's character—by citizens, in public commentary, in scholarly analysis, and in the political arena—are strongly affected by his sexual behavior. If we want to gain perspective by comparing Clinton's character with that of other presidents, we cannot ignore their extramarital sexual behavior any more than we can reasonably ignore Clinton's. If we are to judge presidential character fairly, we cannot turn back the clock to the time before Clinton's impeachment or to the era when the press did not pursue stories of extramarital sexual activity by presidents.

This chapter takes up the issue of sexual fidelity and probity in the modern presidency by examining the known extramarital sexual behavior of Franklin Roosevelt, Dwight Eisenhower, John Kennedy, Lyndon Johnson, and Bill Clinton. Harry Truman was almost certainly true to

Bess when he was president. The 1970s and 1980s were slack years for presidential sex scandals, with Presidents Nixon, Ford, Carter, and Reagan seemingly faithful spouses. George Bush, especially during the 1992 campaign, was dogged by rumors about an alleged sexual relationship with Jennifer Fitzgerald, an aide to Bush at the Republican National Committee and when he was in China, though no improper relationship was ever proved.[4] The chapter concludes with a comparative analysis of these presidents and an assessment of how we might weigh their sexual behavior in evaluating their characters.

Franklin Roosevelt

Franklin Roosevelt married his fifth cousin, Eleanor, against the will of his mother, Sara, on March 17, 1905. They had six children, five sons and a daughter. They lived the life of an ambitious young couple when Woodrow Wilson appointed him assistant secretary of the navy in 1913. In the winter of 1914 Eleanor hired Lucy Mercer to assist her with her correspondence. Lucy was handsome, charming, and very competent with her work. In the summers Eleanor and the children would retreat to Campobello, leaving Franklin in Washington with his official duties. Lucy began to accompany Franklin to dinner parties and then on long car rides in the hills of Virginia; rumors emerged that they were engaged in a sexual affair.

Though Eleanor was uneasy about their relationship, she did not suspect the worst until the fall of 1918. When Franklin returned sick from a trip to Europe, Eleanor was unpacking his bags and found a packet of love letters from Lucy. Eleanor was shattered: "[T]he bottom dropped out of my own particular world & I faced myself, my surroundings, my world, honestly for the first time."[5] Eleanor offered to give FDR a divorce, but his mother, fearful of such a disgrace for the family, said that she would write FDR out of her will and end his financial support if he ended the marriage.[6] In addition, a divorce would probably have terminated FDR's political career. So FDR promised to sever his relationship with Lucy and remain faithful to Eleanor. But the affair had a devastating effect on Eleanor, who felt that sex was "an ordeal to be borne," and the Roosevelts probably did not resume their conjugal relations after his affair.[7] According to their son James Roosevelt, "father and mother sat down and agreed to go on for the sake of appearances, the children and the future, but as business partners, not as husband and wife, provided he end his affair with Lucy at once, which he did. After that, father and mother had an armed truce that endured to the day he died."[8] On the other hand, her psychological distance from FDR allowed Eleanor to pursue her own projects and build her own career. Eleanor and Franklin continued to be partners in his political career and remained affectionate toward each other, but the romantic aspect of their marriage had ended. She once told a friend, "I can forgive but I cannot forget."[9]

The other major woman in FDR's life was Marguerite (Missy) LeHand. She had worked in FDR's vice presidential campaign in 1920 and had so impressed Eleanor that she was asked to come to Hyde Park to help Franklin with his correspondence. In 1921 FDR contracted polio, and Missy stayed on to help with his recovery. They spent several months each winter in Florida on Roosevelt's seventy-one-foot houseboat, the *Larooco*, where FDR relaxed and entertained friends. Eleanor was bored by life on the houseboat and left FDR in Missy's care while she went back to New York.[10] LeHand was his constant companion and hostess on the boat. In 1924, after winter on the boat, both Franklin and Missy moved to the resort community at Warm Springs, Georgia, where FDR underwent rigorous therapy in a futile attempt to regain the use of his legs.

After FDR was elected governor of New York in 1928, Missy moved in with the Roosevelt family in Albany into a bedroom suite adjoining FDR's bedroom, with a connecting door, while Eleanor's bedroom was entirely separate. She carried out all the duties necessary to make his life workable, but more important, she was his friend, confidante, and constant companion, entertaining him and providing moral support. FDR biographer Hugh Gallagher described Missy's role in FDR's life:

> Missy was a member of the family, recognized as such by all the Roosevelts. Where FDR lived, there lived Missy—whether at Warm Springs, in the governor's mansion, or in the White House. Throughout the business day, Missy was at the President's side. She had control of his schedule; determined what letters and papers crossed his desk; monitored his calls and policed his appointments. . . .
>
> When FDR lunched at his desk, she ate with him. When he went for a drive in the afternoon, she would go along. She sat in as the only woman at important political meetings. She hosted many of FDR's political dinners. She invited her guests, he invited his for evening cruises on board the presidential yacht. When bridge was played, they were partners.[11]

According to Geoffrey Ward's set of calculations, in the years from 1925 to 1928, FDR was undergoing rehabilitation from his polio away from New York for 116 of 208 weeks. Of those 116 weeks, Eleanor was with him for 4 weeks, his mother for 2, and Missy spent 116 weeks with him, night and day.[12]

Felix Frankfurter wrote about Missy's role: "Sam [Rosenman] said he always regarded her as one of the five most important people in the U.S. during the Roosevelt Administration.... She was one of the very, very few people who was not a yes-man, who crossed the President in the sense that she told him not what she knew to be his view of what he wanted to hear, but what were, in fact, her true views and convictions."[13]

Whether LeHand and FDR had a sexual relationship is uncertain but plausible. Doctors had determined that after his attack of polio Roosevelt was still potent and capable of sexual relations.[14] FDR's son Elliot concluded that Missy and his father had been lovers. He observed their affectionate behavior on the *Larooco* and was not surprised. On the other hand, James Roosevelt doubts that his father had a sexual relationship with Missy.[15]

At the White House Missy served as hostess when Eleanor was out of town and was FDR's constant aide and companion. Yet Eleanor did not seem to view Missy as a rival for FDR's affection as she had Lucy Mercer. According to his grandson Curtis Roosevelt, it might have been because Missy came from a lower social class: "Eleanor was not threatened by her the way she was with Lucy Mercer."[16] Or perhaps after the affair with Lucy Mercer, FDR's struggle with polio, and the New York governorship, Eleanor was not as concerned with sexual fidelity. According to Eleanor's biographer Blanch Wiesen Cook, "Whatever she actually felt, ER's public attitude toward Missy LeHand was that of first wife to second wife in the culture of extended ruling families.... ER accepted her occasional inability to 'meet the need of someone whom I dearly love,' and in a coded reference to Missy, advised others in her situation: 'You must learn to allow someone else to meet the need, without bitterness or envy, and accept it.'" But more important than whether they had a sexual relationship was that, according to biographer Doris Kearns Goodwin, "it is absolutely clear that Franklin was the love of Missy's life, and that he adored her and depended on her for affection and support as well as for work."[17]

Missy LeHand suffered a stroke in June, 1941, at the age of 43 and had to leave the White House, a blow to FDR. Because of the high cost of her medical treatment and her own lack of resources, FDR changed his will five months after her stroke to set aside one half of his estate to pay her medical bills; the other half went to Eleanor. Upon Missy's death (she died on July 30, 1944), the funds were to revert to Eleanor. FDR said, "I owed her that much. She served me so well for so long and asked so little in return."[18]

Eleanor Roosevelt, despite her psychological distance from FDR, had an affective life of her own, particularly with Lorena Hickok, a lesbian and talented journalist in a time when few women were allowed to write serious news for the papers. Hickok fell madly in love with Eleanor, who returned her affection.[19] The evidence for their affection is plain in the letters from Eleanor to "Hick," who saved all of Eleanor's letters to her. It is obvious that they held great affection for each other, and Hickok lived at the White House for four years during World War II. Whether their love was physically expressed in a sexual relationship is not certain but entirely plausible. According to Goodwin, "the letters possess an emotional intensity and a sensual explicitness that is hard to disregard. . . . Day after day, month after month, the tone in the letters on both sides remains fervent and loving."[20] Eleanor also had a close relationship with her former bodyguard, Earl Miller. According to James Roosevelt's account, "Mother may have had an affair with Earl Miller. . . . [A]s Victorian as mother may have been, she was a woman, too, who suffered from her self-imposed separation from father."[21]

Though FDR had promised not to see Lucy Mercer again, in the 1920s and 1930s they took up their friendship again, though probably not a physical relationship. She was invited to his inauguration in 1933 and viewed it from a limousine that FDR had provided.[22] (At the same inauguration, Eleanor was wearing a ring from Lorena Hickok.[23]) After her husband had a stroke, Lucy visited the White House a number of times.

In April, 1945, Roosevelt was in Warm Springs and called Lucy Mercer almost every day. On April 9 Mercer came to visit at Warm Springs and brought her friend, painter Elizabeth Shoumatoff, to paint a portrait of FDR. Lucy was still there on April 12, when FDR died and had to hurry away so that Eleanor would not discover her presence.[24]

Though the Roosevelt marriage was not a smooth one, both partners held an affection for each other and made a formidable political team. Eleanor traveled and gathered political intelligence for FDR and represented him symbolically. FDR was influenced by her views, even though he sometimes tired of her pressure on social-policy issues. According to Goodwin, "They made an extraordinary team. She was more earnest, less devious, less patient, less fun, more uncompromisingly moral; he possessed the more trustworthy political talent, the more finely tuned sense of timing, the better feel for the citizenry, the smarter understanding of how to get things done."[25] Each had a full career and separate romantic lives, though each was closely bound to the other throughout their careers.

Dwight D. Eisenhower

Dwight Eisenhower was a man of high integrity who lived a life virtually above reproach. His life, however, contains some problems for those who take an absolutist perspective on adultery and who argue that adultery puts a politician beyond the pale of honorable people. During World War II Eisenhower had a romantic relationship with Kay Summersby, a woman twenty years younger than he was. She had been separated from her husband and had volunteered for civilian service in wartime London. She was assigned to drive Eisenhower and other officers around the city. Eisenhower liked her so much that he requested that she be assigned to him as his regular driver.[26]

As she worked for Eisenhower from the summer of 1942 to late 1945, she took on more duties and became his private secretary and assistant. For part of the time she worked for Ike she was engaged to be married to Colonel Dick Arnold. Eisenhower, as a favor to Kay, had arranged for her divorce papers from her first marriage to be sent to Algiers by diplomatic pouch. But Arnold, while in North Africa, was killed as he inspected a minefield.

Rumors of a romance between Eisenhower and Summersby circulated widely in Europe and the United States. General Bradlee's aide, Chet Hansen, said, "there were people who did wonder. . . . If they were sleeping together it was their business. It was none of ours. He was the commander, he knew what he was doing." According to Harrison Salisbury, "There was absolutely no secret about it, so far as—well, let's say anybody in the press corps or anybody in the Red Cross or anybody in headquarters. There are very few secrets in a headquarters of any kind. . . . Practically everybody had boyfriends or girlfriends, regardless of what their marital status was. . . . They enjoyed each other, and it gave them a little interlude in the war. You know, that's the sort of atmosphere that there was there." Eisenhower's son John said of Summersby, "I was very fond of her. . . . Whether she had designs on the Old Man, the extent to which he succumbed, I just don't know."[27]

In Summersby's book *Past Forgetting: My Love Affair with Dwight D. Eisenhower*, she describes their relationship during the three years she worked for him. Over the first year they worked together they gradually fell in love, according to her account. "For over a year, Ike and I had spent more time with each other than with anyone else. We had worked, worried and played together. Love had grown so naturally that it was a part of our lives." It was apparent that they had a romantic attachment to each other, but in her book Summersby claims only one overtly sexual encounter and maintains that their love was not physically consummated because Ike was temporarily impotent. In October, 1945, they were alone together in his house in Germany, and Ike told her that he had arranged for her to become an American citizen. (He had previously arranged for her to become a WAC officer, despite her British citizenship.) They spent the afternoon together: "He had always been very circumspect, but this afternoon he was an eager lover. . . . But it didn't work."[28]

Stephen Ambrose, one of Eisenhower's most admiring and well-known biographers, relates this version of events in his essay on Eisenhower in the book *Character above All*. Summersby also recounted the same events in an interview with Ambrose. Ambrose concluded: "That story certainly rings true to me, but I think his [physical] failure on that occasion was not because he had so much on his mind. I think it was a question of character. I think that he was one of those upstanding men who appear to have been more common in the nineteenth century than they are today."[29] It is entirely plausible that, as Ambrose speculates, Eisenhower was temporarily impotent because of guilt feelings about betraying his wife.

Summersby continued to work for Ike until he left to return to the United States. To help Kay, Ike wrote to both General Beetle Smith and General Lucius Clay; to Clay he wrote, "I hope you will find a really good job for her."[30] In a parting, but formal, letter to her explaining why he would no longer have her on his staff, he said "I particularly request that at any time you believe I can be of help you will let me know instantly. . . . After you come to this country I would be more than glad to do my best in helping you get a job."[31]

She was promoted to captain and worked for General Clay in Berlin for a year, after which she moved to the United States to work in the Women's Army Corps. After she had moved to the United States, she once stopped at the Pentagon to visit Ike. When she told him that she was going to quit the WACs and move to New York, he said: "That sounds sensible. If there's anything I can do to help you about the job, I hope you will let me know when the time comes."[32] Later, when he was president of Columbia University, she arranged to run into Ike again, and he told her, "Kay, it's impossible. There's nothing I can do." "'I understand,' I told him. And I did. We had had a fabulous relationship, but it was over. Completely over." Summersby later married Reginald Morgan and received from Ike a "very sweet note wishing us happiness."[33]

In the early 1970s, when being interviewed by Merle Miller for his oral biography of Truman, *Plain Speaking*, Harry Truman said about Eisenhower:

> Why, right after the war was over, he [Eisenhower] wrote a letter to General Marshall saying that he wanted to be relieved of duty, saying that he wanted to come back to the United States and divorce Mrs. Eisenhower so that he could marry this English-woman. . . . Well, Marshall wrote him back a letter the like of which I never did see. He said that if he . . . if Eisenhower even came close to doing such a thing, he'd not only bust him out of the Army, he'd see to it that never for the rest of his life would he be able to draw a peaceful breath. He said it wouldn't matter if he was in the Army or wasn't. Or even what country he was in. Marshall said that if he ever again even mentioned a thing like that, he'd see to it that the rest of his life was a living hell. General Marshall didn't very often lose his temper, but when he did, it was a corker. I don't like Eisenhower; you know that. I never have, but one of the last things I did as President, I got those letters from his file in the Pentagon, and I destroyed them.[34]

Eisenhower biographer Stephen Ambrose argues that Truman's account of this is "completely untrue" and says that "Truman was approaching senility" when he gave the interview to Miller.[35] Truman's account is also countered by a June 4, 1945, letter from Eisenhower to General Marshall asking that Mamie be permitted to come to Europe to live with him and a number of other letters over the previous several years in which Eisenhower expressed his love for his wife.[36] Eisenhower biographer Peter Lyon calls Truman's account into question because "neither man was likely ever to have written a letter on such a subject, even presuming (which I do not) that such a liaison ever existed."[37] Although Truman's account of the letter seems unlikely, given the other accounts, it still ought to be weighed seriously, if not necessarily believed, because Truman was president and claimed personal knowledge of the letter.

Though Eisenhower was not president during this affair, he was a high officer of the U.S. government and married to Mamie, who was back in Washington, often worrying about the rumors of Ike and Summersby. Ike wrote to reassure her in February, 1943: "Stop worrying about me. The few women I've met are nothing—absolutely nothing compared to you, and besides I've neither the time nor the youth to worry about them. I love you—always."[38] But as Stephen Ambrose points out, "But loving Mamie did not necessarily preclude loving Kay." Mamie was so upset about Truman's story and the publication of Kay Summersby-Morgan's book *Past Forgetting: My Love Affair with Dwight D. Eisenhower* that she allowed her son John to publish *Letters to Mamie*, Ike's wartime letters to her.[39]

The question arises as to whether Eisenhower committed adultery. If we are to believe Summersby's account, and it is at least plausible, Ike did not technically commit adultery because he was impotent at the time and they did not have intercourse. On the other hand, it seems clear that Ike was very affectionate with Summersby and that he probably intended to commit adultery during the session she described. From a moral perspective, his intention to make love with Summersby was frustrated only by his temporary impotence, and he would be morally guilty of adultery. Although he did not have sex by Bill Clinton's definition, that is, sexual intercourse, he did have sex by the definition stipulated in the Paula Jones case—that is, touching with the intent of giving pleasure.[40] With respect to character, it is the moral intention that is crucial, not the failure to consummate due to an unforeseen, temporary condition of impotence.

Some scholars have challenged the credibility of Summersby's account of their relationship, and Summersby's motives might be suspect from several perspectives—glory, money, revenge.[41] But it is important to remember that she did not claim much, only several kisses and one failed attempt at lovemaking. If she had motives other than merely telling the truth as she saw it, she could have claimed much more. The only other witness was dead when her second book was published.

Much of the controversy over the Eisenhower-Summersby relationship has to do with whether Ike really loved her or intended to divorce Mamie and marry her. But for this analysis the question is whether they had a sexual relationship, because if they did, the moral absolutists would have to admit that Eisenhower was not morally fit to be president. If one does not take the moral-absolutist stance, however, the relationship must be understood and evaluated in the context of Eisenhower's life and record of leadership. From this perspective, a lapse such as an affair with Summersby would not be damning; even great leaders are vulnerable to the temptations of extramarital affairs.

John F. Kennedy

John Kennedy's adult life was marked by courage, physical pain, ambition, and charismatic leadership, but there was always an undercurrent of licentiousness, cynicism, and manipulation. His privileged upbringing led him to believe that as long as he performed up to expectations, others would clean up after him. His family had enough money to buy the best lawyers to cover up any predicament into which he might get himself. If he had impetuously married a woman in Florida, the records could be expunged.[42] If he was in the White House swimming pool with several women, the Secret Service would warn him of his wife's arrival.[43]

In contrast to his approach to politics and policy, which was most often marked by caution, in his personal life he took outrageous risks with the confidence that his friends and employees would cover for him, and if the press caught wind of his exploits, they would not be reported.[44] Kennedy's sexual appetite was prodigious throughout his life, and his self-indulgence did not stop when he became president.[45] In the judgment of one scholar, "President John F. Kennedy was a sexual outlaw." According to Kennedy biographer Richard Reeves, "JFK was a wild man and a terrible man on that [sexual] level." According to Kennedy's friend and editor of the *Washington Post*, Ben Bradlee, "It is now accepted history that Kennedy jumped casually from bed to bed with a wide variety of women. . . . Kennedy screwed around. A lot."[46]

In order to understand his ability to get away with his sexual escapades, it is necessary to understand that John Kennedy was a charismatic, seductive, and charming man who made men want to be accepted by him and women want to please him. According to one lover, "It wasn't just the women going ga-ga. It's everybody trying to be good enough, smart enough, witty enough. . . . You had to really work to keep his attention unless . . . he had some thing that he wanted from you. And then, boy, you were the object of extremely focused attention."[47] He exuded power in his professional life and a sense of fun and irreverence in his private life. He hated to be bored, and he constantly needed stimulation and excitement. According to Benjamin Bradlee, "He was fun. That's what you forget. He was fun to be with. He had a great sense of humor and surrounded himself with people with humor. He teased. He liked to be teased. I enjoyed being with him." According to Judith Campbell Exner, "He was an amazing man. When you talked to him, you felt you were the only person on the planet, much less just in the room."[48] Nothing seemed to slow down Kennedy's exploits. On the eve of his inauguration, during the many gala celebrations and after Jackie had gone home, Kennedy slipped off to a private room with actress Angie Dickinson.[49]

For more than a year he had an affair with Mary Pinchot Meyer, the sister-in-law of Ben Bradlee.[50] Between October, 1961, and August, 1963, Meyer was officially signed into the White House many times, usually at about 7:30 in the evening. Their ongoing relationship was social as well as sexual and was successfully concealed from their friends and relatives. Ben Bradlee and his wife, who was Mary's sister, were shocked to discover the affair when they found her diary after she had been murdered in Georgetown. Their reaction was shock: "To say we were stunned doesn't begin to describe our reactions. . . . Like every one else, we had heard reports of presidential infidelity, but we were always able to say we knew of no evidence, none. . . . And so I was truly appalled by the realization of the extent of the deceit involved."[51]

Kennedy saw several women over periods of a year or so, but he would also have trysts with many women who caught his eye or who were brought to him by friends. These sessions might be in the White House, his house in Georgetown, Peter Lawford's home in California, or wherever he might be traveling. One scholar drew up a partial list of Kennedy's sexual partners:

> His affairs involved film stars such as Marilyn Monroe and Jayne Mansfield; would-be actresses like Judith Campbell; White House employees, including Jacqueline's press secretary Pamela Turnure and secretaries Priscilla Wear and Jill Cowen—better known to insiders as Fiddle and Faddle; socialites such as Florence Pritchett, a long-time Kennedy flame married to Eisenhower's ambassador to Cuba, Earl T. Smith, and Mary Pinchot Meyer, the artistic sister-in-law of Benjamin Bradlee and niece of conservationist Gifford Pinchot; and burlesque queens Blaze Starr and Tempest Storm. More alarming, Kennedy occasionally had affairs with casual acquaintances and virtual strangers, who surreptitiously entered the southwest service entrance of the White House as the result of the solicitations of friends and aides.[52]

In 2003 it was revealed that Kennedy had also had an affair with a nineteen-year-old college sophomore who worked in the White House press office. Marion (Mimi) Beardsley Fahnestock (sixty years old in 2003) said, "From June 1962 to November 1963, I was involved in a sexual relationship with President Kennedy."[53] Kennedy once told British Prime Minister Harold Macmillan, "If I don't have a woman for three days, I get terrible headaches."[54]

Even though some of Kennedy's affairs might be considered to be unrelated to his official duties as president, some of them had potential for danger. One such affair was his relationship with Judith Campbell (later Exner), which began in March, 1960, and lasted until March, 1962.[55] Kennedy and Campbell met in the White House, his Georgetown house, and in a number of places when the president was traveling. The potential danger was that Campbell was also an associate (and lover) of the organized crime boss of Chicago, Sam Giancana. The danger was that the relationship might subject Kennedy to blackmail or other influence from organized crime. As historian Michael Beschloss concludes, "If Sam Giancana ever threatened, for instance, to publicize evidence of Kennedy's relationship with Judith Campbell, the President could have been faced with a choice between giving in to whatever demands Giancana made or allowing himself to be driven out of office. What President could survive the revelation that he had knowingly slept with the mistress of a Mafia chief?"[56] But Kennedy was not bothered by the implications of his affair, and according to Exner, she acted as a courier of money and messages between the two men.[57] The affair lasted until FBI director J. Edgar Hoover went to the White House in March, 1962, to warn Kennedy that he had extensive information about the relationship and that it was dangerous.[58]

Another potential danger was Kennedy's affair with Ellen Rometsch in 1963. Rometsch grew up in East Germany and had joined a Communist youth group. Her family escaped to West Germany in 1955, and she later moved to the United States. When Kennedy met her, she was working as a call girl with Bobby Baker, secretary to the Senate and protégé of Lyndon Johnson, who later served eighteen months in jail for tax evasion and fraud. According to Baker, Rometsch pleased about fifty of his friends and was with Kennedy ten times during the spring and summer of 1963.[59] But J. Edgar Hoover heard about her activities and had the FBI conduct an investigation. In August, 1963, Attorney General Robert Kennedy ordered that she be deported to West Germany. According to Seymour Hersh, the Kennedys provided money for her in Germany through LaVerne Duffy, a friend of Kennedy.[60]

Kennedy would not have been able to conduct his many sexual affairs while he was president unless he had had help from the Secret Service.[61] Although the Secret Service has a strict code of silence about the private lives of presidents, several of them agreed to be interviewed by Seymour Hersh in order to correct what they saw as distortions of the history of the Kennedy presidency. According to former agent Tony Sherman, Kennedy's womanizing was constant. "It was just not once every six months, not every New Year's Eve, but was a regular thing. . . When you see nude bodies going down the hall. . . . There were women everywhere." According to former agent Larry Newman, "It was common knowledge in the White House that when the president took lunch in the pool with Fiddle and Faddle, nobody goes in there."[62]

But enabling the president's sexual proclivities also put a strain on the members of the Secret Service. One reason was that one of the many unidentified women who were not cleared to see the president might have been a spy or an assassin. "We didn't know if these women were carrying listening devices, if they had syringes that carried some type of poison, or if they had Pentax cameras that would photograph the president for blackmail." But also grating on the Secret Service was the realization that President Kennedy was not behaving in a mature manner. According to Newman, "It caused a lot of morale problems with the Secret Service. You were on the most elite assignment in the Secret Service, and you were there watching an elevator or a door because the president was inside with two hookers. It just didn't compute. Your neighbors and everybody thought you were risking your life, and you were actually out there to see that he's not disturbed while he's having an interlude in the shower with two gals from Twelfth Avenue."[63]

One does not have to be a prude or a puritan to be dismayed at Kennedy's sexual behavior. It is one thing to have an extramarital romantic relationship with one or even several women; it is another thing entirely to have scores of women procured merely for brief sexual liaisons. His behavior was demeaning to himself, his family, and the women with whom he was carrying on.[64] He often could not recall the names of his lovers. One longtime lover who slept with him the night before his inauguration in 1961 in his Georgetown home recalled that her father was being considered for a political appointment in the administration. During their meeting Kennedy asked her whether "by any chance" she was related to the potential appointee. She was devastated to know that even though they had been lovers for two years, he did not realize who she was.[65] Affairs with Kennedy were often destructive to the women who fell in love with him, thinking that his sexual attention signified a deeper commitment on his side. Marilyn Monroe's affair with Kennedy may very well have played a role in her suicide after Bobby Kennedy went to California in the summer of 1962 to inform her that she had to stop seeing the president.[66]

In addition to the women involved with Kennedy, his behavior compromised those who worked with him and his friends. According to former Secret Service agent Larry Newman, "we loved the man. By the same token, we grieve that he would conduct himself in such a way as to make us so vulnerable and make the country so vulnerable." According to fellow agent William McIntyre, "you feel a little bit used."[67] His male friends were compromised by acting as procurers of women for his pleasure, though most who did, did so willingly and felt privileged to be part of the Kennedy inner circle. His friends often "bearded" for him by going along on social occasions as ostensible escorts for women who were really along for sexual trysts with Kennedy. Sometimes his aides felt used; for example, Secretary of State Dean Rusk was ordered by Kennedy to arrange a villa at Lake Como in Italy for an assignation the night before Kennedy was to see the pope. Rusk felt acutely embarrassed and ashamed about his role, but that did not faze Kennedy, and it probably amused him.[68]

Historian Michael Beschloss sums up some of the risks that Kennedy took: "By pursuing women whose full backgrounds he evidently could not know, Kennedy caused his Presidency to be a potential hostage to any resourceful group in American society that might have wished to bring him down—the Teamsters, the Mafia, the Radical Right—and every hostile intelligence service in the world." According to historian Gil Troy, "His behavior was so outrageous it can only be explained by resorting to psychological speculation: a desire to defeat his illness; a need to outdo his father and brother Joe while punishing his mother and his wife; a self-destructive streak; a feeling of invincibility."[69] Kennedy's friend Ben Bradlee later concluded about Kennedy's conduct as president and the changing rules of press coverage of sexual matters, "I have given a lot of thought to whether Kennedy would have survived these rules, and I have concluded that he could not have withstood the pressure of publicity. If the American public had learned—no matter how the public learned it—that the President of the United States shared a girlfriend, in the biblical sense, with a top American Gangster, and Lord knows who else, I am convinced he would have been impeached. That just seems unforgivably reckless behavior."[70] Despite his many infidelities, at some levels Jack and Jackie probably loved each other. It is likely that Jackie knew about some of his exploits but could not do much about them.[71]

Lyndon Johnson

Lyndon Johnson as a young man was a compelling and charismatic person—tall, dramatic, and driven by ambition. He had a compulsive need to be needed and loved throughout his life, especially by women. He also had a need to dominate others and demonstrate his power over them, which he sometimes acted out sexually. As a young man his physical appearance and ambition helped him in his sexual conquests, and later in life his positions of power and his personal charisma enabled him to fulfill his desires. His willfulness and charisma were apparent in his brief courtship of Lady Bird and his ability to convince her to marry him. Despite his marriage to Lady Bird, "Sex to Johnson was part of the spoils of victory. . . . He collected women like some men collect exotic fish," according to George Reedy, Johnson's press secretary.[72]

Johnson had several affairs with women that lasted over long periods of his life. One was with Alice Glass, the mistress and later wife of Charles March, who was publisher of the *Austin American Statesman*.[73] Their affair began in the mid-1930s and continued off and on for a decade or so when Glass lived at her and Marsh's 800-acre estate, called Longlea, in the Blue Ridge mountains of Virginia. When Johnson was a member of Congress he often visited her on weekends and had a special telephone in the bottom drawer of his Capitol Hill desk that was his private line when he took calls from Glass, whom his staff called the "horse lady." Their affair continued through World War II, and they continued to communicate with each other for the rest of their lives. In 1964 she was invited to a social occasion in the East Room of the White House. As late as 1971 she gave Johnson a present of an antique glass eagle that had reputedly belonged to Thomas Jefferson.[74]

LBJ also had a close relationship with Helen Gahagan Douglas, who was a member of the House of Representatives from California, first elected in 1944.[75] It began when he was in the Senate and she was a member of the House and cooled after she lost her bid for the Senate when she was defeated by Richard Nixon in 1950. According to a friend of the Johnsons, their relationship was an "open scandal," and Johnson would "park his car in front of the house, night after night after night and then would get up in the morning and drive off at 6:30."[76] They would often come to work together in the morning in the same car and walk around Capitol Hill holding hands. In 1964 LBJ saw her at a social occasion and on the spur of the moment asked Douglas to spend the night at the White House. She had not packed any clothes, and, according to Lady Bird's diary, LBJ gave her one of Lady Bird's nightgowns to wear. In the morning Lady Bird was surprised to find Douglas there but never questioned it and invited her to breakfast.[77]

In addition to his longer-term relationships, Johnson also pursued many women for brief liaisons. When he was vice president, reporters called his office in the Senate "the nooky room," and he had affairs with his secretary among other women.[78] In 1965 Johnson had a number of sessions with women alone in the Oval Office that he bragged were sexual assignations.[79] Johnson often felt inferior to the Kennedys, and he was heard to brag, "Why, I had more women by accident than he [Jack Kennedy] ever had by design."[80]

It was humiliating enough for Lady Bird that Johnson had several long-term lovers and a large number of short-term affairs, but Johnson was also gratuitously cruel to Lady Bird in his sexual behavior. He seemed not only to want sexual gratification but also to flaunt it in front of his wife and staff as a display of power. In his offices on the Hill Johnson always had a number of female secretaries whom he liked to intimidate and boss around. He would make obnoxious comments that would now be considered sexual harassment and expect them to meet all of his expectations. According to one of his secretaries, Ashton Gonella, "That was just the way he was. All of us—Lady Bird included—knew it and accepted him." If he wanted a drink, he would merely rattle a glass rather than ask for it, and expect one of his secretaries to bring it. In George Reedy's words, "He could be unbelievably gross, often a miserable human being."[81]

According to Lady Bird biographer Jan Russell, "By the 1960 campaign, most of the people on LBJ's staff understood that Lady Bird and Lyndon had an informal arrangement: he did whatever he liked, and in return for being his wife, Lady Bird pretended not to notice." In 1961, as vice president, Johnson was sent to Paris for a NATO meeting, and he along with Lady Bird and his entourage went to Maxim's for dinner. As the drinking and the evening progressed, the wife of one of the state department officials sat on Johnson's lap, and they began, to everyone's embarrassment, to engage in inappropriate sexual play. Finally, Lady Bird enlisted Johnson aide Horace Busby to convince Johnson that they had to leave the restaurant.[82]

Johnson's cruelty to and humiliation of his wife continued even after he had retired to his ranch in Texas. He would brag to visitors to his ranch: "Ah've had hundreds of women in my life, but let me tell you, nobody is better in that bed than Lady Bird."[83] Former girlfriends would visit him regularly, and he would take them on long walks without Lady Bird. He even told them in her presence that they reminded him of his mother. Once a package was delivered to the ranch, and Lady Bird opened it to find a lavender bikini, obviously not for her. She said to Johnson, "It must be for one of your lady friends."[84]

Given Johnson's boorish and cruel behavior toward women in general and Lady Bird in particular, one wonders how she coped with his infidelities.[85] In a sensitive and sympathetic biography of Lady Bird, Jan Jarboe Russell describes the various ways in which Lady Bird dealt with Johnson's infidelities. One of her reactions was denial. She told friends that she did not believe the rumors about LBJ and Alice Glass: "I never saw that side of him." Her stoicism, lack of self-pity, and grace under pressure were amazing, though she admitted that "He would sometimes say cruel things to me."[86] At another level she accepted Johnson's behavior: "I guess I'm used to it 'cause I like for women to like him, and I like him to like them." "I loved my share of my life with him."[87] Despite his obnoxious behavior, Johnson was clearly dependent on Lady Bird for her unconditional acceptance and love. According to George Reedy, "She knew him inside and out and accepted him for what he was. That acceptance probably gave him the strength to lead—without it, he would have crumbled."[88]

But there was another side to her acceptance of his sexual behavior. Her position and career in politics, from the beginning of their marriage, was dependent on his political success. "His life became my life. I respected it. I wanted to learn from it, excel in it." If she had left him, she would have been abandoning an exciting career, despite all of its humiliation and hardships. Despite her business acumen, it is doubtful that her radio and television stations would have done nearly as well if she had not been Lyndon Johnson' wife. She was also silently complicit in whatever LBJ felt he had to do to gain and keep power. In strategy sessions for Johnson's 1948 campaign, "If she heard something she didn't like or didn't want to know, she would just stand up and walk out."[89]

Her acceptance of his sexual behavior engendered a similar acceptance in his whole staff. Her silence about, and seeming acceptance of, his sexual behavior signaled to his staffers that she condoned it. And if it was okay with her, certainly none of his staffers was going to question it. This protection of LBJ from criticism was symptomatic of other aspects of his presidency, particularly the war in Vietnam. According to George Reedy, "It got to the point that it was a completely closed court and no one could express a doubt about anything, not in the office or in the family quarters. No one could tell Lyndon Johnson to go soak his head. Lady Bird helped perpetuate this. She did not like for Johnson to hear bad news."[90]

Throughout her life Lady Bird, although she at times acknowledged that LBJ behaved poorly toward her, always defended him and found her identity in him, as a partner in his political career and as guardian of his legacy after his death. According to Horace Busby, "The key to understanding Lady Bird is to understand that in her mind her father was the role model for how all men are and should be. . . . She grew up with her father and assumed all men had a wife but also had girlfriends. She didn't attach much importance to it."[91] Later in life she refused to acknowledge the darker side of her husband's behavior. After Johnson's death, when asked by her biographer how she had coped with her husband's infidelities, she responded: "When people ask me these sort of things, I just say, 'Look to your own lives. Look to yourself, everybody. Fix yourselves, and keep your problems to yourself.' The public should weigh what public servants are doing, not their private, innermost feelings. I think we are getting into such a state of intimacy of everyone's lives that we don't judge people by what they are able to do for the country."[92] These incidents of infidelity and denigration of Lady Bird did not mean that Johnson did not love his wife deeply. He was often affectionate to her in public and appreciative of her sacrifices for him and his career, as most of the sources quoted in this section attest.

Bill Clinton

Bill Clinton's active sexual life was covered extensively in the tabloids, in the popular press, and in legal proceedings. Despite years of denial by Clinton and his defenders, it is likely that many of the allegations were true. Clinton was widely rumored to have had a number of affairs when he lived in Arkansas, both before and after he was elected governor. In 1987, when Clinton was considering a run for the presidency, Gary Hart was forced from the race because of his sexual infidelities, and Clinton had to decide whether his own womanizing stories would hurt his possible candidacy. He asked his political advisors Bob Armstrong and Dick Morris how the public might react and how he should respond to probable press inquiries. His loyal political organizer, Betsy Wright, advised against his running because of the effect of the inevitable press inquiries on his family. She had known about his extramarital activities for years and had helped minimize their impact, and she thought that some state troopers had been helping him in his meetings with various women.[93] Clinton took her advice, and Wright said that in 1992 the campaign had hired San Francisco private investigator Jack Palladino to deal with what she called "bimbo eruptions."[94]

The preelection story that was the greatest threat to Clinton's candidacy involved Gennifer Flowers, who claimed that she had had a twelve-year relationship with Clinton, from 1977 to 1989. In her book, *Gennifer Flowers: Passion and Betrayal*, she describes many of their sexual encounters over the years, along with details. In the early 1990s she taped some of her phone calls to Clinton to provide proof of their relationship. The taped conversations were suggestive, but circumstantial.[95]

The Flowers relationship became a campaign issue just before the New Hampshire primary in 1992, when the allegations received wide publicity. In order to deal with the uproar, Bill and Hillary Clinton together went on TV on Super Bowl Sunday in January, 1992, to refute the charges. While admitting that he had caused pain in their marriage, he implied that he had not had a sexual affair with Flowers. When asked about adultery, Clinton said: "I'm not prepared, tonight, to say that any married couple should ever discuss that with anyone but themselves. I have acknowledged wrongdoing. I have acknowledged causing pain in my marriage. I have said things to you tonight that no American politician ever has. I think most Americans who are watching this tonight, they'll know what we're saying. They'll get it, and they'll feel we've been more than candid."[96] Many people interpreted the public session to mean that, although he had strayed in the past, Clinton would give up extramarital sex if he were elected. In the Paula Jones deposition on January 17, 1998, Clinton finally admitted that he had had a sexual relationship with Flowers.

When President Clinton was later accused of various types of sexual misbehavior, one of the arguments of his defenders was that, although he may have been promiscuous, he took "no" for an answer. That is, all of his affairs were consensual and thus not sufficiently serious to be pursued legally while he was president. The primary referent for this defense of Clinton was the Paula Jones incident of May, 1991. Jones was a state employee at a convention where Clinton was speaking. She was told that Clinton wanted to see her in a hotel room, and when she arrived, he propositioned her crudely by exposing himself and asking for oral sex. She refused and left the room. Jones later sued Clinton for sexual harassment, and the case began the unlikely train of events that led to Clinton's impeachment.

Clinton's defense—that his sexual encounters were consensual—was certainly plausible; he was powerful and attractive, and many women were drawn to him. It is also true that some women were offered money for telling certain media outlets about their claimed sexual exploits with Clinton.[97] Kathleen Willey claimed to have had an unwanted sexual encounter with Clinton in the White House, but how reluctant she was about his alleged advances is a matter of dispute. Clinton admitted to only a friendly "embrace" and perhaps a kiss on her forehead. According to Clinton "there was nothing sexual about it."[98] For his book *Uncovering Clinton*, Michael Isikoff interviewed several women who said that they had had sexual invitations of various sorts from Clinton. Some of them took these advances to be harmless flirtations, but others felt they were obnoxious and presumptuous.[99]

Finally, it was Clinton's sexual affair with White House intern Monica Lewinsky that led directly to his impeachment. Lewinsky joined the White House as an intern in the summer of 1995, when she was twenty-one years old; she became a regular White House employee in the Office of Legislative Affairs late in 1995. Their sexual encounters began on November 15, 1995, when she was still working as an intern, and much of the White House staff was not at work because of the government shutdown due to the budget impasse.

The sexual meetings continued to April, 1996, when she was transferred to the Pentagon because White House staffers felt she was spending too much time with the president. Lewinsky continued to try to see the president after leaving the White House, and their sexual relationship resumed briefly in February and March of 1997. The number of their sexual encounters totaled ten over the year and a half, and Clinton ended their affair in May, 1997.[100] Clinton's denial that he had had sex with Lewinsky, both in his Paula Jones case deposition in January and in the grand-jury deposition in August, 1998, led to his impeachment. Chapters 3 and 6 deal with the events of the Starr investigation and Clinton's impeachment.

Throughout the many crises in their marriage over the years in Arkansas and Washington, there is no doubt that Bill and Hillary Clinton shared a love for each other that was able to withstand the pressures of their high positions and an intrusive press. It is also true that their political partnership enabled each to lead a successful political career.

Conclusion

The point of this chapter is certainly not that "everybody does it," but just the opposite. The only commonality in these accounts of the different presidents is the existence of sexual infidelity. There are vast differences among their sexual affairs, their characters, and their conduct of the presidency. It seems, at least on the surface, that FDR acted first out of romantic infatuation and then out of loneliness; Ike became infatuated under wartime conditions; JFK acted out of a sense of entitlement; LBJ was trying to demonstrate his power; and Bill Clinton seemed to be compulsive about sex. At least these are plausible partial explanations of some of their behavior. But the main point is that their motivations were not the same, and their behavior demonstrates the complexity of their characters.

The impeachment and trial of Bill Clinton raises interesting parallels with Eisenhower's behavior after his relationship with Kay Summersby. Was Ike behaving improperly in offering to help Summersby get a job in New York? In Bill Clinton's impeachment, helping to get Monica Lewinsky a job in New York was alleged to be an obstruction of justice. Eisenhower offered orally and in writing to help Kay Summersby get a job in New York. He had already convinced General Clay to give her a job in Germany. The question was one of intent and timing. It was alleged that Clinton was trying to encourage Lewinsky to keep their affair a secret, thus the job efforts were argued to be an obstruction of justice, though his offers of help came before Lewinsky was slated to testify to the grand jury.[101] Asking a person to keep a secret is not an obstruction of justice unless the person is subject to questioning by legal authorities. Eisenhower did not have to worry about Summersby's discretion; she loved him too much to have embarrassed him. Thus his offer to help (or actual help if she had requested it) would presumably not have been an obstruction of justice. Rather it was the type of help any person would offer a loyal subordinate. Nevertheless, the juxtaposition of the two cases is striking. Both men were willing to assist their former lovers to get jobs in New York.

It is also interesting to speculate how Eisenhower would have replied to public accusations of infidelity. Would he have used carefully chosen words to evade direct answers? If he was subpoenaed to testify before a grand jury, would he have freely admitted his indiscretions with Summersby? Would the judge have had to define sex precisely? (Their actions fell within the definition of "sexual relations" specified in the Paula Jones deposition of January 17, 1998.) Of course, that was never necessary because Ike's colleagues protected his personal life, and his relationship was with a person who truly loved him and would not have done anything to hurt him. Bill Clinton was not blessed with such favorable factors, and he suffered the consequences. But part of the responsibilities of leadership and the presidency is to have good judgment about the nature of the times and what is politically possible; Eisenhower had better judgment than Clinton and did not resume his relationship with Summersby after he returned to the United States.

It may seem unfair to Ike to compare his behavior with Bill Clinton's. Ike was clearly a man of high integrity who was a great leader and a near-great president. Bill Clinton was an effective president with many policy and political victories, but he lacked integrity and was willing to lie and engage in reckless sexual behavior. Yet his impeachment boiled down to questions of the definition of his behavior with Monica Lewinsky and his attempts to help her get a job in New York. Eisenhower engaged in similar behavior (i.e., a romantic relationship with a subordinate that included some intimate physical contact and offers of help in obtaining future employment), but without the same consequences.

We evaluate these two cases differently because of the clear differences in the characters of the two presidents. Eisenhower's relationship with Summersby was romantic rather than merely lustful, and it was a one-time occurrence under wartime conditions. Clinton's relationship with Lewinsky was clearly exploitative (even though she was a willing partner) and part of a long-time pattern of extramarital sexual behavior by Clinton. With regard to sexual mores, Clinton did not believe that the rules applied to him, and he sought sex from many women. Eisenhower, on the other hand, was a child of the Victorian era and felt so guilty about being unfaithful to his wife that he was impotent when he had the opportunity.

Sexual probity in presidents is not always associated with presidential competence and trustworthiness, and sexually indiscreet presidents are sometimes effective in their conduct of the office. Franklin Roosevelt, with his acknowledged relationships with Lucy Mercer and Missy LeHand, is generally rated as one of the great presidents. John Kennedy, although sexually irresponsible, was an effective president and continues to be one of our most popular chief executives. There was no hint of any sexual impropriety in Jimmy Carter's presidency, yet he was not considered more effective than FDR or JFK. Richard Nixon was most likely faithful to Pat Nixon in the White House, yet other aspects of his character led to Watergate and campaign abuses.

Thus while sexual probity may be an important aspect of presidential character, it does not guarantee morality or competence in the Oval Office. And sexual impropriety can be found in presidents who are clearly competent in affairs of state.

Although conceding that some presidents were competent even while engaging in sexual activity outside of their marriages, we might still want to judge whether their behavior in this area was appropriate or moral. If the basis of moral judgment is the breaking of marriage fidelity vows, we can make a surface judgment with little understanding of the circumstances. From this absolutist perspective that sex outside of marriage is always wrong, it should not matter in judging presidential character whether the behavior took place before or after election. Adultery is adultery, and character is the bedrock of a person's behavior. Adultery at any time reveals flaws that, according to the absolutist interpretation, brings into question a person's fitness for office. Those who take this perspective must thus admit that Ike may have committed adultery in intent and all but final consummation. Even though this happened before he was president, it would have to be disqualifying from the perspective of the absolutists.

If, however, the moral judgment is based on how a president treats other human beings, a more nuanced response is necessary. For instance, one could argue that affairs of the heart, that is, a long-term romantic relationship, should be judged differently from one-night stands with prostitutes or brief acquaintances. Thus we might look at FDR's long-term romance with Missy LeHand differently from the way we would at JFK's short dalliances with women brought to him solely for his sexual pleasure. We might also consider the relationship between the president and his wife and how the adultery affected their marriage. But in order to make a judgment about these complex relationships one would need to know in some detail the nature of the relationship. This depth of knowledge is difficult to come by except in a detailed historical analysis of the relationship. Doris Kearns Goodwin's *No Ordinary Time* presents such an analysis of Franklin and Eleanor Roosevelt.[102] Her subtle probing of Franklin and Eleanor's relationship over time gives the reader enough information to make some judgments and come to some understanding of the relative responsibility of the couple in their relationships and thus Franklin's level of culpability in his relationships with other women. In this sense, Eleanor's romantic relationships with others are relevant to our judgment of FDR's character. If she had an affective relationship outside of their marriage, the effects of FDR's unfaithfulness were mitigated, though not excused.

A similar depth of analysis of the relationship of Warren and Florence Harding is available in *Florence Harding* by Carl Sferrazza Anthony.[103] Anthony concludes about their relationship: "They made some sort of agreement. . . . In every way except through sexual fidelity, and his honesty about that . . . [h]e would honor, cherish, and obey if she asked no questions. Her jealousy never actually abated, but her attempts to keep him from other women became more a matter of protecting his career and their work on the career's behalf. There was what one friend gently termed 'the perfect understanding' which existed between them."[104]

This sort of arrangement also seemed to characterize the dual careers of Lyndon and Lady Bird Johnson and of Bill and Hillary Clinton. These wronged women always had the option of leaving their husbands, but they would have paid an enormously high price. They would have had to give up their own power and position and at the same time effectively end their husbands' careers, the goals of which they had spent good portions of their lives supporting. Power, prestige, wealth, and political ideals were too high a price to pay for the satisfaction of divorcing their husbands. Thus it is not surprising to find these intelligent, powerful, and competent women putting up with the obnoxious behavior of their philandering spouses. In addition, each of these couples was bound by strong ties of love, despite the many problematic parts of their marriages.

Even if we set aside Bill Clinton's insensitivity to his wife in his various adulteries, we can still judge his sexual behavior harshly. The basis for judgment, rather than an absolute prohibition of adultery or the morality of relationships, would be a question of prudential judgment and self-restraint. Even though conceding that we might not know enough to be able to judge the relationship between two people, we might still make harsh judgments about a president's sexual behavior outside of marriage.

This judgment would be based on the premise that public morality, however hypocritical it might be, proscribes adultery and sexual profligacy. And it is predictable that public reaction to discovered sexual impropriety will be harsh and threaten the reputation of a president and his administration. Given this reality of American politics, any president who violates these public norms is liable to judgment for risking his reputation and the success of his policy and political agenda.

Any person who runs for the presidency after the 1970s ought to realize that any sexual indiscretion while in office may very well be uncovered, and if it is, much more is at risk than personal reputation; the political and policy legacy of the administration is also in jeopardy. The predictable ensuing political scandal will at the least distract him and at the most engulf his administration. He will be spending time plotting with lawyers how to confront charges rather than pursuing public-policy goals.

It is from this perspective that we can judge Bill Clinton; we can judge his sexual relationship (of whatever kind) with a young woman in the White House to be reckless and irresponsible. His actions were doubly reckless, given that Paula Jones's lawyers were actively seeking to undermine him and that he might well be called to testify in her case. At a personal level, Clinton's indiscretions were predictably embarrassing to his wife and daughter. In satisfying his own pleasure he undermined public trust in him; he made himself vulnerable to the distractions of defending himself, and he put at risk his political agenda and legacy.

This helps explain the bitterness of many of his followers who felt betrayed by Clinton's recklessness. They felt that all of their work and hopes over the years were put in jeopardy because of the personal self-indulgence of the president. In the words of one member of his administration, "What a shame it would be if he was remembered for having sex with some kid from Beverly Hills. It just makes me sad. All that opportunity lost. And I blame him. Who else is there to blame?"[105] Former Clinton confidant George Stephanopoulos wrote: "But if the Lewinsky charges are valid, I know this: I'm livid. It's a terrible waste of years of work by thousands of people with the support of millions more." Former press secretary Dee Dee Myers said, "We don't know everything but we know that she visited the White House 37 times. We know they exchanged gifts. I don't need to know any more than that to know that he put himself at risk. It was reckless."[106]

Morally, Kennedy and Johnson were more culpable than Clinton, but they accurately judged that their sexual behavior would not be reported. Thus they were better judges of American politics than was Clinton, and they both got away with behavior morally worse than Clinton's when he was president. They failed the moral test, but Clinton failed both the moral test and the political judgment test.

In a person aspiring to be president, past extramarital sex may be wrong, but it should not, in and of itself, be disqualifying. That is, adultery in itself is not so reprehensible that it is beyond the pale of normal (though not admirable) human conduct, and it is common in all societies. But if extramarital sexual behavior is compulsive and entails elaborate, sustained deception or unusual risk taking, it raises serious questions about the judgment and self-control of a person who is to be entrusted with a large degree of political and governmental power. Extramarital sex by a president is almost by definition reckless behavior. The unwillingness to give up extramarital sex when running for the presidency would indicate a serious lack of self-restraint, as it did in the case of Gary Hart in 1987. If the candidate is not willing to sacrifice extramarital sexual pleasure, how serious is the person's commitment to public office?[107] Ben Bradlee argues that the rules of reporters covering politicians have changed: "[T]he press had been accused of covering up Kennedy's fooling around, which had become increasingly well documented since his death. They had silently decided they were never going to be accused of covering up the fooling around of any subsequent candidate."[108]

In American society, issues of sexual fidelity are important, and the failure of some presidents and presidential candidates to forgo this illicit pleasure legitimately calls into question their judgment, self-restraint, and commitment to the duties of public office. But in judging their behavior in retrospect, we ought to judge their sexual behavior in balance with other important aspects of their character and contributions to the country.

CHAPTER 5

Character, Consistency, and Campaign Promises

—ɯ—

I stick by my principles, and one of my principles is flexibility.
—EVERETT DIRKSON

Presidential promises and consistency are important because of the basic democratic premise that citizens need to know what politicians intend to do in office in order to make informed judgments before casting their ballots. If politicians did not regularly keep their promises, voters would have much less information upon which to base their electoral choices.

Conventional wisdom in American public opinion holds that politicians cannot be trusted and that they seldom keep their promises. A skeptical public, reinforced by negative press coverage, heavily discounts campaign promises, yet feels that it is important for candidates to be consistent and to fully intend to keep their promises.[1] But contrary to the conventional wisdom, presidents most often do make serious efforts to keep their campaign promises. This chapter deals with the two issues of consistency and promise keeping in presidential candidates. First discussed is the issue of consistency, with Lincoln and Franklin Roosevelt providing examples of inconsistency. Then the chapter takes up campaign promise keeping in general and specific examples of promises kept and promises broken.

Consistency

Promise keeping and consistency are important because they reflect on the character of a candidate. If a person continually shifts positions on important issues and does not keep promises, how can we trust that person in other matters? Stephen Carter states this position well in his book *Integrity*:

Surely we want to believe that our politicians have come to their principles after careful and sustained thought, in some cases a career's worth; and if they jettison too quickly what we thought they believed, we have before us the evidence that they lack the first ingredient of integrity: the ability to think long and hard before making difficult moral decisions.

Why does a change of tune cause us to admire our leaders less? The reason must be that when politicians are able to change so thoroughly what they have claimed to stand for, we begin to question whether their previously stated views were preceded by anything like the degree of moral reflectiveness that is necessary for us to have faith in what they say.[2]

That is, consistency is an important dimension of integrity, and we want leaders of integrity. One of the most devastating charges that can be made against politicians is that they flip-flop on important issues. Presidential candidates of the 1980s and 1990s had to deal with the divisive issue of governmental control of abortion. They had to walk fine lines between the two sides, knowing that extremists at both ends of the spectrum would attack them for changing or moderating their stance on this contentious issue. A change of position would surely bring down the wrath of one side or the other.

Yet electoral victories in American politics are created by forging coalitions of various factions that stretch political support from the core of their political party to the independents and moderates in the middle of the political spectrum. Thus candidates often see ambiguity on issues and a shifting of position to reflect public opinion as necessary in order to be elected. Voters often admire those whose convictions are numerous, explicit, firm, and unyielding, but these politicians seldom win elections in the United States. The reasons that candidates for office may waffle on issues during a campaign include their own possible uncertainty about the best policy to solve a problem and the need to keep their options open in order to adapt to changing circumstances. Elected presidents might reverse a policy position because of changing circumstances, exposure to new information, or a genuine of change of mind after careful thought. Besides, contentious issues in American politics often have compelling arguments on both sides.

This chapter's premise is that consistency, as desirable as it might be, is often very difficult to maintain if one is to succeed in American politics. An example that illustrates this point is Abraham Lincoln's public statements on the slavery issue over the course of his political career. Although ultimately as responsible as any other single American for abolishing slavery and considered one of our greatest presidents, Lincoln in his public statements seemed to be inconsistent about the status of blacks and what the U.S. government ought to do about slavery. After looking at Lincoln, the chapter turns to another of our great presidents, Franklin Roosevelt, and argues that FDR did not have a consistent, coherent plan to deal with the Great Depression and that his policies were often inconsistent. Finally, the chapter analyzes a number of presidential promises, both broken and kept.

LINCOLN AND SLAVERY

Leadership is paradoxical in that it presumes followers. It is paradoxical in the sense that we often think of leaders as people of fixed convictions who sway the masses to their point of view through the courage of their convictions, soundness of reasoning, and force of personality. But in a democracy the reality is often in conflict with this easy stereotype. Leaders must often tailor their own views to those that their followers (or potential followers) are willing to accept or be persuaded of. In high office this is a continual and iterative process throughout an individual's career or campaign.[3]

The case of Abraham Lincoln is an interesting and instructive one. Lincoln is generally considered to have been the preeminent U.S. leader who led the country through its greatest crises, the Civil War and the abolition of slavery. He is also considered by a consensus of contemporary scholars to be one of our greatest presidents (even surpassing Washington in some recent surveys of experts).[4] Yet Lincoln was not consistent in his statements on the slavery issue throughout his career, and abolitionists often denounced him as being too sympathetic toward the slave-owning South. William Lloyd Garrison declared of Lincoln in 1861, "He has evidently not a drop of anti-slavery blood in his veins."[5]

One of Lincoln's most-remembered statements about the slavery issue came on June 16, 1858, in the speech in which he accepted the Republican nomination to run against Stephen Douglas for the Senate seat from Illinois. Lincoln declared: "A house divided against itself cannot stand. I believe this government cannot endure, permanently half slave and half free."[6] On July 10, Lincoln stated in Chicago: "Let us discard all this quibbling about this man and the other man—this race and that race and the other race being inferior. . . . [A]ll men are created free and equal."[7]

During the campaign Lincoln traveled 4,350 miles and gave sixty-three speeches, but he was not consistent in such strong antislavery statements.[8] There were seven formal debates between the two candidates, and in the fourth Lincoln backed off from his earlier firm statement against slavery.

That debate was on September 18, 1858, in Charleston in southern Illinois, which tilted to the Southern side on the slavery issues, while the sympathies of northern Illinois were against slavery, though not abolitionist. Democrats had displayed a banner hostile to Lincoln that said "Negro Equality" and had a picture of a white man and a black woman with a mulatto boy. This was clearly an inflammatory banner intended to imply that Lincoln favored racial equality and full integration. Lincoln intended to assure his conservative audience that he was not a threat:

> I will say then that I am not, nor ever have been in favor of bringing about in any way the social and political equality of the white and black races,—that I am not nor ever have been in favor of making voters or jurors of Negroes, nor of qualifying them to hold office, nor to intermarry with white people; and I will say in addition to this that there is a physical difference between the white and black races which I believe will for ever forbid the two races living together on terms of social and political equality. And inasmuch as they cannot so live, while they do remain together there must be the position of superior and inferior, and I as much as any other man am in favor of having the superior position assigned to the white race.[9]

Lincoln biographer David Herbert Donald argues that Lincoln's statement was made out of political expedience because of the anti-black sentiments of his audience in southern Illinois.[10] David Zarefsky argues that Lincoln's statement in Charleston was not inconsistent with his position against slavery as economic oppression. Zarefsky's argument is that Lincoln was always consistent in his statements that slavery constituted economic oppression and was thus wrong.[11]

Lincoln's political expedience, pragmatism, or fine parsing of language is also reflected in his first inaugural address, in which he said, "I have no purpose, directly or indirectly to interfere with the institution of slavery in the States where it exists, I believe I have no lawful right to do so, and I have no inclination to do so."[12] Lincoln thus distinguished his personal moral convictions from the actions he felt he could legitimately take as president of the United States.

His priorities as president were reflected in a letter he wrote to the *New York Tribune* in response to an editorial by Horace Greeley:

> My paramount object in this struggle *is* to save the Union, and is *not* either to save or to destroy slavery. If I could save the Union without freeing *any* slave I would do it, and if I could save it by freeing *all* the slaves I would do it; and if I could save it by freeing some and leaving others alone I would also do that. What I do about slavery, and the colored race, I do because I believe it helps to save the Union; and what I forbear, I forbear because I do *not* believe it would help to save the Union.[13]

Donald argues that Lincoln here is expressing his conviction that the preservation of the Union would necessarily contain slavery and inevitably lead to its extinction. Lincoln also reaffirmed in this letter his "oft-expressed *personal* wish that all men every where could be free."[14]

Despite Lincoln's principle that all humans were equal before God and that blacks were "my equal and the equal of Judge Douglas, and the equal of every living man," he may very well have thought that whites were superior to blacks in ability.[15] Because of Lincoln's background in his parents, the geography of his birth, the politics of his time, and the scarcity of blacks where he grew up (Springfield had 171 blacks of 5,000 total inhabitants),[16] we might expect him to reflect the social attitudes of his times.[17] Donald, although admitting that Lincoln's harsh Charleston declaration ("I am not, nor ever have been . . .") was based in political expedience, also judged that it "represented Lincoln's deeply held personal views, which he had repeatedly expressed before."[18]

Perhaps the harshest portrayal of Lincoln with respect to race is presented by Lerone Bennett in *Forced into Glory: Abraham Lincoln's White Dream*, which argues that Lincoln was thoroughly a racist who wanted to preserve slavery and deport blacks to a foreign colony. In his judgment, "*Lincoln was shockingly indifferent and insensitive to the plight of the slaves in particular and African-Americans in general*" (italics in original).[19] Bennett argues that the Emancipation Proclamation was not a truly liberating document but carefully limited and that Lincoln was forced into issuing it by circumstances and events rather than by personal conviction. Lincoln's personal preference, mentioned in his first annual message to Congress (December 3, 1861), was to establish a colony for blacks "at some place or places in a climate congenial to them" (probably in Central

America or the West Indies).[20] This had long been the preferred remedy to the slavery issue for the American Colonization Society, which saw this as a just way to end slavery in the United States. While Lincoln favored colonization, he wanted it to be voluntary. The problem with this proposal, which Lincoln eventually understood, was that it was impractical; neither blacks nor Southern slaveholders favored it, and Northern states did not want to pay the heavy costs involved.[21]

Historian Allen C. Guelzo argues that contemporary historians must come to terms with Lincoln's differing public stances toward the slavery issue. Guelzo argues that Lincoln approached slavery as a political-economic problem as much as a moral problem. "Lincoln came to emancipation at last, but by a road very different from that taken by the abolitionists." Lincoln "preferred gradualism and compensation for emancipated slaves." And he "would proceed against slavery no further than the Constitution allowed."[22] According to Guelzo, Lincoln never doubted that slavery was wrong, but he was keenly aware of the limits the Constitution imposed on him and his ability to alter the political reality of the intense Southern feelings about slavery and the power of the Southern states. Thus Lincoln resented "the self-righteousness of the abolitionists" as he sought to preserve the union and end slavery in a politically realistic way.[23] That his efforts led to the Civil War demonstrates the recalcitrance of the slavery controversy in American politics.

In Garry Wills's opinion Lincoln's various and changing positions on the race issue were necessary for the eventual liberation of African Americans. He argues that Lincoln's Charleston declaration was necessary for his election. "But for that pledge Lincoln had no hope of winning office."[24] From this perspective, Lincoln's true feelings were expressed in a letter he wrote in 1864: "I am naturally anti-slavery. If slavery is not wrong, nothing is wrong. I can not remember when I did not so think, and feel, and yet I have never understood that the Presidency conferred upon me an unrestricted right to act officially upon this judgment and feeling."[25] Thus in Wills's analysis, Lincoln had to be expedient in order to be elected so that he might work to eradicate slavery. His problem, according to Wills, was that he "had no clear expression of popular will to implement. He had to elicit the program he wanted to serve."[26] He had to forge a constituency among abolitionists, some defenders of slavery, and many who wanted to avoid the issue altogether. Thus Lincoln's changing statements on the slavery issue were necessary, and his deviousness had the ultimate purpose of a free America. Wills approvingly quotes G. K. Chesterton's observation about Lincoln: "He loved to repeat that slavery was intolerable while he tolerated it, and to prove that something ought to be done while it was impossible to do it. . . . But for all that this inconsistent consistency beat the politicians at their own game, and this abstracted logic proved most practical of all. For, when the chance did come to do something, there was no doubt about the thing to be done. The thunderbolt fell from the clear heights of heaven."[27] According to Wills, "Without his immense skills for hesitating, obfuscating and compromising where necessary, Lincoln could not have been in a position to define the great moral issues of the war."[28]

Lincoln's critic, Lerone Bennett, feels that Lincoln "should have been consistent."[29] But Wills's argument is that inconsistency was necessary for Lincoln to achieve office in that society at that time and that he had to temporize all along until he could achieve his final goal of emancipation. Bennett would argue that Lincoln was a racist and that emancipation was never his goal but that he was forced into it by circumstances, that is, "forced into glory." He quotes Lincoln as saying of emancipation, "*It must be done. I am driven to it.* . . . [B]ut though my duty is plain, it is in some respects painful." Bennett concludes that Lincoln "was literally dragged, protesting every step of the way, to the mountain top."[30]

Thus when we judge contemporary politicians for flip-flopping or inconsistency, we should keep in mind that one of our greatest presidents did not pursue his greatest achievement along a straight, unwavering course. Rather, insofar as he sought to free the slaves, he pursued a circuitous, sometimes devious, course of action. The fundamental challenge was that he had to convince others that it was in their own best interest to go down this path. Lincoln's general approach was one of pragmatism: "My policy is to have no policy" was a motto for him. As he explained, "The pilots on our Western rivers steer from point to point as they call it—setting the course of the boat no farther than they can see; and that is all I proposed to myself in this great problem."[31] Even if some historians can plausibly argue that Lincoln remained consistent in all of his public statements about race and the slavery issue, one must admit that some of his public statements at least seem inconsistent.

The important point is not whether Lincoln was pure in motive or merely an expedient politician but rather what is possible for political leaders in the United States. The implication of this analysis is that politicians cannot always pursue fixed purposes and be consistent and expect to win office and attain their goals. The case of Lincoln is particularly compelling because of the near-universal agreement that he was one of our greatest presidents. In the end he emancipated the slaves and achieved the abolition of slavery through the Civil War and the Thirteenth Amendment to the Constitution. Even though Lincoln's arguable inconsistency does not justify inconsistent statements by contemporary politicians, we ought to think carefully about holding them to a higher standard than we would Lincoln.

FRANKLIN ROOSEVELT AND THE NEW DEAL

Just as Lincoln was inconsistent in his public stance toward the most pressing issue of his day, slavery, so also did another great president, Franklin Roosevelt, often vacillated on important issues in his day. His lack of consistency was based at least partly in his personality and his need to please people, which was both his strength and his weakness as a politician. In addition to his natural politician's desire to please everyone, he wanted to keep his options open until the right course of action was determined. His political flexibility contrasted with his more principled wife. He once chided Eleanor, "When you take a position on an issue, your backbone has no bend!"[32]

During the campaign of 1932 one reporter conceded that he was sure that FDR was against prohibition, but "You could not quarrel with a single one of his generalities; you seldom can. But what they mean (if anything) is known only to Franklin D. Roosevelt and his God."[33] Roosevelt had no overall set of policy plans to deal with the Great Depression once he entered office. His campaign, rather, decried the state of the economy and promised to improve it. According to James MacGregor Burns, "He was trying to win an election, not lay out a coherent philosophy of government. He had no such philosophy." A frustrated Herbert Hoover said that Roosevelt was "a chameleon on plaid." When Raymond Moley offered him two different and opposing drafts on tariff policy, Roosevelt told him to "weave the two together."[34]

Shortly after his election (November 8, 1932) he went to visit President Hoover, who wanted Roosevelt's support for a measure before Congress. After the meeting, Hoover was sure that he had Roosevelt's support, but when there was no public statement forthcoming from FDR, Hoover felt betrayed and said that he would never again talk with him alone. In Roosevelt's mind, however, he had only been agreeable with Hoover but had not agreed to support the measure.[35]

The New Deal contained a wide range of measures to ameliorate the worst effects of the Depression, but it did not constitute a coherent approach. According to FDR biographer James MacGregor Burns, Roosevelt "could be bold or cautious, informal or dignified, cruel or kind, intolerant or longsuffering, urbane or almost rustic, impetuous or temporizing, Machiavellian or moralistic. Most political leaders embody contrasting traits; the baffling question about Roosevelt was what kind of internal standard, if any, determined which of his qualities would appear in what situations. . . . [W]as there a discernible core of ideas and values behind the glittering facades? What kind of crucible would prove the iron in the man?"[36]

"The president [Clinton] has kept all of the promises he intended to keep."
—GEORGE STEPHANOPOLOUS

Presidential Promises

The chapter now takes up the issue of campaign promises in general, followed by an analysis of specific presidential campaign promises, including Franklin Roosevelt's 1932 promise to balance the budget and his 1940 promise to keep the United States out of war, Eisenhower's and Nixon's promises to end wars, Reagan's 1980 promise to balance the federal budget, Bush's 1988 promise not to raise taxes, and Clinton's promise of a middle-class tax cut. The chapter concludes that consistency and promise keeping are admirable and desirable in presidential candidates but that they are not always possible, and at times it may be wise policy to change one's mind and reverse a policy position.

CAMPAIGN PROMISES

Despite general public cynicism about whether presidential candidates keep their campaign promises, most presidents do in fact try to keep their promises, once elected. Any careful consideration of promise keeping must exclude those general, vague statements of campaign themes such as Kennedy's promise to "get the country moving again" or Carter's intention to "restore the trust of the American people in their government" or Reagan's promise "to get the federal government off of the backs of the people" or Clinton's promise to "put people first." These are all such broad statements of sentiment that they are functionally and programmatically meaningless. But presidential candidates make a number of much more specific campaign promises against which their actions, once in office, can be measured.

Scholar Jeff Fishel has made such a study, and in his book *Presidents and Promises,*[37] he measures quite rigorously the performance of recent presidents in keeping their promises. Contrary to the conventional wisdom, he convincingly concludes that most presidents keep their promises most of the time. By promise keeping he does not mean that presidents in office were necessarily successful in achieving their goals. Clearly the U.S. political system divides power, and presidents do not control policy making. Most important, Congress, which may be controlled by the political party that is not the president's, has the final say in which proposals finally become law. Thus Fishel counts as promise keeping all serious efforts by presidents to keep their promises.

First, Fishel counts as promises statements that are concrete enough to be categorized as pledges of continuity, expressions of goals and concerns, pledges of action, or detailed pledges. In his count of campaign pledges from Kennedy to Reagan he finds the following totals:[38]

Kennedy:	133 promises
Johnson:	63 promises
Nixon:	153 promises
Carter:	186 promises
Reagan:	108 promises

But, of course, for the purpose of judging character, the number of promises is much less important than the relative proportion that presidents genuinely try to keep. In judging good-faith efforts to keep presidential promises, Fishel uses the following categories: fully comparable, partially comparable, token action, contradictory action, no action, mixed action, and indeterminate. Combining the top two categories of fully comparable and partially comparable actions to fulfill campaign promises and excluding token action and the other categories, Fishel finds the following percentages for good-faith efforts to fulfill campaign pledges:

Kennedy:	67 percent
Johnson:	63 percent
Nixon:	60 percent
Carter:	65 percent
Reagan:	53 percent (through 1984)

Kathleen Hall Jamieson takes up the issue of campaign promise keeping and focuses particularly on the 1992 and 1996 elections. Despite general voter skepticism in public-opinion polls and media focus on several campaign promises that President Clinton did not keep (e.g., the middle-class tax cut and Haitian refugee status), Clinton's overall record on promise keeping was quite good. One study that replicated Jeff Fishel's earlier study found that Clinton attempted to keep sixty-nine percent of his promises, slightly better than his predecessors as measured by Fishel.[39] Several systematic newspaper accounts also found that Clinton had attempted to keep most of his promises.[40] Thus despite minor variation, systematic analysis reveals an impressive record of presidential effort to fulfill campaign promises, especially given the number of relatively specific campaign promises of these presidents.

Even though this record is significant and indicative of good faith on the part of politicians, not all promises are of equal import. Some are clearly major promises on important policy issues facing the country, whereas others are merely attempts to fix things at the margin. We can conclude from the preceding data and careful analysis that presidents in general try to keep their promises and that major character differences among these recent presidents cannot be discerned from merely looking at the totals. But some promises on important issues clearly outweigh others and ought to be seriously considered in evaluating any president's record of consistency and promise keeping. Thus we turn now to some of the specific campaign promises of the modern presidents.

FDR'S CAMPAIGN PROMISE TO BALANCE THE BUDGET

In 1932 the United States economy was in a shambles, with productivity decreasing and unemployment approaching twenty-five percent of the workforce. President Hoover was well aware of the problem and briefly considered deficit spending but rejected that approach in favor of balancing the budget in hopes of restoring business confidence in investment. In the Revenue Act of 1932 he proposed significant tax increases. The eventual deficit for fiscal year 1932 was $2.7 billion, the largest peacetime deficit relative to total outlays (about sixty percent) in U.S. history to that point.[41]

In his campaign for the presidency, Franklin Roosevelt called for new and innovative thinking and governmental action to deal with the devastating effects of the Depression on the working classes. But on the issue of balancing the budget, Roosevelt was right in the mainstream with Hoover. In fact, he attacked Hoover for not balancing the budget and promised to balance it if elected.[42] After he was inaugurated in March, he sent a message to Congress asking for discretion to cut the budget where needed. He said, "Too often in recent history liberal governments have been wrecked on rocks of loose fiscal policy."[43]

Business interests and conservatives, of course, did not trust FDR to behave responsibly in fiscal policy. They were fearful that the inflation that had wracked Germany in the 1920s would come to the United States if the federal budget were not brought into balance. Business leader Bernard Baruch thought the government had to stop borrowing: "Balance budgets . . . stop spending money we haven't got. Sacrifice for frugality and revenue. Cut government spending—cut it as rations are cut in a siege. Tax—tax everybody for everything."[44] Conservative Democrats as well accepted the conventional wisdom that the budget had to be balanced. Despite FDR's intentions to balance the budget, the economy was still too anemic to bring in tax revenues that were necessary for balance, and Roosevelt, when confronted with cutting funds for relief, refused to balance the budget by cutting relief for the poor. In 1936 he told reporters, "A balanced budget isn't putting people to work. I will balance the budget as soon as I take care of the unemployed. . . . Hell, I can stop relief tomorrow. What happens? . . . It isn't any joke."[45]

Despite FDR's unwillingness to cut government expenditures for relief for the poor, he continued to rank balancing the budget as one of his high priorities. In his 1936 campaign for reelection, he again promised to balance the budget, and in 1937 he said, "I have said fifty times that the budget will be balanced for the fiscal year 1938. . . . If you want me to say it again, I will say it either once or fifty times more."[46] But the budget was not balanced in 1938, and in 1940, in order to move toward balance, Roosevelt did not propose much new spending for the poor and those displaced by the continuing depression. Only World War II and its unprecedented deficit spending finally brought the nation fully out of the Depression and renewed the health of the economy. Even though John Maynard Keynes was writing about how government borrowing could be used as a fiscal tool to prime the economic pump during an economic downturn, it was not until after World War II that his ideas became an accepted part of conventional economics. As Richard Nixon is famously said to have declared after he became president, "We are all Keynesians now." But Franklin Roosevelt never accepted Keynes's new theory and continued to try to balance the federal budget while he was president, though he was never able to do it.

How then should we evaluate Roosevelt's campaign promise in 1932 to balance the budget? FDR clearly accepted the conventional economic wisdom that balancing the budget was the best way to cope with a poor economy, and he did not abandon that belief during his presidency. The promise was not merely a campaign expedient, meant to palliate some electoral constituency; he clearly believed it, and he severely disappointed his progressive supporters in 1940 for his failure to support more public works because he wanted to balance the budget.[47]

Thus FDR's promise to balance the budget was not kept, but not for lack of trying. FDR clearly felt that other priorities, particularly providing aid to those severely hurt by the Depression, was a higher priority, and he refused to cut back on relief spending, even though he did not spend as much as many of his supporters thought ought to be spent on relief for the poor. But a balanced budget was not his highest priority; he considered the operation of the government, the maintenance of defense spending, and aid for those stricken by the economic disaster as more important priorities than balancing the budget. FDR might be faulted for his priorities but not for lack of trying to keep his promise to balance the budget. In the future it would become accepted economic doctrine that deficit spending is appropriate during an economic downturn.

FDR'S 1940 CAMPAIGN PROMISE NOT TO GO TO WAR

During his 1940 campaign for a third term, Roosevelt tried to assure Americans that he did not want to take them into the European war. Yet clearly FDR's sentiments, and those of most Americans, were on the side of England and France and against the aggressions of Hitler. Throughout the campaign he had assured the country that the United States would not go to war "except in cases of attack." On October 30, just before the 1940 election, Republican candidate Wendell Willkie charged that Roosevelt would break his promise and the United States would be at war within six months.[48]

The day after the president presided over the drawing of the selective service numbers, he was traveling to Boston to give a speech, and it seemed that Willkie's attacks were having an effect. During the train ride to Boston the campaign received hundreds of messages from Democratic politicians throughout the country that Roosevelt was in danger of losing the election unless he firmly promised to keep the country out of war.[49]

In light of the importuning messages from Democratic politicians and recent opinion polls showing Willkie rapidly gaining on him, Roosevelt grudgingly yielded to his advisers' advice. "How often do they expect me to say that? . . . I've repeated it a hundred times."[50] So in his speech in Boston Garden, Roosevelt went further than he had before in trying to reassure the country after the beginning of the draft that the newly inducted soldiers would not have to fight:

> Very simply and honestly, I can give assurance to the mothers and to the fathers of America that each and every one of their boys in training will be well housed and well fed. . . . And while I am talking to you fathers and mothers I give one more assurance. I have said this before, but I shall say it again, and again, and again. Your boys are not going to be sent into any foreign wars.[51]

When asked by his speechwriters why he dropped the usual qualifying phrase they had inserted in his speech, "except in cases of attack," he said, "It's not necessary. . . . It's implied clearly. If we're attacked, it's no longer a foreign war."[52]

Roosevelt's promise in the Boston speech on October 30 must have been a campaign expedient in the face of Willkie's gaining in the polls. How else can we explain FDR's dropping his usual qualification "except in cases of attack"? Thus Roosevelt was misleading in making the statement since he knew that it was quite likely that American troops would have to fight, and he was clearly convinced that the United States had to back England and France in the historic war against Hitler's aggression. (Ironically, Willkie was an interventionist and was only posing as an antiwar candidate in order to win votes and beat Roosevelt. After FDR was reelected Willkie testified before the Senate in favor of FDR's lend-lease plan to help England.)[53]

But FDR's culpability might have been mitigated by the probability that the American public knew that war with Hitler was likely and that the draft was necessary. When public-opinion polls asked whom people would vote for if there were no war, Willkie received a 5.5 percent plurality. But if asked whom they would vote for if the country had to go to war, Roosevelt was highly favored. Given the outcome of the election, it is likely that American voters believed that war was likely. They gave Roosevelt a victory because if war came, they wanted an experienced president in charge and because economic news was beginning to look a little brighter, with unemployment dropping to 14.6 percent, the lowest it had been in the past ten years.[54]

Thus Roosevelt's misleading promise may not have accurately represented his expectations, but in historical perspective the decision to go to war was the right one. In addition, the United Stated did in fact get attacked by Japan in 1941, and it is likely that most Americans saw the attack as sufficient to break any promise about not going to war.

EISENHOWER'S AND NIXON'S PROMISES TO END WARS

It might be interesting to juxtapose the campaign promise of Dwight Eisenhower to end the war in Korea with Richard Nixon's campaign promise to end the war in Vietnam. On the surface, one might argue that Eisenhower kept his promise but that Nixon's insistence on "peace with honor" doomed more U.S. soldiers and many more Vietnamese to die as he negotiated with the North Vietnamese in Paris. It would be interesting, but it would not be accurate. Neither candidate explicitly promised to end the war; each kept his options open.

Several weeks before the 1952 election, on October 24, in a campaign speech in Detroit Eisenhower announced that he would "forgo the diversions of politics and concentrate on the job of ending the Korean war. . . . That job requires a personal trip to Korea. I shall make that trip. Only in that way could I learn how best to serve the American people in the cause of peace. I shall go to Korea."[55] Though he said that he would concentrate on the job of ending the Korean war, Eisenhower did not say what he would do or the time frame in which he expected to act. Nixon biographer Stephen Ambrose argues that this purposeful ambiguity helped in winning votes (though he was confidently ahead of Stevenson at the time) by implying that the war would be ended soon. It also kept his options open in negotiations with the North Koreans.

In 1968 the war in Vietnam was the major issue, and President Johnson had dropped out of the race in order to focus on ending the war. Nixon and the Republicans had been critical of Johnson, and the political right argued that Johnson was not strong or decisive enough. But the war was dragging on, and a significant portion of the electorate wanted it ended, one way or another. In the spring of 1968 in his campaign speeches Nixon regularly pledged that "New leadership will end the war and win the peace in the Pacific."[56] On August 6, 1968, speaking at the Republican national convention to Southern delegates, Nixon reassured them about Vietnam: "How do you bring a war to a conclusion? I'll tell you how Korea was ended. We got in there and had this messy war on our hands. Eisenhower . . . let the word go out diplomatically to the Chinese and the North [Koreans] that we would not tolerate this continual ground war of attrition.

And within a matter of months, they negotiated. Well, as far as negotiation [in Vietnam] is concerned that should be our position. We'll be militarily strong and diplomatically strong."[57] When the press asked Nixon about specific details on how he would deal with Vietnam, Nixon refused to provide any, allowing others to speculate about what plans he might have.

Nixon speechwriter William Safire, who formulated Nixon's campaign wording on the issue, explained that Nixon's primary opponent, George Romney, upset at Nixon's challenge to him, demanded to know "Where is your secret plan?" Thus it soon became widely accepted that Nixon had a secret plan to end the war, though Nixon had never said the words. As Nixon explained in his memoirs, "As a candidate it would have been foolhardy, and as a prospective President, improper, for me to outline specific plans in detail. . . . To some extent, then, I was asking the voters to take on faith my ability to end the war."[58]

Thus Eisenhower and Nixon both behaved appropriately with respect to campaign promises. Each was faced with an unpopular war that they would inherit if they were elected. Each made ambiguous statements about the war, implying though never stating that he would move with dispatch to end the war. And each kept his options open for decision making once he was in office and had access to the full range of information available to the commander in chief. If one wants to criticize Nixon for prolonging the Vietnam war in a futile search for "peace with honor" at the cost of the lives of thousands of U.S. soldiers and uncounted Vietnamese, the argument has to be made on the merits of his decisions, not on the basis of his breaking of a promise for an early end to the war.[59]

PRESIDENT REAGAN PROMISES TO BALANCE THE BUDGET

In the 1970s the federal-budget situation had been deteriorating rapidly. The economy was plagued with "stagflation," simultaneous stagnation (low growth) and inflation, which in the past had been thought to vary inversely. Richard Nixon imposed wage and price controls, but when they were lifted, prices jumped. The OPEC oil cartel raised oil prices sharply in 1973, aggravating inflation considerably. President Carter dealt with the unemployment resulting from the mid-decade recession with a stimulative fiscal policy. The policy was successful in reducing unemployment, but along with a second oil shock from OPEC in 1979, it contributed to increased inflation. In 1979 Carter appointed Paul Volcker to be chairman of the Federal Reserve Board to contain the money supply and wring inflation out of the economy. Thus in the 1980 campaign for the presidency Ronald Reagan had considerable ammunition with which to criticize the Carter administration. With inflation at thirteen percent and interest rates approaching twenty percent, Reagan was easily able to convince the country that a change was needed, and he made the economy a centerpiece of his campaign.

One important appeal of Reagan was that he would balance the budget. He blamed the budget deficit on wasteful spending by the Democratic administration and Congress and promised to balance the budget if elected: "Balancing the budget is essential. . . . I support a requirement that the federal government balance its budget except where temporary periods of war or national emergency require otherwise. My preference is that the balanced budget requirement be implemented legislatively, but, if it is necessary, I would support a constitutional amendment to that effect."[60] In his first inaugural address Reagan declared: "But great as our tax burden is, it has not kept pace with public spending. For decades, we have piled deficit upon deficit, mortgaging our future and our children's future for the temporary convenience of the present. To continue this long trend is to guarantee tremendous social, cultural, and political upheavals. . . .We must act today in order to preserve tomorrow. And let there be no misunderstanding—we are going to begin to act, beginning today."[61] Reagan was appealing to the traditional fiscal conservatives of the Republican party as well as to moderate Democrats who believed in fiscal prudence.

But another of Reagan's priorities was the desire to cut taxes, which he believed were an excessive confiscation of private property by the government, which encouraged wasteful spending. The problem was that decreasing tax revenues would put the budget further out of balance. In order to square this circle Reagan adopted the "supply side" argument of some economists. They argued that tax cuts, especially at the higher end of income scales, would put more money in the hands of those who would invest it in business. These new investments would put unemployed workers back to work, which would increase production, thus increasing tax revenues to the government and balancing the budget.[62] Reagan proposed an income tax cut of ten percent for three years to "get the government off the backs of the American people" and to stimulate the economy and achieve a balanced budget.

The other major policy proposal of the new Reagan administration was a sharp increase in defense spending. Reagan argued that, since the

Vietnam War, the United States had let its defense forces fall into decline, and he proposed significant increases if he were elected. President Carter reacted to the Reagan campaign promises by matching Reagan's proposals with his own proposal of defense increases of five percent per year. Reagan had to distinguish himself from Carter and upped his proposed increases to seven percent. After Reagan took office, the details of the defense increases were negotiated between Secretary of Defense Casper Weinberger and David Stockman. Weinberger maneuvered Stockman into agreeing to the seven-percent increase from the elevated base of defense expenditures for fiscal year 1982 rather than the lower base of previous Carter budgets, which were the basis of Reagan's campaign promises. The implication was a five-year, defense-budget total of $1.46 trillion, according to David Stockman's calculations.[63]

In addition to the increased tax revenues predicted by the supply-siders, the early Reagan administration intended to cut from the budget "fraud, waste, and abuse" and some domestic social service programs that it argued sapped the initiative of poor people. The estimates of savings from cutting "fraud, waste, and abuse" proved to be highly optimistic, as did the administration's hopes of cutting domestic-welfare programs. When the public and members of Congress became concerned about the effect of domestic cuts, the administration cordoned off a "safety net" of programs that broadly benefited Americans. The safety net included seven programs; among them were Social Security, veterans benefits, Medicare, and the Head Start program, which amounted to forty percent of social spending. Thus domestic cuts would have to come from other programs, such as food stamps, Aid to Families with Dependent Children (AFDC), Supplemental Security Income, subsidized housing, Medicaid, employment training, community services, legal services for the poor, the Women, Infants, and Children food program, and so on. The problem was that these cuts, as significant as they were for the poor, who were recipients of their benefits, amounted to only about $35 billion toward deficit reduction, nowhere near enough to move the budget toward balance.

After manipulating the numbers and using the "magic asterisk" to designate budget cuts that would be specified in the future, the Reagan administration still had to admit that budget deficits would rise to the $100 to $200 billion level "as far as the eye could see," in David Stockman's words. On November 6, 1981, after Treasury Secretary Donald Regan conceded that the budget could not be balanced before 1984, Reagan admitted the fact but said, "I've never said anything but that it was a goal."[64] The cumulated deficits resulted in an increase of the national debt from $1 trillion in 1981 to $2 trillion in 1985 to $3 trillion in 1989 to $4 trillion in 1994 to more than $5 trillion before the budget came into balance, and the debt began to decline briefly in the late 1990s. The fiscal implications of interest payments on the national debt would continue to crowd out other spending priorities well into the twenty-first century.

How should we evaluate Reagan's breaking of his campaign promise to balance the budget? His promise was most probably not a cynical one; he truly wanted to bring the budget into balance, and he probably thought that he could, even well into his first year in office. But his desire to balance the budget ran smack into his two other major priorities: increasing defense spending and cutting taxes. Since Reagan did not understand the budget implications of these policies according to most inside accounts, he probably did not believe that he had to make any trade-offs. He resisted the idea that he might have to compromise any of his goals and did not attempt to reconcile in his mind economic data that conflicted with his own convictions.[65]

The supply-side economists promised increased tax revenues because of the large tax cuts. Military-expenditure hawks framed any change in defense spending as going back on Reagan's promise to make America strong again. In the public-relations battle over these policies and their budget implications David Stockman and administration spokesmen continued to argue that the budget would be brought into balance by 1984 until it was too late to make any serious changes in order to accomplish that goal. And when the political implications of balancing the budget by severe cuts in domestic spending were faced, they were too daunting to undertake.

Thus Reagan can be faulted for not keeping his promise to balance the budget, and he can be criticized for not taking the trouble to fully understand the fiscal and economic consequences of his policies. But his defenders would argue that his other priorities of increased military spending and cutting taxes were more important to him than bringing the budget into balance. That is certainly what happened. In addition, social spending programs, particularly Social Security and Medicare, which were indexed to inflation, made it difficult to cut overall expenditures. And the serious recession of 1981 and 1982 significantly cut tax revenues at the same time as it increased spending on unemployment and social programs. One might criticize Reagan's priorities and the effects of his policy choices, but criticisms of his broken promise would also have to include an element of disagreement about his policy priorities. Reagan intended to balance the budget. But when faced with the trade-offs necessary to actually do it, he chose other priorities.

PRESIDENT BUSH'S PROMISE OF "NO NEW TAXES"

In 1988 George Bush was President Reagan's vice president and heir apparent to the Republican nomination for the presidency. But Bush was not the overwhelming favorite of all Republicans. After seven years of low visibility and subjugating his own political views to those of President Reagan, some Republicans began to ask whether he had the requisite stature and toughness to be president. The national news media even raised explicitly the issue of the "wimp factor," with the implication that Bush might not be tough enough to be president.

Ronald Reagan had built an important part of his presidential persona by fighting taxes, from his twenty-five-percent supply-side tax cut in 1981 to his 1984 campaign against Walter Mondale, who made the political blunder of admitting that a tax increase might be necessary to deal with the unprecedented budget deficits and accumulating national debt of the 1980s. Even though Reagan had backed significant tax increases in 1982 and 1983,[66] his anti-tax rhetoric was so firmly embedded in voters' minds that he continued to be seen as the hero of anti-tax conservatives.

But George Bush did not have the conservative credentials that Reagan had and had always been under suspicion from the right wing of the Republican party. In order to shore up his conservative credentials for the New Hampshire primary, he felt he had to "take the pledge" that, if elected, he would not increase taxes. New Hampshire was particularly crucial after Bush had come in third behind Senator Robert Dole and evangelist Pat Robertson in the 1988 Iowa caucuses. Thus Bush emphasized his no-taxes pledge and attacked Dole as "Senator Straddle" for not promising unequivocally that he would not increase taxes as president. Bush's firm stand on taxes helped him to win the New Hampshire primary and go on to win the majority of the remaining primaries, sewing up the nomination before the Republican national convention in July, 1988.

While Bush's no-tax pledge helped him win the Republican primary, a strategic decision had to be made as to whether it should be an important part of his campaign. In the summer of 1988 Bush was running behind Democratic candidate Michael Dukakis, and Bush decided to position himself as a true conservative versus a "liberal" Michael Dukakis. One of the defining moments of the 1988 campaign came when Bush gave his acceptance speech at the Republican convention.

Former Reagan speechwriter Peggy Noonan was recruited to draft the speech, and she sought to present Bush as bold and assertive. She also wanted to assure Republican conservatives that Bush would be true to his word. When she put in lines promising no new taxes, some of Bush's advisers, particular Richard Darman, deleted the lines as being "stupid and irresponsible," that is, too absolute and leaving no wiggle room for change. Darman knew the budget numbers and expected that some tax increases would be necessary to deal with the increasing deficit.[67] According to Darman's memoirs, "it was imprudent to be absolutist. . . . [A] President should never lock himself in a box." But "I was indulging in the fantasy of governing without attending to the prior imperative of winning."[68]

Noonan and other aides who were more concerned with winning the election than with the economic consequences of increasing deficits argued that Bush needed to sound decisive. Bush was worried about Dukakis's lead in the polls and agreed to include the words "The Congress will push me to raise taxes, and I'll say no, and they'll push and I'll say no, and they'll push again. And all I can say to them is read my lips: No New Taxes."[69] She said that she insisted on the words "Because it's definite. It's not subject to misinterpretation. It means, I mean this."[70] Noonan was right about the impact of the words, and even Darman admitted that Bush "exuded [macho movie actor Clint] Eastwood's power, directness, and absolute firmness."[71]

Bush's intent was to take his statement about not increasing taxes out of the normal category of campaign promises and harden it into a commitment that would be perceived as irrevocable and thus more credible to voters who cared strongly about taxes. The statement in the speech at the national convention was carefully rehearsed and managed to achieve maximum effect. It was perceived as successful by the campaign, and Bush soon began to gain on Dukakis and won the election convincingly in November.

After taking office, President Bush formulated his first budget proposal aimed at keeping his pledge, but it was based on optimistic economic assumptions and a number of gimmicks. The actual deficit turned out to be much higher than predicted.[72] For his second budget, in the spring of 1990 (for fiscal year 1991), President Bush used a similarly optimistic set of assumptions, but in the late spring it became clear that the actual deficit would be more than twice as large as the initial projected deficit.

Pressure mounted from Congress, the business community, and Federal Reserve Board chair Alan Greenspan to reduce the deficit. The Democrats in Congress were willing to consider tax increases to reduce the deficit but were unwilling to be the first to propose them, fearing that the Republicans would blame them for any tax increases and take credit for deficit reduction. The Republicans were willing to close the deficit gap by cutting entitlements and domestic spending, but the Democrats were unwilling to allow domestic spending to take the full load for reducing the deficit. Thus initial talks about deficit reduction were at a stalemate in the spring of 1990. The Democrats were willing to use spending cuts as part of a deal to reduce deficits, but they insisted that the president take part of the blame for any tax increases (knowing that breaking his pledge would hurt him politically). This situation set the stage for the budget summit between the White House and Congress at Andrews Air Force Base in July.

It was clear to the White House negotiators, including President Bush, that any agreement to increase taxes would hurt the president with the Republican right wing, but the president decided that the long-term health of the economy was more important than keeping his promise. If there were no budget agreement, the current law would have forced across-the-board cuts in defense and domestic spending that were unacceptable to both parties. If the deficit were allowed to continue to increase with no significant spending cuts or tax increases, the situation would have been seen as inflationary by Wall Street, and interest rates would have begun to rise just as the economy was beginning to slow. By mid-June, Republicans in Congress had come to the conclusion that some agreement was necessary and that a tax increase was an essential part of any viable agreement.[73]

On June 26, 1990, Democratic House Speaker Tom Foley proposed an agreement that included entitlement reform, decreases in domestic and defense discretionary spending, budget-process reform, and tax increases. President Bush, with the concurrence of his top aides, agreed to the deficit-reduction formula and ordered that a press release be issued, including the phrase "tax revenue increases."[74] The Democrats agreed to cuts in entitlements, caps on spending, and growth incentives.[75] The total package amounted to a reduction in the deficit of about $500 billion over the next five years.

From the political perspective, abandoning his pledge was a major mistake for Bush. In Bush press secretary Marlin Fitzwater's words it was "perhaps the biggest mistake of the administration. . . . Our political world exploded."[76] Some even blame Bush's defeat at the polls in 1992 to his reneging on his promise (though it is doubtful that conservative voters would have voted for Clinton or Perot merely because Bush had agreed to a tax increase). But from the economic perspective, the concession was necessary to ensure a sound economy. The business world was supportive as well as both parties in Congress, even though the initial agreement had to be renegotiated over several months because of a revolt by Newt Gingrich and conservatives who did not want any tax increases and liberals who thought that domestic programs were cut too much.

On June 29, 1990, after the agreement was announced, former President Nixon wrote to Bush to say that he had done the right thing. He compared Bush's breaking his pledge to his own trip to China, saying "You are taking heat on the tax issue. . . . What mattered most [when Nixon went to China] was not that I had changed my mind, but that I had done what I thought was best for the country and for the cause of peace in the world."[77]

In retrospect, it seems that the responsible thing for the president to do was to break his pledge and agree to the deficit-reduction package. It led to fiscal discipline through the negotiated spending caps throughout the 1990s and helped prepare the way (along with President Clinton's deficit-reduction policies in 1993) for the unprecedented economic boom of the late 1990s.

If one concedes that Bush made the difficult but courageous decision to agree to a tax increase and thus break his promise, what moral weight should be given to his initial promise? He made the promise because he thought it was necessary to win the election in 1988, even though his usual prudence would ordinarily have led him to avoid such a promise. So any judgment critical of Bush should be directed against the initial promise made from political expedience rather than from his difficult decision to do the right thing for the economy and the country in 1990 by breaking his promise. Sometimes the test of character is to break a promise in order to do the right thing in spite of political harm to one's self.

BILL CLINTON ABANDONS HIS
PROMISED MIDDLE-CLASS TAX CUT

Bill Clinton ran for the presidency promising a range of programs and priorities. He kept some of his promises, such as cutting the deficit in half, "ending welfare as we know it" (by signing a Republican bill), signing gun-control legislation, increasing the minimum wage, beginning a national-service program, and cutting the White House staff by twenty-five percent.[78] In some areas he tried to fulfill promises but was thwarted by Congress, most notably his health-care reform proposals but also his proposal to allow homosexuals to serve openly in the armed forces.[79] This section takes up one significant campaign promise that he abandoned early in his term: his promise of a middle-class tax cut. This issue is instructive because it was a fairly clear commitment that he explicitly abandoned. But it is also comparable to President Bush's pledge of "no new taxes," not so much in the vehemence with which it was stated but in the justification for it and the positive economic consequences of breaking the promise.

The major theme of the campaign had been the state of the economy, and Clinton had promised to stimulate the economy, cut the deficit, invest in worker training and infrastructure, cut taxes for the middle class, and reform health-care financing. With all of the preparation in December and with his economic team carefully chosen, many expected that Clinton would have a plan ready early in his administration, even if not on "day one" of his presidency. But the policy was not ready to go because Clinton had not yet made up his mind whether the economy needed to be stimulated to pull it out of the recession or whether the deficit had to be attacked to ensure the longer-term health of the economy. The first several months of the administration were a fight for the mind of the president over this issue.

In one corner were the consultants who had run the campaign and who continued to be actively involved in policy deliberations and advising the president. Even though they did not hold official positions in the government, James Carville, Paul Begalla, Mandy Grunwald, and Stanley Greenberg were trusted advisers to the president and first lady. They argued that Clinton should stick to his campaign promise for a middle-class tax cut and investments to help people deal with economic dislocations caused by a globalizing economy and layoffs.[80] In the other corner were the "deficit hawks," who believed that the long-term health of the U.S. economy was dependent on reducing the deficit. The national debt had climbed from $1 trillion in 1981 to $4 trillion in 1993; the annual deficit would be nearly $300 billion if no changes were made; and interest on the debt approached $200 billion per year and fourteen percent of budget outlays. The country was eating the seed corn rather than investing it in the future.

The deficit hawks argued that an economic recovery depended upon keeping interest rates down and inflation in check. If the bond markets (moneylenders) thought that the Clinton economic plan would encourage inflation by continuing to increase the deficit, they would demand higher interest rates to lend money, and these higher rates would cut short the recovery. On the other hand, steep deficit reduction would not guarantee a robust recovery in the short term.

The deficit hawks included Treasury Secretary Lloyd Bentsen, OMB director Leon Panetta, NEC staff director Robert Rubin, and OMB deputy director Alice Rivlin. Chairman of the Federal Reserve Board Alan Greenspan was perhaps the most important deficit hawk, though his role was indirect since "the Fed" was nominally an independent agency. His advice to Clinton implied that if there were sufficient deficit reduction, the Fed would not raise interest rates in order to head off potential inflation. He made this clear to Clinton in personal meetings with the president-elect and White House staffers.[81] Greenspan was reinforcing the same message that the deficit hawks were arguing. Clinton understood both sides of the economic arguments well and was clearly ambivalent, realizing the necessity of deficit reduction but not eager to sacrifice his other policy initiatives and devote much of his initial political capital to fighting the deficit battle.

One of the key turning points came during the transition in a meeting of Clinton with his main economic advisers (including Gore, Bentsen, Rubin, Tyson, and Alan Blinder) on January 7, 1993. They warned that the deficit would soar to $360 billion in 1997 and $500 billion in 2000 if nothing was done to curb it. They admitted that in the short term the cuts and taxes might slow the economy, but in the longer term the economy would benefit. The key importance of the psychology of the bond market was made clear to the president. If the lenders thought that Clinton was not serious about deficit reduction they would demand higher interest rates, which in turn would slow the economy, and the Fed might also raise interest rates in order to head off anticipated inflation. The problem was that it was not yet clear that the economy was in a strong recovery. It might still need a stimulus.

Clinton was facing the unfortunate dilemma of being forced to impose economic pain during his presidency so that economic benefits would accrue in the future, possibly under his successors. "You mean to tell me that the success of the program and my reelection hinges on the Federal Reserve and a bunch of f——— bond traders?" he asked. The answer was yes.[82] But the consultants argued that the deficit hawks were taking over and that Clinton was betraying the coalition that had elected him. They urged him to spur the economy by spending on infrastructure, retraining workers, and cutting taxes for the middle class rather than paying a heavy political price for deficit reduction by increased taxes and spending cuts. Stanley Greenburg, one of the consultants, complained that "The presidency has been hijacked."[83]

In a series of all-day sessions in early February, 1993, the outlines of the Clinton economic plan were hammered out. Clinton decided to drop his promise for a middle-class tax cut, increase tax rates on the affluent, and propose a broad-based energy tax. The combination of tax increases with spending cuts would reduce the deficit by about $500 billion over five years, and in the short run the economy would be stimulated by a separate investment package.

Clinton's campaign to get Congress to pass his budget was fraught with difficulties and misjudgments. On March 18 the House passed the budget resolution on a party-line vote of 243 to 183, with eleven Democrats defecting. The vote in the Senate was tougher, but after six days of lobbying and forty-five roll-call votes to defeat Republican amendments, the Senate passed the budget resolution 54 to 45 with Senator Shelby (D-Ala at the time; in 1995 Shelby switched to the Republican party), the only Democrat voting no. The fight for the reconciliation bill to enforce the budget resolution was just as intense. Finally, after a grueling fight and giving out many favors, the president won the battle on May 27 by a vote of 219 to 213, with thirty-eight Democrats defecting and no Republican votes in favor. On June 24, after another exhausting fight, during which the tax on British thermal units was dropped and replaced with a 4.3-cent-per-gallon gas tax, the Senate passed its bill with Vice President Gore breaking a 49 to 49 tie.

But the fight was not over. Both the House and the Senate had passed different versions of the reconciliation bill, and the differences had to be ironed out in conference committee and brought back to the floors for final votes before it could go to the president for his signature. Clinton won in the House with a 218 to 216 win and no votes to spare. The Senate voted on August 6, and the final Senate vote was 51 to 50, with the vice president again casting the tie-breaking vote.[84] Clinton had pushed the Congress as far as it could go toward deficit reduction at that time. The budget votes were important in that they made a significant contribution to deficit reduction, but they also demonstrated how fragile congressional support was for the president. The reconciliation packages were the only major pieces of legislation since World War II that were adopted without one vote from the opposition party.[85]

Clinton's decision to abandon his promise of a middle-class tax cut and replace it with a tax increase of 4.3 cents per gallon and tax increases on the wealthy was an important turning point in his administration. He had made a crucial decision and was severely criticized by an important part of the coalition that had elected him, represented by his top campaign aides (Greenwald, Greenberg, Carville, and Begalla), not to mention Republicans, who denounced the plan as irresponsible. But Clinton felt that the long-term health of the economy was at stake and decided to seek deficit reduction. In retrospect, it seems clear that he made the right decision. Interest rates did not spike up, and the country entered its longest economic expansion in history, wiping out the deficit and beginning to pay down the national debt with the first budget surpluses in decades. Clinton, along with George Bush, deserves credit for making the right economic policy decision, despite his earlier campaign promise.

Conclusion: Character, Consistency, and Campaign Promises

The intent of this chapter is not to discount the importance of consistency in politics. Consistency, particularly in significant policy choices, is important as a signal to voters in a democracy. Both consistency and promise keeping are important aspects of character and rightly admired in politicians as well as other people. If politicians cannot be counted on to keep their promises, how can voters decide how to cast their ballots?

But the point of this chapter is that these general rules of conduct—promise keeping and consistency—are not absolute. Merely declaring that a politician is inconsistent or has broken a campaign promise is not sufficient to prove that the elected official is not worthy of respect. The context of the inconsistency, the sincerity of the promise made, and the reasons for breaking a promise are essential components of any conscientious moral judgment. The examples in this chapter illustrate these points.

President Lincoln's public position on the slavery issue was certainly not consistent, yet in the end he engineered historic changes that led to the elimination of slavery and to the Civil War constitutional amendments. He was able to decide to abolish slavery only by carefully gauging public opinion and what was possible at any given time. Politics is the art of the possible, and in a democracy with a political process open to opposing forces, consistency is not always possible.

Franklin Roosevelt did not have a consistent approach to the New Deal, but his experimentation was ultimately successful in alleviating many of the worst effects of the Great Depression. He was not successful in balancing the budget but made serious efforts to do so. His promise in the heat of the 1940 campaign not to send U.S. soldiers to war was imprudent and expedient; yet he was right in his efforts to convince the American people that Hitler had to be confronted.

Candidates Eisenhower and Nixon were appropriately ambiguous in their campaign statements about ending the wars in Korea and Vietnam. President Reagan wanted to keep his promise to balance the budget but was unwilling to admit that he could not cut taxes deeply and increase defense spending greatly at the same time. George Bush made an imprudent and expedient promise in the 1988 campaign that he thought was necessary to get elected, yet he was right to break that promise in order to reduce the deficit. Bill Clinton made his commitment to a middle-class tax cut when he thought the economy needed a stimulus; the decision early in his term to undertake deficit reduction was the right one for the economy. Both Bush and Clinton deserve credit for breaking their promises and thereby helping to create the unprecedented economic expansion of the late 1990s.

In short, consistency and keeping campaign promises are important, but they are not absolute measures of character.

CHAPTER 6

Three Presidents in Crisis

—୬ୟଠ—

*I gave them a sword. And they stuck it in, and they twisted it with relish. And
I guess if I had been in their position, I'd have done the same thing.*
—RICHARD NIXON

Three major crises of confidence have shaken the modern presidency—
Watergate, Iran-Contra, and President Clinton's impeachment. Each of
them was caused not by external threats but by presidential decisions.
Each of them led to serious consideration of impeachment and removal
of the president from office: Nixon resigned in the face of virtually certain impeachment, Reagan saved himself by getting the truth out, and
Clinton was impeached but not removed from office.

These crises were rooted in the character of the presidents involved.
Watergate was based in Richard Nixon's resentment of his political "enemies" and his paranoia about how they were thwarting him. He was
willing to use illegal tactics in order to get back at his political enemies,
and he was willing to lie to cover up the illegal actions. The diversion of
funds to the Contras was allowed to happen because President Reagan
either did not care or did not bother to find out what his subordinates
were doing in his name. Bill Clinton was impeached because he was
willing to risk an illicit relationship and unwilling to take responsibility
for his behavior. He was willing to lie about it and encouraged others to
lie for him.

This chapter examines each case from the perspective of the president's
motives, what happened in the crisis, and its consequences. We then compare the three cases with respect to the key presidential decisions, the
ironies of the outcomes, the personal culpability of each president, and
finally the relative threats to the Constitution and the polity presented by
the crises. The conclusion is that each of the three presidents was guilty of
serious missteps but that President Reagan handled his crisis better by
taking serious steps to get the truth out and that President Clinton's trans-
gressions did not present as serious a threat to the Constitution as the

other two crises. Previous chapters deal with the lies surrounding these three crises, and Chapter 4 considers Clinton's sexual behavior. This chapter, however, analyzes the full context of these self-inflicted wounds to Nixon, Reagan, and Clinton.

Watergate

President Nixon's willingness to use unethical and illegal means to get back at his political enemies reflected his character. His presidency was tragic in the sense that his potential for greatness was undermined by his own actions. The seeds of his destruction were present in his character.

PRESIDENT NIXON'S MOTIVES

The deeper roots of Watergate can be found in Richard Nixon's early resentment of those who grew up in privileged circumstances and did not have to work as hard as he did to achieve success. In Nixon's mind a privileged upbringing became associated with people who thwarted him in his political career; these people included the "Eastern establishment elite," intellectuals in general (especially from Harvard and other Ivy League schools), and the media (especially the *New York Times* and *Washington Post*). President Nixon's resentment also focused on the Democratic political party, the Democratically controlled Congress, the bureaucracy of career civil servants, think tanks (especially the Brookings Institution), antiwar protesters, and civil-rights activists.

Although Nixon was paranoid (in the nontechnical sense of the word) in that he attributed to his enemies powers greater than they actually had and saw threats greater than in reality existed; he did in fact have political enemies. Certainly the Democrats wanted to embarrass him and see him defeated; certainly those who disagreed with his policies wanted to thwart him.[1] But that is the nature of politics, and in a democracy disputes over policy and political power are appropriate and necessary. In Nixon's mind, however, the distinction between the loyal opposition and enemies of the state blurred, and he thus felt justified in using the power of the government to "screw our enemies" (in John Dean's terms). Nixon justified his actions by arguing that Democratic presidents had used various unethical means to their political advantage. But the scale, scope, and means of Nixon's abuse of power were much broader than those of any of his predecessors. Thus President Nixon's character led to the unethical and illegal actions of Watergate.

WHAT HAPPENED

One key turning point came early in his administration when Daniel Ellsberg, a former defense analyst, leaked to the media a lengthy internal analysis of early U.S. policy toward Vietnam. The collection of documents became known as the "Pentagon Papers" and were all concerned with policy making before Nixon became president. Nixon decided that the release of the documents was an unacceptable breach of security and ordered his aides to do something about it. In 1969 he told John Ehrlichman to establish "a little group right here in the White House. Have them get off their tails and find out what's going on and figure out how to stop it."[2] This "little group" became the "plumbers," who were supposed to figure out how to stop leaks and carry out other tasks of political intelligence and sabotage.

In order to discredit Daniel Ellsberg, Nixon operatives broke into the office of Ellsberg's psychiatrist in Los Angeles. Though they did not find anything useful, their intention was probably to find and release embarrassing information about Ellsberg in order to affect his trial for violating security regulations. Breaking and entering is, of course, a crime, and this attempt to deprive Ellsberg of his civil rights was included in Article II of the House Judiciary Committee impeachment charges. Nixon also encouraged breaking into the Brookings Institution to seize documents of those he thought were working on the Pentagon Papers.

The plumbers, who were funded from campaign funds and through the Committee to Reelect the President (CREEP), were to undertake a number of political intelligence operations including the bugging of Larry O'Brien's office at the Democratic National Committee (DNC) headquarters in the Watergate building. The national headquarters of political parties are not the most likely place to find valuable political intelligence, and the Nixon people were probably more interested in finding an illegitimate connection between Larry O'Brien and Howard Hughes. After the 1968 election Nixon had received an illegal campaign contribution from Howard Hughes. But at the same time Hughes also paid Larry O'Brien a retainer. Thus information about the O'Brien-Hughes connection could be used to counter any Democratic disclosure or condemnation of the Nixon-Hughes connection.[3]

On the night of June 17, 1972, five of the plumbers, under the direction of Howard Hunt and Gordon Liddy, broke into DNC headquarters in the Watergate building to repair a listening device they had previously set.

After they were discovered and arrested, investigators learned that the trail led back to the Committee to Reelect the President and the White House. The cover-up of this break-in eventually brought President Nixon down.

In addition to these events, the Nixon White House and reelection campaign undertook a number of other measures that are broadly covered under the rubric of Watergate. Among these were "dirty tricks" to affect the 1972 Democratic primary elections. Since Nixon believed that Senator Edmund Muskie would be his strongest opponent, his operatives tried to undermine Muskie's campaign by disrupting campaign rallies, forging letters, and financing his opponents.[4] White House officials tried to get the IRS to undertake audits on Democratic opponents and their supporters. A plan for political intelligence and operations, the "Huston plan," was approved by Nixon but never implemented.[5] Nixon's counsel John Dean and others drew up lists of political enemies who were to be targets of political retaliation.

Of all of these illicit activities, what eventually caused President Nixon's downfall was his involvement with the cover-up of the crimes. Nixon never seemed to consider seriously the possibility of denouncing the break-in and promising that the White House would not conduct any such activities in the future. Nixon's lawyer, Leonard Garment, recalled

> The transition from bungled break-in to cover-up took place automatically, without discussion, debate, or even the whisper of gears shifting, because the president was personally involved, if not in the Watergate break-in then by authorizing prior Colson and plumber activities like the Ellsberg break-in and a crazy Colson plot to firebomb the Brookings Institution in order to recover a set of the Pentagon Papers. These were potentially more lethal than Watergate. Other factors contributed to the cover-up, but I have no doubt that the main motive was Nixon's sense of personal jeopardy. His decision was not irrational, though it turned out terribly wrong.[6]

In retrospect, Nixon argued that the actions of Watergate themselves were minor but that the cover-up was his big mistake.[7] But he was wrong in this judgment; the illegal activities, including breaking and entering conducted by a secret White House intelligence unit, were serious abuses of power. This is why Nixon felt that the Watergate break-in had to be concealed at all costs. A thorough investigation of Watergate would have opened up the whole "can of worms" that included the other illegal abuses of power in the Nixon White House. And that, in fact, is what happened to the Nixon administration.

THE CONSEQUENCES

When the Watergate burglars were arrested, they did not admit that they were working for Nixon's reelection campaign because Gordon Liddy had assured them that they would be taken care of and their prison sentences would be minor if it came to that. But Judge "Maximum John" Sirica gave them long prison sentences because he suspected that their silence was protecting their superiors. This led to John Dean's discussion with the president about hush money for the jailed plumbers. Dean told the president that it might cost $1 million to keep them quiet. Nixon replied: "We could get that. On the money, if you need the money you could get that. You could get a million dollars. You could get it in cash. I know where it could be gotten."[8] John Dean testified that $500,000 went to Liddy and his men.[9]

The Senate Watergate Committee investigated many aspects of the White House activities and found out that President Nixon had set up a taping system in the White House. The tapes were subpoenaed by the special prosecutor and the House Impeachment Committee. Nixon sent to the committee transcripts of the tapes, but they had been altered in key places. Finally, the Supreme Court ruled that Nixon could not withhold the evidence on the tapes. The turning point in the House came when the "smoking gun" tape was discovered. Until that time, many Republican members of the committee had argued that the evidence against Nixon was not conclusive and that impeachment was so serious a step that only conclusive proof of a crime was sufficient to vote in favor of impeachment.

In the tape of a conversation on June 23, 1972, just five days after the Watergate break-in, H. R. Haldeman told the president that FBI investigators were tracing the money carried by the Watergate burglars and were about to discover that it had come from CREEP and White House safes. He suggested that the way to stop the FBI investigation would be to have the CIA tell the FBI that further investigations would jeopardize CIA operations and they should drop the money trail. Haldeman suggested that "the way to handle this now is for us to have Walters [of the CIA] call Pat Gray [director of the FBI] and just say, 'Stay the hell out of this . . . this is ah, business here we don't want you to go any further on it.'" After this suggestion, Nixon told Haldeman to tell CIA director Richard Helms that "the president believes that it is going to open the whole Bay of Pigs thing up again. And . . . that they [the CIA] should call the FBI in and [unintelligible] don't go any further into this case period!"[10]

The release of the tapes and their damning evidence provided the final impetus for the House Judiciary Committee to vote articles of impeachment. Article I charged the president with failure to fulfill his oath of office and obstruction of justice. It specifically mentioned the break-in of Ellsberg's psychiatrist's office, misuse of the CIA to obstruct the Justice Department investigation, withholding evidence, and counseling perjury, among other things. Article II charged the president with failing to faithfully execute the laws by using the IRS to harass his political opponents, by using the FBI to place unlawful wiretaps on citizens, by maintaining a secret investigative unit in the White House paid for by campaign funds, and by impeding criminal investigations, among other things. Article III charged the president with refusing to honor congressional subpoenas lawfully issued by the House Judiciary Committee and impeding the Congress from constitutionally exercising its impeachment powers. But before the articles could be represented to the full House for action, President Nixon resigned and left office on August 9, 1974.

Iran-Contra

President Reagan's character allowed the Iran-Contra affair to happen. He was not plagued with the resentment that Nixon felt, but it was Reagan's commitment to his policy goals and his unwillingness to oversee his subordinates carefully that led to the scandal that almost caused his downfall.

PRESIDENT REAGAN'S MOTIVES

Despite his relatively humble beginnings, President Reagan did not suffer from the resentment of "the establishment" that had characterized Richard Nixon, and he did not have a similar hatred of his political enemies He was not paranoid about his political enemies and did not seek their destruction. His character, including his motives and personal predispositions, however, contributed to the Iran-Contra affair and seriously damaged his presidency. Reagan held strong convictions about his political values and goals, but he did not often inquire into the implications of the actions necessary to carry out his objectives. His tendency to delegate to his subordinates the responsibility to implement his goals was in some cases good management practice. But on important issues of state and major policy his refusal to look more closely into the means they would use to accomplish his ends could be seen as an abdication of his responsibility as president.

In the Iran part of the Iran-Contra affair, President Reagan let his personal concern for the hostages override his own stated convictions and the policy of the United States government that giving in to terrorists will only lead to more terrorism. This inconsistency on the president's part is understandable and in some ways admirable; his concern for the human beings involved overrode his rational mind. He might have taken more seriously, however, the concern of his secretary of defense that sending arms to Iran was a breach of law.

In the Contra part of the Iran-Contra affair, President Reagan's personal ideological convictions were that the Sandinista government of Nicaragua was a threat to U.S. national-security interests and that the United States should support the Contras. There is nothing wrong or sinister about these convictions, but his concerns set a tone in the White House that led his National Security Council (NSC) advisers to break the law in order to carry out what they were sure were his wishes. Here, the president's failure to inquire more closely into how his White House staff was carrying out his policies can be seen as a serious problem.

If the diversion of funds had been framed as a question and put to him by his aides about whether to break the law, President Reagan would almost certainly have said no (though he was willing to break the law to free the hostages[11]). But if the diversion issue was framed as "we're taking care of the Contras," Reagan might not have inquired too closely as to exactly how they were doing it. Thus President Reagan's character led him to entrust his goals to his subordinates but not to pay sufficient attention to what they were doing in his name.

WHAT HAPPENED

In 1984 and 1985 seven U.S. hostages were kidnapped in Lebanon by Shiite Muslims closely connected to the leaders of Iran. Iran and Iraq were at war, and Iran desperately needed military equipment and spare parts to fix its weapons, many of which had come from the United States during the period when it supported the shah of Iran. Intermediaries proposed a deal that would include the release of the hostages in exchange for the United States supplying spare airplane parts and missiles to Iran.

President Reagan had become extremely concerned with the plight of the hostages, one of whom was a CIA station chief. His concern was reflected by NSC staffers, who made arrangements to exchange U.S. arms and spare parts for Iranian intervention to have the hostages in Lebanon released. NSC staffers also argued that it was important to try to reestablish U.S. ties to moderates in Iran, so that when the Ayatollah Khomeini died, the United States would have some influence in Iran, which the United States did not want to fall under Soviet influence. Israel also wanted to support Iran in its war with Iraq, which Israel considered a greater security threat. So Israel agreed to ship arms to Iran, which would then be replaced by the United States. The United States also shipped TOW missiles and HAWK missiles directly to Iran.

The president's decision to trade arms for hostages can be questioned on several grounds. First, the surface rationalization for the policy was to open relations with moderates in Iran. But it is doubtful that there were any moderates in powerful positions in Iran at the time. The CIA believed that Khomeini was in charge and that no one else would be allowed to negotiate with the Americans, especially about weapons.[12] Second, the United States had a firm policy not to negotiate with terrorists. In a 1985 speech President Reagan said that Iran was part of a "confederation of terrorist states . . . a new international version of Murder Inc. America will never make concessions to terrorists."[13] The Reagan administration had launched "Operation Staunch," a diplomatic campaign to stop U.S. allies in Europe from selling arms to Iran or Iraq.[14]

In a number of meetings in the White House, Secretary of State George Shultz and Secretary of Defense Casper Weinberger argued strenuously against trading arms for hostages (e.g., on August 6 and December 7, 1985, and also on January 7, 1986).[15] Even though Weinberger and Shultz may have been right on the merits of the arguments, the president was elected and clearly has the authority to set policy in the executive branch. Members of the cabinet are merely advisers to the president and implementers of policy, and the president has no obligation to take their advice. On the other hand, sending arms to Iran raised the issue of the Arms Export Control Act of 1976, which prohibited the sale of U.S. arms to nations designated as sponsors of terrorism. Iran had been so designated since 1984. George Shultz asked his legal adviser, Abraham Sofaer, to consider the legality of the arms sale, and Sofaer concluded that such sales would not be legal.[16] In the December 7, 1985, meeting with the president and his top aides, Casper Weinberger argued against the sale of arms and contended that it would violate the Arms Export Control Act.[17]

In addition, the National Security Act specifies that covert actions are to be taken only after an official finding by the president that such actions are important to national security.[18] NSC adviser John Poindexter testified before Congress that President Reagan had signed such a finding for the earlier approaches to Iran but that Poindexter had later destroyed it to save the president from possible embarrassment. President Reagan also signed a finding on January 17, 1986, that authorized U.S. direct arms sales to Iran. The law requires that Congress be notified before covert actions are undertaken or, if that is impossible, "in a timely fashion."[19] Congress did not learn of the arms-for-hostages initiatives until they were disclosed in the Lebanese newspaper *Al-Shiraa* on November 3, 1986.

The Reagan administration's actions to gain the release of the hostages over the course of several shipments of arms turned out to be futile. Several hostages were released, but three more were captured. The courting of moderates in Iran was not successful because first, there were no moderates in power, and second, some of the missiles were inferior equipment for which they were charged artificially high prices.

In the Contra dimension of the Iran-Contra affair, White House aides, particularly NSC adviser Admiral Poindexter and NSC staffer Oliver North undertook to use the "profits" received from the sale of missiles to Iran to aid the Contras in Nicaragua. The problem was that Congress had passed—and President Reagan had signed—a law prohibiting U.S. aid to the Contras. The Boland amendment stated: "During fiscal year 1985, no funds available to the Central Intelligence Agency, the Department of Defense, or any other agency or entity of the United States involved in intelligence activities may be obligated or expended for the purpose or which would have the effect of supporting, directly or indirectly, military or paramilitary operations in Nicaragua by any nation, group, organization, movement or individual" (Public Law 98-473, 98 STAT 1935–37, sec. 8066). The law had not been passed without due deliberation in Congress. From the early 1980s, the Regan administration had believed the Sandinista government of Nicaragua posed a serious threat to U.S. national-security interests, and support of the Contra opposition was a high priority of the administration, which provided financial and operational aid to the Contras. Military aid, however, was subject to a series of limitations written into public law between 1982 and 1986. Despite the best arguments of the Reagan administration, Congress was dubious of the wisdom and efficacy of continuing to arm the Contras. Thus the Boland amendment was passed for fiscal year 1985.[20]

Despite the law the administration was committed to continuing support of the Contras. President Reagan told NSC adviser Robert McFarlane to keep the Contras together "body and soul."[21] NSC staffer Oliver North proposed the "neat idea" of using the money from the sale of arms to Iran to support the Contras by diverting it from the U.S. Treasury, where it should have gone. To carry this out, North and his associates set up secret bank accounts to handle the money.

THE CONSEQUENCES

The secret attempt to fund the Contras was in direct violation of public law and a serious breach of the Constitution. The president's aides decided that what they could not achieve through the public constitutional process (continuing aid to the Contras) they would accomplish through secret means. There was no doubt about what the law prohibited; throughout the 1980s a high-level public debate had raged over aid to the Contras, and the administration had not been able to convince a majority of the Congress that continued military aid to the Contras in 1985 was essential to U.S. security. But White House aides decided that aid to the Contras nevertheless ought to continue. There is no doubt that President Reagan strongly supported aid to the Contras and that he communicated this directly to his staff. Reagan, however, denied any knowledge of the diversion of funds to the Contras, and there is no evidence that he knew about it before Attorney General Edwin Meese discovered it.

Public revelation of arms-for-hostages deals and the diversion of funds to the Contras threw the administration into chaos for a number of months. Opinion polls showed that most Americans believed that President Reagan was lying when he denied that he had traded arms for hostages, and public approval of the president and his administration dropped significantly. George Shultz, Reagan's secretary of state, concluded that Poindexter and North

> had entangled themselves with a gang of operators far more
> cunning and clever than they. As a result, the U.S. government
> had violated its own policies on antiterrorism and against arms
> sales to Iran, was buying our own citizens' freedom in a manner
> that could only *encourage* the taking of others, was working
> through disreputable international go-betweens, was circum-
> venting our constitutional system of governance, and was

misleading the American people—all in the guise of furthering some purported regional political transformation, or to obtain in actuality a hostage release. And somehow, by dressing up this arms-for-hostages scheme and disguising its worst aspects, first McFarlane, and then Poindexter, apparently with the strong collaboration of Bill Casey, had sold it to a president all too ready to accept it, given his humanitarian urge to free American hostages.[22]

Congress held hearings on the affair and concluded that it was a disaster:

In the end, there was no improved relationship with Iran, no lessening of its commitments to terrorism, and no fewer American hostages.

The Iran initiative succeeded only in replacing three American hostages with another three, arming Iran with 2,004 TOWs and more than 200 vital spare parts for HAWK missile batteries, improperly generating funds for the Contras and other covert activities (although far less than North believed), producing profits for the Hakim-Secord Enterprise that in fact belonged to the U.S. taxpayers, leading certain NSC and CIA personnel to deceive representatives of their own Government, undermining U.S. credibility in the eyes of the world, damaging relations between the Executive and the Congress, and engulfing the President in one of the worst credibility crises of an Administration in U.S. history.[23]

Although the possibility of impeachment was discussed in both the executive and the legislative branches, Congress did not pursue it. The feeling in Congress was that the country was not ready to go through another trauma so soon after Watergate. In addition, Congress had no evidence to support the most likely grounds for impeachment—that President Reagan had known about the diversion of funds to the Contras before it happened. The other aspects of the opening to Iran, despite its possible illegality, were not serious enough for impeachment proceedings. In addition, President Reagan did not stonewall the investigations as President Nixon had done and Clinton later did. He established the Tower Board to investigate the matter; he brought in Special Counsel David Abshire to ensure that no cover-up would occur; and when Howard Baker became chief of staff, an exhaustive internal investigation ensued.[24] Reagan refused to claim executive privilege and turned over documents to the independent counsel and congressional investigators. Thus he salvaged his presidency from what might have been much worse consequences. The positive dimensions of his character prevailed in the end and saved his presidency.

President Clinton's Impeachment

President Clinton's impeachment in 1998 grew directly out of his character. His unwillingness to accept responsibility for his actions and tell the truth allowed the Republicans to convince a majority of the House of Representatives that he should be impeached. Even though the Senate voted not to remove him from office, his impeachment left a permanent stain on his presidency and his reputation.

PRESIDENT CLINTON'S MOTIVES

For all of his talents and electoral victories, Bill Clinton still felt like a victim. When the press wrote stories about his past sexual affairs, he felt that they and his enemies were out to thwart him and ruin his career. According to his long-time associate and adviser, Dick Morris, Clinton "was constantly trying to escape blame for anything. Denial spread into a ubiquitous pattern where everything that went wrong was somebody else's fault. Never his."[25] According to scholar Stephen J. Wayne, "When things do not go right, Clinton tends to see himself as victim. He rarely blames himself, however. Clinton not only lashes out at his staff, but also demonizes his opponents."[26]

On January 17, 1998, Clinton testified in a deposition for the Paula Jones case that he had not had sex with Monica Lewinsky. On January 21 the story was made public in the Washington Post. After the story broke about Clinton's affair with Monica Lewinsky, the turning point seemed to be when Clinton decided to lock himself irrevocably into lying about his relationship with Lewinsky. Clinton's motive was to avoid personal embarrassment and injury to his standing with the public. As he later considered whether to admit that he had lied, his motives came to include avoiding the legal ramifications of admitting that he had broken the law. Clinton's character became evident in his willingness to lie rather than to accept responsibility for his actions.

WHAT HAPPENED

Shortly after graduating from college in June, 1995, Monica Lewinsky came to work in the White House as one of many interns. While in a new job at the Pentagon, she made friends with a former White House secretary, Linda Tripp, who had been the source for a news story about an encounter between President Clinton and Kathleen Willey in the White House. When the president's lawyer questioned Tripp's credibility in the fall of 1997, Tripp began to tape her phone conversations with Lewinsky. The tapes contained assertions by Lewinsky about her relationship with the president and her frustration because he was not calling her.

In the meantime, the suit brought against the president by Paula Jones had been under way for several years. Jones alleged that, in a 1999 encounter in a Little Rock hotel room, then Governor Clinton had crudely propositioned her and that she had turned him down. The suit was a civil action alleging sexual harassment. In the course of building their case, Jones's lawyers were gathering evidence about other women with whom Clinton might have had relationships over the years in order to demonstrate a pattern of sexual harassment.

The president gave a deposition in the Paula Jones lawsuit on January 17, 1998. With knowledge of the Tripp-Lewinsky tapes, the lawyers for Paula Jones asked Clinton whether he had had sex with Lewinsky. When asked about an affair, Clinton denied a sexual relationship. His denial would provide grounds for charges of perjury and eventual impeachment if independent counsel Kenneth Starr could prove that Clinton and Lewinsky had in fact had a sexual relationship. Having sex with an intern is not illegal (however wrong it might be), but intentionally lying about it in a civil deposition could constitute perjury. Thus the question by Jones's lawyers about Lewinsky set Clinton up for a possible perjury charge. Because of the tapes, Starr suspected that Clinton might have tried to illegally cover up their affair.

After Clinton publicly denied the affair, Kenneth Starr's investigation continued through the spring and summer of 1998. In July Starr came to an agreement with Monica Lewinsky that assured her of immunity from prosecution based on her testimony about her relationship with Clinton. Lewinsky testified in detail about their relationship and provided evidence that convinced the grand jury that she and Clinton had had a sexual relationship. With the evidence from Lewinsky's testimony, Starr sought to subpoena the president to testify before a grand jury.

THE CONSEQUENCES

In the face of the subpoena, President Clinton agreed to testify "voluntarily" before Kenneth Starr's grand jury on August 17, 1998, about his relationship with Lewinsky. During four hours of close questioning by Starr's lawyers President Clinton carefully answered most questions but still maintained that he had not lied in his denial of a sexual relationship with her. The president was clearly equivocating in his answers to some of the questions about their relationship.

In the evening after his deposition the president made a statement about his testimony in a nationally televised broadcast. He told the nation that he regretted his relationship with Lewinsky and its consequences. "Indeed, I did have a relationship with Miss Lewinsky that was not appropriate. In fact, it was wrong. It constituted a critical lapse in judgment and a personal failure on my part for which I am solely and completely responsible. . . . I know that my public comments and my silence about this matter gave a false impression. I misled people, including even my wife. I deeply regret that." In his statement Clinton also criticized Starr for his relentless pursuit of evidence: "It is time to stop the pursuit of personal destruction and the prying into private lives and get on with our national life."

Several weeks later, on September 9, Starr sent his report to Congress concerning possible impeachable offenses by President Clinton. The list of charges included allegations that the president had lied under oath in his deposition in the Paula Jones sexual harassment case and in his testimony on August 17, that he had urged Lewinsky and his secretary to lie under oath, that he had tried to obstruct justice by having his secretary hide evidence, and that he had tried to get Ms. Lewinsky a job to discourage her from revealing their relationship.

On October 5 the House Judiciary Committee voted 21 to 16 along party lines to recommend impeachment hearings. Three days later, on October 8, the full House voted 258 to 176 (with thirty-one Democrats voting in favor and no Republicans against) to open an impeachment inquiry. On December 11 and 12 the committee voted along party lines in favor of four articles of impeachment. The Republicans easily defeated a Democratic motion to censure the president, and the articles were reported to the full House.

The formal impeachment debate opened on December 18 on the floor of the House of Representatives, with the Republicans arguing that Clinton had corrupted the rule of law by committing perjury and obstructing justice and the Democrats arguing that he should be censured but not impeached. Democrats and moderate Republicans who felt that Clinton's actions were reprehensible but not impeachable wanted to vote to censure Clinton. Democrats proposed censure language that harshly condemned Clinton for making "false statements concerning his reprehensible conduct" and for "violat[ing] the trust of the American people, lessen[ing] their esteem for the office of the President, and dishonor[ing]" the presidency.[27] But the motions for censure were not successful.

The House of Representatives met on December 19, 1998, and adopted two articles of impeachment. Article I charged that President Clinton had "willfully provided perjurious, false and misleading testimony to the grand jury" on August 17, 1998, concerning his relationship with Monica Lewinsky and his attempts to conceal it. Article II charged that President Clinton had "prevented, obstructed, and impeded the administration of justice" in order to "delay, impede, cover up, and conceal the existence of evidence and testimony" in the Paula Jones case by encouraging a witness to lie, concealing evidence, and trying to prevent truthful testimony by finding a job for Lewinsky. Each of these articles concluded that "William Jefferson Clinton has undermined the integrity of his office, has brought disrepute on the Presidency, has betrayed his trust as President, and has acted in a manner subversive of the rule of law and justice, to the manifest injury of the people of the United States." The two articles charging both perjury in the Paula Jones deposition of January 17 and failure to respond adequately to congressional inquiries were defeated.

The trial in the Senate opened on January 7, 1999. The House impeachment brief argued that the president had indeed committed the crimes charged in the two articles—that he had lied under oath before the grand jury investigating him on August 17, 1998 (Article I), and that he had attempted to obstruct justice by encouraging Lewinsky to lie about their relationship, concealing evidence, and getting Lewinsky a job. On February 12, 1999, the final votes were taken, and both articles failed to receive the two-thirds majority necessary for conviction and removal from office.

Comparing Three Presidents in Crisis

When confronted with potentially damaging public revelations about his behavior, each one of these presidents faced a crisis of character. Each acted initially to limit the political damage to himself and his administration, and each chose a course of behavior that would threaten his presidency. Admitting to the truth of the alleged improper behavior would have damaged their administrations, but their failures to respond truthfully led directly to much worse damage.

At a deeper level each president could not initially admit to himself that he had done anything wrong. Richard Nixon rationalized his administration's actions by arguing that Democratic presidents had done the same thing and that his enemies were out to destroy him. Ronald Reagan rationalized his trading of arms for hostages by arguing that the hostages were merely a side issue in a strategic opening to Iran. Bill Clinton rationalized his lies by arguing that his enemies were out to get him, that other presidents had done worse, that his private life was not the public's business, and that he was technically telling the truth. Each of these sets of rationalization allowed the presidents to choose a path that would end up damaging them more than an initial admission would have.

THE KEY DECISIONS

Each president made initial key decisions that reflected character flaws that got them in trouble.

When he first heard about the Watergate break-in Richard Nixon did not hesitate; he followed his first instinct, which was to limit the political damage and cover up the incident. His decision was based in part on a rational calculation that publication of the incident would hurt him politically and might uncover other damaging evidence of illegal behavior by other White House and reelection committee aides. His character flaw was his resentment of his political adversaries, which led him to put his short-term, partisan interests above telling the truth and obeying the law.

Ronald Reagan's initial reaction when the McFarlane trip to Iran was made public was to deny that a problem existed. He argued that the actions of his highest aides were merely intended to bring about an opening to Iran. His character flaw was to be so confident in his own good intentions that he could not admit his true motives, and he did not devote sufficient energy to overseeing the actions of his subordinates. He knew he did not approve of trading arms for hostages, so he concluded that he could not have done so. After weeks of publicity and press reports and after strong prodding by David Abshire and George Shultz, he was finally convinced that he had to tell the truth. He saved himself from further damage from the diversion of funds to the Contras by fully cooperating with the investigations, refusing to invoke executive privilege, and turning over requested documents. He thus stemmed the damage to his presidency in a way that the other two presidents did not. Although the diversion of funds was a grave constitutional issue, it was done without President Reagan's knowledge.

Bill Clinton's character flaw stemmed from his resentment of his political enemies and his unwillingness to admit his own culpability. His first instinct was to deny his sexual relationship with Monica Lewinsky, just as he had with previous allegations of sexual impropriety. He seemed to consider the possibility of telling the truth after the allegations became public, but after the poll by Dick Morris, he concluded that confessing to a lie would hurt him too much politically, so he embarked on a firm policy of denial that resulted in his impeachment.

IRONIES

The initial irony is that each president's denial and cover-up hurt him more than they would have if he had immediately admitted the truth about his previous behavior. The cost would have been quite high for each, but the truth came out in the end and caused more harm at that late stage than an early admission would have.

The more profound irony, however, is that none of the three breaches of trust by these presidents or their aides was necessary or achieved the goals they had hoped for.

Richard Nixon did not need illegal help to get reelected in 1972. Even if Edmund Muskie was the Democratic candidate, Nixon's foreign and domestic policy record was sufficiently popular to put him in a strong position. Thus the actions that led to the cover-up and other illegal actions were unnecessary; it was only Nixon's paranoia and the tone he set that encouraged his aides to undertake the actions that eventually caused his downfall.

Ronald Reagan's selling of arms to Iran did not achieve freedom for the hostages; those who were freed were replaced by others. The selling of inferior arms at inflated prices did not endear the United States to Iran. Iran also had its own security reasons for not wanting to be pulled into the Soviet orbit. The diversion of funds from Iran to the Contras did not make a big difference in their ability to resist the government of Nicaragua. Only a small percentage of the funds intended for the Contras actually got to them.

Bill Clinton did not need to lie in his deposition in the Paula Jones case. The judge dismissed the case several months later even though it had been revealed that Clinton had lied. Neither did he need to lie directly to the American people in his finger-pointing statement. As became evident after his lies were revealed, public support for him was strong enough to weather that storm. Clinton's highest public-approval ratings came during his impeachment and trial. His treatment of Kenneth Starr as his nemesis became a self-fulfilling prophesy when Starr pursued Clinton and revealed his most private and embarrassing actions.

THEY DID IT TO THEMSELVES

Each president felt that his political enemies and the press were the cause of his troubles, but in fact each of these presidents was the primary cause of his own problems. A character flaw was the fundamental cause of their self-inflicted wounds.

Richard Nixon had developed deep suspicions about his political enemies and the tactics they would use to get him. But these suspicions were often projections of the tactics he used to get his enemies. Certainly Nixon had political enemies and they wanted to beat him politically, but that is the nature of politics. Nixon's overreaction and actions against his enemies were the very things that accomplished what his enemies never could have: his resignation from the presidency in disgrace. Nixon's epiphany came in the last moments of his presidency in his farewell remarks just before leaving for California: "[A]lways remember, others may hate you, but those who hate you don't win unless you hate them, and then you destroy yourself."[28]

Ronald Reagan felt that the press was guilty of embarrassing him and undermining his attempts to repair relations with Iran. He felt that Congress tried to obstruct his policies and was generally irresponsible. Certainly Congress had policy preferences that differed from Reagan's and passed laws of which he did not approve. But it was neither the press nor Congress that initiated the doomed arms-for-hostages initiative, and it was not their fault that North and Poindexter felt justified in breaking the law. It was Ronald Reagan's decision to trade arms for hostages, and it was his approach to policy direction and the way in which he managed his White House that allowed his subordinates to pursue their illegal actions.

Bill Clinton had long blamed his enemies for working to bring him down. He felt that the press was hostile to him, and his wife blamed a "vast right-wing conspiracy" for attempting to orchestrate his downfall. Certainly Clinton had political enemies who were doing their best to undermine him. But it was not his political enemies who initiated his affair with Monica Lewinsky or led him to lie about it. His own denial of his actions as well as his refusal to take responsibility for his behavior caused his disaster. Even if LBJ and JFK had engaged in similar behavior, it was wrong for them also. But the press had changed, and Clinton should have understood that. He was wrong on both moral and prudential grounds.

THREATS TO THE CONSTITUTION AND THE POLITY

The central themes in each of these crises of the presidency are the rule of law, accountability to the Constitution, and abuse of power. The major threat in Watergate was to the domestic political process, the integrity of elections, and the civil rights of citizens. The major threat in Iran-Contra was to the constitutional role of Congress, the president's obligation to faithfully execute the laws, and accountability to the Constitution. The major threat in the Clinton case was to the president's respect for the judicial process and his obligation to obey the law.

The Watergate activities constituted a major threat to civil liberties and the integrity of the political and electoral process. White House aides paid a secret unit that was unaccountable to anyone but its political directors to intimidate Nixon's political enemies and illegally gather information. President Nixon used governmental agencies, such as the U.S. Treasury, FBI, and CIA for illegitimate and illegal activities. His campaign operatives illegitimately interfered with the political and electoral process. In addition to his own lies and illegal actions, President Nixon set the tone so that his campaign and White House aides thought he wanted them to undertake illegal and unethical activities in support of his reelection, which they did.

The Iran-Contra case presented a major threat to the rule of law and the constitutional balance between the president and Congress. Secretary of Defense Weinberger warned the president that the arms-for-hostages deal might violate the law and was unwise policy. The president's failure to notify Congress about the covert action was even more troubling. But the most serious problem was the diversion of funds to the Contras in direct violation of the law. The president's aides also destroyed evidence, produced false chronologies, and lied to Congress to hide their actions. William Casey intended to set up "the Enterprise" to generate money that could be spent at his direction entirely unaccountable to the Congress, the Constitution, or the law.

The threat to the Constitution was not merely the sidestepping of the legitimate role of Congress in making foreign policy in the violations of the Arms Export Control Act and the failure to notify Congress as the National Security Act requires. These violations of the law were serious but probably did not rise to the level of "high crimes and misdemeanors." The diversion of funds to the Contras, however, violated the law and constituted a serious breach of the Constitution by allowing the executive to make policy unilaterally in contravention of the explicit will of Congress as expressed in public law signed by the president. If such practices were permitted, they might indeed lead to the tyranny of the executive that the framers of the Constitution had feared. If the president had known and approved of the diversion of funds, impeachment proceedings would likely have resulted.

As it was, there was no evidence that President Reagan had knowledge of the diversion of funds until the attorney general's aides discovered it. Thus Congress took no impeachment actions. President Reagan's actions in the aftermath of the public disclosures were clearly superior to the reactions of Presidents Nixon and Clinton to their crises. He ordered that the truth be found, and he cooperated with the investigative authorities.

On the other hand, despite the independent counsel's conclusion that "President Reagan's conduct fell well short of criminality which could be successfully prosecuted," he failed to carry out all of his duties as president.[29] The congressional committee that investigated the Iran-Contra affair concluded:

> [T]he ultimate responsibility for the events in the Iran-Contra
> Affair must rest with the President. If the President did not know
> what his national Security Advisers were doing, he should have.
> . . . It was the president's policy—not an isolated decision by
> North or Poindexter—to sell arms secretly to Iran and to maintain
> the Contras "body and soul," the Boland Amendment notwith-
> standing. . . . The President created or at least tolerated an environ-
> ment where those who did know of the diversion believed with
> certainty that they were carrying out the President's policies.[30]

What President Reagan was guilty of was setting a tone in the White House that encouraged his most senior aides to believe that they were carrying out his wishes when they undertook to violate the law by giving aid to the Contras. With respect to selling arms to Iran, Reagan was willing to continue even after his secretaries of state and defense argued that it might be illegal.

The major issues that President Clinton's impeachment raises are not so much his personal behavior, which was deplorable, but his lying about it under oath in legal proceedings. His lies undermined the judicial system, which depends on the truthful testimony of all, particularly government officials. His lies to the American people also undermined the trust of citizens in the president and the government more generally. President Clinton was also guilty of setting the tone in his White House, where lying was acceptable insofar as his aides and appointed officials also lied to the public in his defense, even though they probably privately suspected that the president was lying. His lies and actions were corrupting.

Clinton's behavior was thus corrupting of several members of the executive branch, and he did not take care to faithfully execute the laws. His actions were deplorable and wrong but did not constitute the same level of institutional threat to the polity that Watergate and Iran-Contra did.

CHAPTER 7

Character Complexity

—ɯɯ—

If they sometimes lie in the strenuous task, it is regrettable but understand-
able. If they sometimes truckle, that is despicable but tolerable. If they are
sometimes bribed, that is more execrable but still not fatal. The vices of our
politicians we must compare not with the virtues of the secluded individual
but with the vices of dictators. . . . People elsewhere get killed in the conflicts of
interest over which our politicians preside with vices short of crimes and with
virtues not wholly unakin to magnanimity.

—T. V. SMITH

Presidents are complex human beings with many admirable attributes but who often exhibit less commendable traits. They are, after all, human. This chapter presents illustrations of presidential character complexity, beginning with the paradox of Richard Nixon's anti-Semitism. It then takes up George Washington and the issue of slavery. How do we evaluate the character of a man so sterling in most respects, yet who owned, bought, and sold human beings? Next we weigh the important contributions of Presidents Lyndon Johnson, Ronald Reagan, and Bill Clinton against their faults. The point of doing so is that, in evaluating presidential character, we ought not to focus solely on the negative but rather consider the full range of a president's contributions (though this does not mean that we overlook or excuse immoral behavior). The chapter concludes by urging that we aspire to realism in our expectations of presidential behavior.

When tapes of President Nixon's Oval Office conversations were released, they contained a number of anti-Semitic remarks. "The Jews are all over the government," he complained to H. R. Haldeman in 1971.[1] He was concerned that the Bureau of Labor Statistics was out to undermine him by releasing economic data showing that unemployment was increasing, and he asked his aides to investigate: "They are all Jews?" He also asked about a junior national security aide of Henry Kissinger, "Is Tony Lake Jewish?" (He wasn't.)[2] Nixon wondered about the 1968 demonstrators in Chicago: "Aren't the Chicago Seven all Jewish?" he asked Haldeman. (They weren't.)[3] Nixon suspected that liberals and Democrats were out to get him and thought that many of them were Jewish. "Now here's the point, Bob, please get me the names of the Jews, you know, the big Jewish contributors of the Democrats. . . . All right. Could we please investigate some of the [expletive]? That's all."[4]

On the face of it, Nixon's remarks are disturbing. Given centuries of persecution of Jews and Hitler's "final solution," any expression of anti-Semitism should be a matter of concern, especially in a person who wields great power. But in Nixon's case, anti-Semitic remarks did not lead to negative public-policy actions toward Jews. Jewish columnist Charles Krauthammer argues that internal attitudes ought not to matter in public officials. What counts is their actions and public policies: "[B]oth in his personal relations and in his public actions as president, he was a friend of Jews."[5] Nixon's defenders point in particular to his support of Israel during the 1973 Yom Kippur war.

Nixon's statement that "Most Jews are disloyal. . . . You can't trust the bastards" was belied by some of his top-level appointments: Alan Greenspan and Herbert Stein as CEA chairs, William Safire as speechwriter, Arthur Burns as adviser, and Leonard Garment as counsel. Garment wrote that Nixon "was a champion equal-opportunity hater" and that his anti-Semitic remarks were merely part of his general paranoia. But "[h]is anti-Semitic outbursts in the private conversations found virtually no correspondence in his speech or actions outside those explosions."[6]

Nixon's anti-Semitic remarks, if known before an election, might justify voting for his opponent because of the potential for misuse of power by one so evidently prejudiced. But in retrospect, Nixon's expressed feelings did not seem to affect his policy judgment, which was favorable toward Israel, or his appointment of prominent Jews to high-level positions. Thus the remarks should not be weighed as heavily in our evaluation of his presidency as his actions, both positive and negative. Yet his comments, in light of twentieth-century history, are still disturbing. As Michael Beschloss concluded, "the voice on the tapes rankles still."[7]

George Washington and Slavery

George Washington's character was recognized as sterling during his lifetime, and the assumption that he would be the first president played a key role in the formulation and adoption of the Constitution. Even during his lifetime he was revered by many, and after his death he was exalted almost to the point of apotheosis. At the dedication of the Washington Monument in 1885, Robert C. Winthrop declared: "Does not that Colossal Unit remind all who gaze at it . . . that there is one name in American history above all other names, one character more exalted than all other characters, . . . one bright particular star in . . . our firmament, whose guiding light and peerless lustre are for all men and all ages . . . ?"[8]

More recently, scholars have also written of Washington's admirable character. Seymour Martin Lipset argues that Washington's character was essential to the founding of the Republic because of his personal prestige, his commitment to the principles of constitutional government, and his key precedent of leaving office after two terms.[9] David Abshire argues that Washington was not perfect but that he learned from his experience and that his public character was not different from his private behavior.[10] Joseph Epstein writes that Washington's "genius was perhaps the rarest kind of all: a genius for discerning right action so strong that he was utterly incapable of knowingly doing anything wrong." Epstein laments: "Each generation of our politicians today, at the end of their careers, happily peddle their influence in large law firms, or simply set up as straight lobbyists for causes in which they can have no real belief. Washington would have been aghast."[11] Perhaps Washington would have been aghast if he had known about modern politicians cashing in on their government experience. But then, modern politicians do not have slaves to provide for their economic well-being. The question we address here is, What light does slavery shed on the nature of Washington's character?

WASHINGTON'S CHANGING ATTITUDE TOWARD SLAVERY

George Washington was born into a slave-holding family, and he continued to increase his human property until late in his life. When he was eleven years old (in 1743), Washington's father died and left him 10 slaves. When Washington's half-brother died in 1752, he inherited a larger number of slaves. In an agreement with his half-brother's widow, Washington acquired Mount Vernon along with 18 more slaves; he eventually added 5,600 acres of land to Mount Vernon. In 1759 Washington married Martha Dandridge Custis, a widow who brought with her several hundred more slaves. The slaves who came with Martha were legally "dower slaves," and Washington kept them separate in his financial accounting, though for practical purposes they were used as Washington's property in the running of Mount Vernon. Although the counts may not be exact due to conflicting records, Washington's slave holdings steadily increased during his lifetime, from 49 in 1760, to 87 in 1770, to 135 in 1774, to 317 when he died in 1799.[12]

Through most of Washington's life up to the Revolutionary War his attitude toward slavery was much like that of most slave owners in the American South. He fed them adequately as important components of the operation of his plantation at Mount Vernon.[13] Though Washington did not encourage the whipping of slaves by his overseers, he condoned it when deemed necessary for discipline.[14] He bought and sold slaves and threatened to sell disruptive slaves to owners in the West Indies as the ultimate enforcement of discipline. Conditions in the West Indies were even harsher than in the United States, and the tropical climate and probability of disease made the threat a serious one. For instance, in 1766 Washington wrote to Captain Joseph Thompson, a slave trader, that "With this Letter comes a Negro (Tom) which I beg the favour of you to sell . . . for whatever he will fetch. . . . This Fellow is both a Rogue & Runaway . . . [though] he is exceeding healthy, strong, and good at the Hoe. . . . and [I] must beg the favour of you (least he shoud [sic] attempt his escape) to keep him handcuffd till you get to Sea."[15] Nor did Washington hesitate to pursue slaves who escaped his plantation.

It appears that Washington's attitude toward slavery, though not his public position, began to change during the Revolutionary War, when he left Mount Vernon to lead the Continental Army.[16] Washington's change of perspective may have stemmed from the necessity of extending to slaves the opportunity to enlist in the Continental Army. Initially, when Washington went to Massachusetts to lead the Continental Army in 1775 he removed the free black soldiers from the army.[17] Southern slave owners did not want to take the risk of allowing slaves to join the army and bear arms. But in 1775 Lord Dunmore, the royal governor of Virginia, issued a proclamation that any black who joined the British forces would be granted freedom. Washington thus felt compelled to allow the free blacks to reenlist and fight with the revolutionary forces, lest they constitute an effective force for the British against their former owners.[18] During the war, with blacks constituting twenty percent of his army, Washington treated them as human beings and with the respect due to any soldier.[19] He also witnessed their willingness to fight and die for the revolutionary cause. After the war, perhaps because of his experience, Washington's attitude toward slavery began to change, though his public position did not.

In the winter of 1778–1779 Washington considered selling his slaves and investing the capital, in part because he did not want to "traffic in the human species," but he didn't seriously pursue the idea.[20] In 1783 the Marquis de Lafayette proposed that he and Washington establish a small estate and work it with free blacks as tenants rather than slaves and added that "Such an example as yours might render it a general practice."[21] Washington praised Lafayette's character, but nothing ever came of the proposal. In 1786 Washington wrote to Robert Morris, "I can only say that no man living wishes more sincerely than I do to see the abolition of [slavery] . . . by slow, sure, and imperceptible degrees."[22] Washington's contemporary David Humphreys quoted Washington as regretting the institution of slavery: "The unfortunate condition of the persons whose labors I in part employed has been the only unavoidable subject of regret."[23] Though Washington had resolved not to engage in the buying or selling of slaves, when he returned to Mount Vernon after the war, he continued to manage his estate, fully utilizing the slave labor that was essential to its economic viability.

When Washington went to Philadelphia to preside over the Constitutional Convention, it was widely known that he was one of the largest slaveholders in Virginia. At the convention his prestige and reputation were second to none, and he weighed his actions and words carefully because he was aware of their political effect. His acceptance of the institution of slavery and his refusal to make any public statement against it undoubtedly influenced the deliberations of the delegates against taking any steps against slavery, despite strong arguments to do so.[24] But it is also probable that if the Constitution had contained proscriptions on slavery the Southern states would not have ratified it.

As president, Washington was careful to stay neutral on the slavery issue. His only official act on the issue was to sign the Fugitive Slave Law, which Congress passed in February, 1793. In 1791, as president in Philadelphia, Washington feared that if he were considered legally a resident, his household slaves might be automatically freed under local laws. He ordered Tobias Lear to take some of his slaves back to Mount Vernon. "I wish to have it accomplished under a pretext that may deceive both them and the public. . . . I request that these sentiments and this advice may be known to none but *yourself* and *Mrs. Washington*."[25]

In 1793 Washington "entertained serious thoughts" of dividing his Mount Vernon estate and renting the land to English farmers who would employ his slaves as free laborers. Washington could thus live off of the rent. His purpose was "to liberate a certain species of property which I possess very repugnantly to my own feelings, but which imperious neces- sity compels, and until I can substitute some other expedient by which expenses not in my power to avoid (however well disposed I may be to do it) can be defrayed."[26] Washington was not able to find suitable English farmers to rent Mount Vernon.

Despite Washington's private reservations about slavery, as late as 1796, when he was president, Washington sought the return of Oney Judge, a slave who had escaped to New Hampshire. Denouncing "the ingrati- tude of the girl," he wrote in a letter that she "ought not to escape with impunity if it can be avoided."[27] On the day in 1797 that Washington left Philadelphia after his presidency to return to Mount Vernon, one of his other slaves escaped rather than return to work on Washington's plan- tation. Washington sought his return but feared he would have to re- place him by buying another. He wrote to Major George Lewis, "The running off of my cook has been a most inconvenient thing to this fam- ily, and what renders it more disagreeable, is, that I had resolved never to become the master of another slave by *purchase*, but this resolution I fear I must break."[28] He continued to seek the return of his property into 1798, the year before his death, though he did not purchase another slave.

HOW GENERAL WAS THE ACCEPTANCE OF SLAVERY?

It has been argued that Washington grew up in an era when and in a part of the country where slavery was taken for granted and widely accepted by the white population; thus he should not be held accountable for his behavior with respect to owning slaves. This perspective maintains that we should not impose twentieth-century values on eighteenth-century people and blame them for violating what are only recently accepted as human rights. Although this argument might be accepted with respect to some aspects of changing attitudes toward human rights, such as eco- nomic and political rights, the issue of slavery is much more basic. The owning and disposition of other human beings as property, despite vari- ous precedents in human history, is such a basic breach of human values that it is hard to excuse.[29] Other forms of economic or social exploitation pale in comparison with the evil of slavery. Thus we must acknowledge that Washington, even though he was more humane than some other slave owners, may have had a character flaw in his behavior with respect to slavery.

His culpability for his behavior might be mitigated if slavery was so universally accepted that no one was speaking out against it. But from the earliest days of the European colonization of North America, religious groups such as the Methodists, the Puritans, the Quakers, and the Mennonites and individuals such as James Oglethorpe, William Penn, and Roger Williams had raised their voices against slavery.[30] In 1785 a Virginia Quaker, Robert Pleasants, wrote a letter to Washington, saying in part:

> How strange then must it appear to impartial thinking men, to be informed, that many who were warm advocates for that noble cause during the War, are now siting down in a state of ease, dissipation and extravigance on the labour of Slaves? . . . It seems highly probable to me, that thy example & influence at this time, towards a general emancipation, would be as productive of real happiness to mankind, as thy Sword may have been: I can but wish therefore, that thou may not loose the opertunity of Crowning the great Actions of thy Life, with the sattisfaction of, "doing to Others as thou would (in the like Situation) be done by," and finally transmit to future ages a Character, equally Famous for thy Christian Virtues, as thy worldly achievements. [Spelling as in the original][31]

There is no record that Washington ever responded to the letter. Later in his life, in 1796, Edmund Rushton wrote to Washington:

> Shame! Shame! That man should be deemed the property of man or that the name of Washington should be found among the list of such proprietors. . . . Ages to come will read with Astonishment that the man who was foremost to wrench the rights of America from the tyrannical grasp of Britain was among the last to relinquish his own oppressive hold of poor unoffending negroes. In the name of justice what can induce you thus to tarnish your own well earned celebrity and to impair the fair features of American liberty with so foul and indelibile [sic] a blot."[32]

Washington's unwillingness to abandon slavery or even speak out publicly against it can be contrasted with some of the other founders at the Constitutional Convention, such as Luther Martin and Gouverneur Morris, both of whom denounced slavery at the convention. John Adams was a consistent opponent of slavery.[33] George Mason, a slave owner who was a close friend and neighbor of Washington, sought the end of slave trading, declaring: "This infernal traffic originated in the avarice of British Merchants. . . . Every master of slaves is born a petty tyrant. . . . By an inevitable chain of cause & effects providence punishes national sins, by national calamities. . . . [T]he Genl. Govt. Should have the power to prevent the increase of slavery."[34] But Mason's position against the slave trade did not mean that he favored giving the national government the authority to abolish slavery. Virginians had an economic interest in the continuation of slavery, and their own slave property would multiply naturally; thus they would benefit from the ending of the slave trade in the United States but did not want their own slaves to be freed.[35]

Yet not all Virginians accepted slavery as natural and inevitable. The Commonwealth of Virginia passed a law in 1782 providing that owners of slaves could grant them freedom if they wished; by 1790 more than 12,000 slaves had been freed, and by 1800 there were 20,000 free blacks in Virginia.[36] Most of the Northern states had declared slavery illegal in the late 1770s and early 1780s and had abolished it by 1804.[37] A number of antislavery motions were introduced in the U.S. Congress as well as the Virginia legislature. In 1790 Benjamin Franklin, who was president of the Pennsylvania Society for Promoting the Abolition of Slavery, signed an antislavery document brought to the House of Representatives.[38] Though Franklin had owned and traded slaves in the 1730s, he came to see slavery as unwise as well as immoral. He wrote and spoke out on the evils of slavery from the 1750s until his death.[39]

Although many of the abolitionists did not benefit from slavery personally and had little to lose in advocating its abolition, such was not the case with Robert Carter III, grandson of the notorious Robert "King" Carter, who "seasoned" his newly arrived slaves from Africa by a "minor dismemberment—perhaps a finger or a toe."[40] The grandson was a correspondent of Jefferson, Madison, Mason, and Patrick Henry and a neighbor of Washington. He was a significant member of the landed gentry who owned more land, slaves, and books than either Washington or Jefferson. He lent money to Jefferson and hesitated to allow his daughter to marry into the Washington family.[41] In 1791 Carter decided that "Slavery is contrary to the true Principles of Religion and Justice, and that therefor it was my duty to manumit them."[42] Over a period of years Carter proceeded to free his slaves, at least 280 and probably many more, possibly as many as 500.[43]

Thus slavery was not universally accepted in Washington's time, even by Southern landholders, and many voices were raised against it, some of them directed personally at Washington.

WASHINGTON FACES THE SLAVERY ISSUE

Toward the end of his life Washington privately expressed opinions critical of slavery. In 1797, in a letter to his nephew, Washington confided: "I wish from my soul that the Legislature of this State could see the policy of a gradual Abolition of Slavery; it would prevt. much future mischief."[44] John Bernard talked with Washington about slavery in the summer of 1798 and quoted him as saying that the end of slavery was "an event, sir, which, you may believe me, no man desires more heartily that I do. Not only do I pray for it, on the score of human dignity, but I can clearly foresee that nothing but the rooting out of slavery can perpetuate the existence of our union, by consolidating it in a common bond of principle."[45]

Finally, at the end of his life, Washington fully faced the implications of his changed attitude toward slavery. When he was drawing up his will in the summer of 1799 he made "the first and only tangible commitment . . . to the emancipation of the slaves."[46] Washington decided to free those slaves who belonged completely to him at the death of his wife, Martha. The dower slaves that she had brought to the marriage would remain in her estate. His will provided:

Item Upon the decease of my wife, it is my Will & desire that all the Slaves which I hold in *my own right*, shall receive their freedom . . . it not being in my power, under the tenure by which the Dower Negroes are held, to manumit them. . . . [T]hey . . . shall be comfortably cloathed & fed by my heirs while they live . . . taught to read & write; and to be brought up to some useful occupation. . . . And I do hereby expressly forbid the Sale, or transportation out of the said Commonwealth, of any Slave I may die possessed of.[47]

Washington set up a fund for their support as long as they lived. Martha Custis Washington, however, decided to free his slaves after a year rather than waiting until her death, fearing that there might be motive on the part of some to speed their freedom by quickening her demise. But Martha still possessed about 150 dower slaves in her own right whom she left, along with Mount Vernon, to her heirs.[48]

How then should we evaluate Washington's character with respect to slavery? His motives for freeing his slaves at the end of his life probably ranged from guilt to a recognition that abolition was inevitable if the United States was to survive, to an act of personal generosity toward those who had served him during his life.[49] But the deeper reality was that Washington benefitted from his slaves all of his life. Slavery made his wealth possible, and he was unwilling to make the serious economic sacrifice of freeing his slaves as long as he depended on their work for his income.

His public silence on the issue along with his own slave holdings, given his reputation, must have had an important effect on the willingness of others to go along and not question the status quo. Washington's reputation was so great that even a small public gesture or statement might have made a large difference. Scholar Joseph Ellis argues that regarding slavery Washington, "perhaps alone, possessed the stature to have altered the political context if he had chosen to do so." Observing that Washington had what John Adams called "the gift of silence," Ellis concludes that "this was one occasion when one could only have wished that the gift had failed him."[50] Thus Washington's vice, as well as his virtues, had important public effects.

The most persuasive argument that Washington's lack of public opposition to slavery was based on admirable motives might be that any sudden move to abolish slavery would have alienated the Southern states so much that the Union would have been in peril. At the time of the Constitutional Convention any public move by Washington in the direction of emancipation might have jeopardized the willingness of the Southern states to join the Union and ratify the Constitution. His silence as president, particularly in his farewell address, in which he spoke out against sectionalism generally, might be attributed to a prudential judgment that a public statement hostile to slavery might have inflamed sectionalism enough to jeopardize the Union.[51]

But this explanation for his failure to speak out is more persuasive when applied to the time Washington was in public office than it is about the time after he retired from the presidency, when he refused to favor publicly even a gradual phasing out of slavery. The argument of this explanation is that Washington's character was flawed in that he failed to speak out publicly against slavery after leaving the presidency at the end of his life. His private statements clearly demonstrate that he knew slavery was wrong, yet he was unwilling to associate his personal prestige to public criticisms of slavery. The argument that Washington had a character defect with respect to slavery does not vitiate all of the other admirable aspects of his character. Despite his public attitude toward slavery, he was still a great president and a great man. We must admit, however, that his greatness existed alongside his buying and selling of human beings.

Historian, Pulitzer Prize winner, and civil-rights activist Roger Wilkins argues that Washington's ownership of slaves was understandable because it was only the work of the slaves that enabled Washington to have the time to become a statesman and to lead the United States in its founding period.[52] "Washington became *the* indispensable man" necessary to the survival of the early Republic, and the success of the new Republic played an important role in the expansion of human freedom over the past two centuries. Wilkins continues, "Isn't it a wonderful coincidence that he was present and out front each step of the way?" Wilkins concludes, "The founding slave owners were more than good men; they were great men. But . . . myth presents them as secular saints, and . . . whitewash[es] their ownership of slaves and the deep legacy of racism that they helped to institutionalize."[53]

In an article in *The New York Times* in 1998 historian Robert F. Dalzell Jr. implicitly contrasts Washington with more recent presidents.[54] The question Dalzell publicly discusses is how could President Clinton act effectively as president at the same time that he was engaging in unbecoming conduct with Monica Lewinsky? Dalzell's explanation of Clinton's ability to do these seemingly incompatible things at the same time (sometimes simultaneously) is that Clinton could mentally compartmentalize the contrasting aspects of his personality and thus be capable of contradictory behavior.

Dalzell argues that in deciding to free his slaves in his will Washington was giving up a lot. "Washington had no talent for compartmentalizing the separate parts of his life. Nor did he wish to."[55] This is an argument that Washington's character was seamless, with no disjunction between his private and his public lives. But the fact that Washington's slaves would not be freed until after he was dead proves just the opposite of Dalzell's claim. Washington had to be capable of extreme compartmentalization in order to continue owning slaves at the same time as he was fighting for the ideals expressed in the Declaration of Independence and presiding over the newly created Republic. Especially toward the end of his life, when he began to reflect more seriously about the implications of slavery and privately express his distaste for it, his source of economic support must have weighed heavily on his mind.

Dalzell also makes the point that in freeing his slaves, Washington was giving up quite a bit since it necessarily implied the break-up of his beloved Mount Vernon. But the fact that Washington had no children of his own may have played a role in his final decision. If he had had biological heirs, would he have dissipated their patrimony on the principle of the injustice of slavery? Neither Thomas Jefferson nor George Mason, both of whom spoke out publicly against slavery, freed their slaves when they died.

We can thus reasonably conclude that Washington's failure to speak out publicly against slavery late in his life was a character flaw. But he must be given credit for freeing his slaves and providing for them after his death, an action that some other, more outspoken, founders, failed to take. At the same time, if we are to be honest with ourselves, we must accept the negative dimensions of Washington's decision to embrace slavery (until after his death) along with his many accomplishments that were essential to the founding and establishment of our Republic. The point here is not that Washington was a bad person or president, merely that his character was complex and not seamless.

Character Complexity in Three Presidents

Much of this book has dealt with essentially negative aspects of presidential character, and too much of the public rhetoric about presidential character focuses on negative character traits. But the absence of sexual indiscretion and lying is no guarantee of effectiveness in the White House. Presidents are elected to lead the country in public policy, and the quality of this leadership ought to weigh heavily in our judgment of presidential character. This section considers three presidents whose characters were complex and who have both positive and negative character traits: Lyndon Johnson, Ronald Reagan, and Bill Clinton. If we are going to attribute the failings of these presidents to faults in their character, we must also credit their accomplishments to their character strengths. Even if we personally disagree with the policy or political goals of these presidents, we should recognize their accomplishments in terms of their policy goals.

LYNDON JOHNSON

The negative aspects of Lyndon Johnson's character are recognized in both scholarly and popular judgments. His personal behavior was often obnoxious, and he took a domineering approach to most of his personal and professional relationships. His behavior toward women was often

boorish and crude. His misleading of the American people during his
escalation of the war in Vietnam had severe consequences and has been
analyzed earlier. But the emphasis on the negative aspects of his character
also obscures the positive dimensions of Johnson's character.

Those who knew him testified to the complexity of Johnson's personality. His White House aide, Joseph Califano, said that

> The Lyndon Johnson I worked with was brave and brutal, compassionate and cruel, incredibly intelligent and infuriatingly
> insensitive, with a shrewd and uncanny instinct for the jugular of
> his allies and adversaries. He could be altruistic and petty, caring
> and crude, generous and petulant, bluntly honest and calculatingly devious—all within the same few minutes.[56]

His press secretary, George Reedy, said that Johnson "was a man of too
many paradoxes. . . . Almost everything you find out about him you can
find out a directly contrary quality immediately."[57]

Historian Robert Dallek summarizes Johnson's contradictions: "Driven,
tyrannical, crude, insensitive, humorless, and petty, he was also empathetic,
shy, sophisticated, self-critical, uproariously funny, and magnanimous."[58]
In his biography, *Flawed Giant*, Dallek adds, "throughout his Senate and
vice-presidential years, he remained an exhibitionist and a philanderer
who didn't mind flaunting his conquests." But

> Johnson's neediness and abuse of people around him was not the
> sum total of the man. . . . To the contrary [people close to him]
> describe Johnson as a wonderfully funny, almost zany character,
> who loved his friends and associates and took pains with their
> well-being. He had an exceptional gift for storytelling and mimicry, which made him a superb entertainer. He was also a highly
> sentimental and emotional man whose compassion for human
> limitations and suffering made him especially generous toward
> people less fortunate than himself.[59]

Some of the negative aspects of Johnson's character may be found in the
psychological insecurity that characterized him from the time of his
youth.[60] He felt compelled to dominate any situation in which he found
himself. He had a need to feel loved and accepted, especially by the Eastern elite establishment that he resented (as did Richard Nixon).

But his childhood, which exhibited some of the negative traits that would characterize his adult personality, also laid the experiential basis for his future commitment to policy accomplishments. In rural Texas he saw firsthand the nature of poverty and the limits it put on the lives of those who were caught in its grind. He also witnessed the ravages of racism on the self-esteem and life opportunities of minorities in the South. Despite his own pretensions and condescension toward some of the less privileged, Johnson was also able to identify with their affliction. When he became president his empathy for the less privileged, and particularly black Americans, drove his policy agenda along with his own need for personal achievement.

As a Southerner, Johnson was able to accomplish more progress in civil rights than a Northern liberal would have been able to. He knew the South firsthand and understood intimately the nature of prejudice and political opposition he would have to overcome if he were to succeed. One of his greatest legislative victories as majority leader in the Senate was his orchestration of the Civil Rights Act of 1957. Even if its provisions were primarily symbolic, it was important symbolism: It was the first civil-rights bill Congress had passed since 1875.

After John Kennedy's death in 1963 Johnson committed himself to the passage of the civil-rights bill, then under consideration in Congress, to end segregation in public accommodations. Senator Richard Russell of Georgia warned him that his championing of the bill would "cost you the South and cost you the election." Johnson replied, "If that's the price I've got to pay, I'll pay it gladly."[61] Throughout the spring of 1964 Johnson demonstrated his skills as an orchestrator of the legislative process in dealing with the Senate filibuster and convincing Senate minority leader Everett Dirkson to support the bill. Johnson signed the historic law in August, 1964.[62]

Even though it is true that Johnson calculated the impact of civil-rights legislation on his political opportunities and historical legacy, it is also true that he felt strongly about the issue and was genuinely committed to equal opportunity for African Americans. His commitment to civil rights was not necessarily in his short-term political interest; that is, it took political courage to press for historic changes in the public treatment of blacks in the United States. Civil-rights leader Andrew Young said that "it was not politically expedient" for Johnson to back the 1964 Civil Rights Bill.[63] After Johnson signed the bill on July 2, 1964, he told his aide, Bill Moyers, "I think we just delivered the South to the

Republican party for a long time to come."[64] His prediction came true over the next several decades as Republicans came to prevail in Southern elections and eventually controlled a majority of Southern seats in Congress.[65]

Johnson was committed to expanding political equality to African Americans and worked to pass the Voting Rights Act of 1965. When he went to Congress to advocate passage of the act, he said: "Their cause must be our cause too. Because it is not just Negroes, but really it is all of us, who must overcome the crippling legacy of bigotry and injustice."[66] The Voting Rights Act of 1965 had a huge impact on the political complexion of the South. Johnson was also responsible for the passage of the many programs his Great Society agenda created, including Medicare, Medicaid, food stamps, aid to education, public housing, environmental cleanup, and consumer protection laws, among others.[67]

Thus, despite the negative aspects of Johnson's character and the disastrous war in Vietnam that he deceptively led the country into, he must be given credit for the many positive accomplishments of his presidency. John Kenneth Galbraith had been a friend of Johnson's but opposed his reelection because of the war, and the two men never spoke again. But Galbraith concluded in 1999 that Johnson's reputation had to be balanced. He called Johnson "the most effective political activist of our time" and said that he would place Johnson "next only to Franklin D. Roosevelt as a force for a civilized and civilizing social policy essential for human well-being and for the peaceful co-existence between the economically favored (or financially fortunate) and the poor."[68] Even George McGovern, the antiwar presidential candidate in 1972, had words of praise for Johnson in retrospect: "But despite his involvement with the war, Johnson used his remarkable political skills to build the most far-reaching progressive domestic program since the New Deal."[69]

RONALD REAGAN

Ronald Reagan's character was closely related to his strengths and weaknesses as a politician and his successes and failures as president. Part of his popularity with the American public was due to his frequent appeals to traditional American values. His American values included a suspicion of government, the national government in particular, but also a conviction that America was still destined for greatness. Optimism was one of his major strengths; he believed that there was a solution to every problem.[70] Part of Reagan's appeal was that he was confident in himself and projected his optimism about the United States, if it could only be brought back to its traditional values. Importantly, he did not feel the same insecurity and resentment that Lyndon Johnson and Richard Nixon did.

Reagan's rhetorical abilities were impressive, in part because of the professional skills he had honed as an actor and in part because he personally believed what he was preaching. His simple vision of the country was a strength in that it corresponded with his own values and vision and Americans easily understood it. But the weakness of his vision was that its simplicity did not always correspond with reality. His executive style was to set the overall direction of a policy but to delegate the details and implementation to his subordinates. This conforms to good management theory, as long as the executive has a thorough knowledge of the policy and the tenacity to oversee and ensure that his subordinates are faithfully carrying it out. But Reagan often neglected the follow-through part of this approach to management and thus was vulnerable to the entrepreneurial tendencies of his subordinates. We now examine these aspects of Reagan's character in the context of three major policy areas of the Reagan presidency: the initial economic agenda of his first year in office, the Iran-Contra affair, and the end of the Cold War.

Reagan's First-Year Budget Victories

Ronald Reagan ran for office in 1980 by arguing that the economy was a mess, with 12-percent inflation and 20-percent interest rates. He promised to cut taxes, balance the budget, and make America strong again militarily. In addition, he appealed to social conservatives who were concerned with moral issues such as abortion, crime, and prayer in school. But after he won the election he decided to limit his policy agenda to his economic priorities and put the agenda of the social conservatives on the back burner, a wise strategic choice.[71] Reagan substantially increased military spending and effected the largest peacetime military buildup in history. He also succeeded in getting Congress to cut income taxes by 25 percent. His promise to bring the budget into balance was undercut by these two policies, and the cuts in domestic programs were not sufficient to make up the difference.

The supply-side theory that tax cuts would result in new investments and spur the economy to produce sufficient revenues to balance the budget did not work. Thus one of the Reagan legacies was a string of $200 billion deficits and a tripling of the national debt from $1 trillion to $3 trillion. Reagan deserves credit for his resolute leadership and political skills in pushing his initial agenda through Congress, but his failure to try to understand the flaws in supply-side theory or how his economic policies would hurt poor Americans made him blind to the negative implications of his economic policies.

Iran-Contra

Although Reagan's hands-off approach to management worked in his first term, in part because he chose James A. Baker to be his chief of staff, it led to disaster in his second term. Baker left the White House to become Secretary of the Treasury, and Treasury Secretary Donald Regan came to the White House to be chief of staff. Regan was a domineering chief of staff and did not have the political instincts or skills that Baker had.[72] Thus the plan for trading arms to Iran in hopes of freeing the hostages held in Lebanon was allowed to go forward despite the vehement objections of Secretary of State George Schultz and Secretary of Defense Casper Weinberger.

When Lt. Colonel Oliver North had the "bright idea" to use the profits from the arms sales to Iran to support the Contras in Nicaragua even though it was forbidden by law, no system was in place to stop him. Reagan had made it clear that he wanted the United States to support the Contras, and even though he did not specifically order North to break the law, his national-security adviser, John Poindexter, concluded that Reagan would have approved the illegal aid. So Poindexter had North go forward with the plan but did not inform Reagan so that the president would have deniability if he were asked. Thus the delegation approach to management failed to prevent disaster in this case. Either Reagan was unwilling to ensure that the actions of his subordinates were adequately overseen, or he purposefully allowed them to accomplish his goals through illegal means without his direct knowledge.

The End of the Cold War

Ronald Reagan's hostility to the Soviet Union had long been a central part of his political persona. When he came to office his actions were prudent, but his rhetoric was often bellicose, condemning the "evil empire" of the Soviet Union. Nevertheless, when Gorbachev came to power in 1985, Reagan was able to develop a relatively trusting relationship with him and engage in a dialogue about the reduction of nuclear forces on each side. Reagan's optimism and willingness to take bold steps led him to take seriously the possibility of deep cuts in nuclear arms and bring Gorbachev along with him.

The deep-cuts option came close to an agreement between the two leaders at the 1986 Reykjavik summit (a possibility that alarmed the national-security establishments of both nations), except that Reagan refused to consider abandoning the Strategic Defense Initiative (SDI). The plan for the SDI envisioned an antimissile system that was space based and would enable the United States to intercept and destroy any hostile missiles fired at the United States. Computer specialists concluded that such a system was not technologically feasible in the foreseeable future, but Reagan believed that it could be created. Fortunately, so did the Russians, and part of the final push that led to the breakup of the Soviet Union was the expectation that the United States could develop an effective SDI and that the Russians could not afford to keep up with the expenditures necessary to counter such a system.[73]

Even though we might fault Reagan for his rigid and hostile attitude toward the Soviet Union, we must give him credit for his open relationship with Gorbachev. Although a wide range of historical forces having to do with the internal contradictions of a nation that suppressed political freedom and tried to run its economy through central control precipitated the downfall of the Soviet Union, part of the credit is due to Ronald Reagan and his relationship with Gorbachev.[74]

Ronald Reagan's character played a role not only in the victories of his presidency but also in his shortcomings as a leader. His optimism and conviction helped him lead his administration to the impressive budget victories of his first year in office. But his simplified vision made him blind to the consequences of his policies for the national debt or their effects on the poor. In the Iran-Contra affair, Reagan's staff took his steadfast commitment to aid the Contras despite the Boland amendment as a green light to pursue the illegal actions that left greatest stain on the Reagan presidency. Reagan's unselfconscious belief in his own good intentions blinded him to the reality that he was trading arms for hostages in the Middle East and that he was deceiving the American people about his policies there. In relations with the Soviet Union, Reagan's consistency blended into rigidity in his hostile statements, but his personal connection to Gorbachev allowed the Cold War to end more peacefully than it might have otherwise. Edwin Hargrove, in evaluating President Reagan, concludes that "The appeal to illusion, which characterized his entire life, was his great political strength, but also his greatest weakness as a political leader."[75]

BILL CLINTON

President Clinton was the poster boy for defective character in the 1990s. In both the 1992 and 1996 campaigns the character issue was raised in attacking Clinton. He picked up the nickname "Slick Willie" when he gave misleading answers to questions during the 1992 campaign about his draft status in 1968 and 1969 and about his previous affair with Gennifer Flowers in Arkansas. His waffle on alleged marijuana smoking in college became emblematic of his deviousness when he claimed not to have inhaled.[76] But the most important breaches of trust attributed to his character failures were his affair with Monica Lewinsky while he was president and his lies in public and under oath in denying their affair.

Even though Clinton's weaknesses were well known, his character was not unidimensional.[77] Analysts and observers point out that strengths and weaknesses exist side by side in Clinton's character.[78] *New York Times* reporter Todd S. Purdum observes: "One of the biggest, most talented, articulate, intelligent, open, colorful characters ever to inhabit the Oval Office can also be an undisciplined, fumbling, obtuse, defensive, self-justifying rogue.... In a real sense, his strengths are his weaknesses, his enthusiasms are his undoing and most of the traits that make him appealing can make him appalling in the flash of an eye."[79] According to one of his aides, "It's almost impossible not to be charmed by him, and it's almost impossible not to be disappointed by him."[80]

Clinton's talents and failures of judgment alternated throughout his political history. From the 1992 election victory to an ineffective transition; from his budget victories to his health-care disaster; from the 1994 election defeats to his 1996 reelection; from the solid fifth year to the disaster of impeachment; and from his acquittal in the Senate to his last-minute pardons of some dubious characters, Clinton's presidency was on a roller coaster from beginning to end. Fred Greenstein describes this syndrome as "his tendency to oscillate between an uninhibited, anything-goes approach to leadership and a more measured operating mode in which he sets attainable goals and proceeds skillfully in his efforts to realize them."[81]

Long-time Clinton consultant and associate Dick Morris describes Clinton's dichotomous personality:

> The Sunday-morning President Clinton is the one we have all
> seen so often on television. Pious, optimistic, brilliant, principled,

sincere, good-willed, empathetic, intellectual, learned, and caring, he is the president for whom America voted in 1992 and again in 1996. But the Saturday-night Bill who cohabits within him is pure id—willful, demanding, hedonistic, risk-taking, sybaritic, headstrong, unfeeling, callous, unprincipled, and undisciplined.[82]

Scholar Stephen J. Wayne observes:

Driven by limitless ambition and desires, Clinton says more than he should, promises more than he can deliver, or behaves in an excessive manner. Stymied by political defeat, legal constraints, and/or public admonishment, he recovers. He does so by moderating his words and actions and making compromises when necessary and carefully and consciously orchestrating his public persona to be more closely in accord with mainstream opinion and the political feasibility that it permits. But the corrective is short lived and becomes undone when ambition and desire take over again.[83]

Critics of President Clinton, even when admitting that he had some political skills, could find few redeeming character traits and saw Clinton's policy positions as merely poll-driven opportunism.[84] But in several important policy battles, Clinton did what he judged to be best for the country, despite serious political opposition (e.g., the 1993 deficit reduction, NAFTA, intervention in Haiti, bailout of the Mexican peso, and intervention in Bosnia and Kosovo). One might criticize any one of these decisions on policy grounds, but it is hard to argue that they were all merely poll-driven, craven adherence to the path of least resistance. Thus, despite Clinton's faults, his character led him to take some tough policy stands and achieve some significant victories.

Deficit Reduction in 1993

For instance, Clinton's decision to pursue deficit reduction early in 1993 rather than the middle-class tax cut that he had promised in his campaign has been criticized as demonstrating a lack of trustworthiness.[85] But, as described earlier in this book, Clinton decided in February of 1993 that he had to abandon his campaign promise and pursue deficit reduction in his first budget. His budget combined a gas-tax increase with an increase in the tax rate on high-income individuals and with program cuts to achieve about $500 billion in deficit reduction over five years.[86] He was convinced that a failure to address the deficit seriously would lead Wall Street financiers to anticipate inflation and raise interest rates. This in turn would slow the economy and prolong the recession. Clinton would rather have increased spending on social programs but was convinced that deficit reduction was necessary for the health of the economy.

Although some might argue that Clinton should have kept his campaign promise, one can also argue that the deficit hawks were correct and that the economic boom of the latter 1990s would not have occurred without the 1993 deficit reduction. One might argue that it took strength of character for Clinton to change his mind in light of rational arguments that economic conditions had changed between his campaign and the spring of 1993. Even though making the initial decision was tough, it was not nearly so tough as convincing Congress to pass his first budget. Yet Clinton applied all of his political skills to win the thinnest of victories without any Republican votes and by a margin of two in the House and with Senate votes that depended on tie-breaking votes by Vice President Gore. In this case, Clinton pushed the political system as far as it would go and won an important policy victory. Regardless of whether one thinks this was good public policy, it was Clinton's commitment and perseverance that made the difference.

Middle-East Peace

Clinton's powers of persuasion were also demonstrated in negotiations over Middle East peace at Wye Plantation in the fall of 1997, when he convinced Prime Minister Benjamin Netanyahu and Palestinian leader Yasir Arafat to sign an agreement that neither felt was fully fair to his side and that political adversaries in their own countries attacked. This achievement pushed the political possibilities for peace in the Middle East about as far as they could go at that time. Clinton demonstrated his ability to empathize, his powers of persuasion, his patience, and his tenaciousness in the Wye Plantation negotiations. His commitment to peace in the Middle East was recognized by Jordan's King Hussein, who interrupted his cancer treatment at the Mayo Clinic in Minnesota to help facilitate the final agreement. Hussein, who had dealt closely with every president since Eisenhower on Middle East peace issues, said to Clinton: "With all due respect and all the affection I held for your predecessors, [I have never] known someone with your dedication, clear-headedness, focus and de-

termination to help resolve this issue."[87] This was high praise from someone who could speak with authority on the Middle East.

Confronting the 104th Congress

Another aspect of Clinton's character was the resoluteness he demonstrated when faced with the severe budget and programmatic cuts the
Republican 104th Congress had passed in 1995. The Republicans, led by
Newt Gingrich, believed that they had a mandate from the people in the
1994 elections and set out to dismantle important elements of the federal
government establishment. They proposed to eliminate three cabinet de-
partments, cut EPA funding by half, make severe cuts in Medicare and
Medicaid, cut educational funding, and make deep cuts in other social
programs.

Since President Clinton was politically vulnerable at the time, the Republicans felt they could force him to sign the budget bills in the fall of
1995. Clinton, although he agreed to move to a balanced budget, refused
to go along and vetoed the bills, allowing much of the government to be
shut down temporarily for lack of funding. After several months of fruit-
less negotiations, the government was shut down again until Senate majority leader Robert Dole finally decreed that "enough is enough" and
ended the shutdown. Regardless of whether one agrees that the programs were worth saving, one must admit that Clinton's actions took
courage, skill, and tenaciousness. In contrast to Clinton's health-care
fiasco in 1994, his opposition to the 104th Congress was a major policy
victory for him.

The argument here is that despite President Clinton's spectacular character failings (recklessness, lying, and lack of sexual restraint), positive
aspects of his character allowed him to win significant policy victories.
Although in part due to his character, his asserted lack of "moral com-
pass" and his vacillation between the left and the right wings of the political spectrum were also affected by the political situation in the country in the 1990s. Clinton was internally torn because he could sympa-
thize with and articulate both sides of the arguments about major policy
issues of the 1990s. His lack of a fixed star of policy preference or a unified
vision of the future reflected not only his personal ambivalence but also
the political reality of deep divisions in American politics. Clinton attempted to straddle the fissures of American political cleavages and was
not fully successful. Erwin Hargrove has observed that "President Clinton

has incorporated the seemingly intractable political conflicts of his time without finding a way to transcend them."[88]

Conclusion: Character Complexity

In this conclusion I will first deal with the consequences of calling attention to the flaws in presidents' characters. Then I address the relationship of character to political survival in the United States. As I have argued in this book, the winners of the biggest prize in U.S. politics are seldom paragons of virtue on the same terms by which we judge ordinary people. That is, we may yearn for political leaders who exhibit the traditional moral virtues of truthfulness, fidelity, and promise keeping by which we judge ordinary people.

But the reality is that the types of people who seek power at the highest levels often engage in behavior that is necessary to be successful. This reality of American politics makes it unlikely that our most effective presidents will also be saints in their personal behavior. This does not mean that we have to approve of or condone presidential behavior that ought to be unacceptable. Their position does not give them license to break the rules of normal, civilized behavior. On the other hand, a realistic examination of presidential behavior should lead us to expect that these successful power wielders will not always play by the rules and that the path to power in U.S. politics is biased against those who scrupulously tell the truth and never change their minds.

FINDING FAULTS IN OUR POLITICAL LEADERS

Some might argue that to investigate a litany of presidential misbehavior and abuse merely reduces the stature of our former leaders and thus leads to cynicism. Others might argue that pointing out flaws in our leaders stems from an excessive egalitarianism and is intended to "cut them down to our size," that is, to see them as no better than ourselves. The feared result is that if we fail to honor heroes of the past we will undermine the conditions that give rise to future virtuous rulers. Thus this "muckraking" will encourage our descent from the glorious days of the past and lead us to certain decline because it encourages the cynical argument that virtuous leaders are not possible.

But my perspective is just the opposite. Insofar as we exalt past leaders to the point of apotheosis or creating icons of them, it is easy to see them as superhuman. In looking at current leaders and finding them wanting in comparison with paragons of the distant past (e.g., Washington, Lincoln, FDR), we might despair of the ability of current real-life humans to achieve their stature. Thus an unrealistic understanding of our past leaders can lead to defeatism.

My purpose, rather, is to present a more realistic picture of our presidents so that our current expectations of the possibilities of political leadership are more achievable. Pointing out that some past heroes had character flaws does not detract from their true accomplishments, which should be appreciated for what they are. The implication of my argument is that human character, and especially that of political leaders, is complex. The purity of a saint is not often conducive to effective political leadership, especially in a democracy. In a sense, we are stuck with mere human beings for our political leaders; there are few paragons without flaws. But the positive side of this perspective is that mere human beings are sometimes capable of great things, as were our great presidents.

To argue that our great heroes were faultless can easily lead us on the one hand to despair that any contemporary can ever measure up to them and on the other hand to fall prey to the cynicism of "they all do it" when we discover that they do in fact have flaws. A realistic understanding of the combination of virtues and flaws in past heroes can lead to an appreciation of the range of people who are capable of providing effective political leadership.

Pointing out that George Washington was a conventional slaveholder who did not show much ambivalence about slavery until late in his life does not detract from the greatness of his many acts of political leadership. It merely calls attention to the fact that he was not perfect. That is, he was human. Thus his virtues should impress us even more—his courage, his sense of duty, his self-restraint, and his ability to learn from past mistakes. We should not shrink from admitting that the father of our country had faults by trying to minimize his actions as a slaveholder. But we should also give him credit for recognizing the evils of slavery at the end of his life, for freeing and providing for his slaves in his will, and for living a virtuous (if not perfect) life.

To realize that Lincoln's public statements on the slavery issue were ambiguous does not detract from his final victory and the emancipation of all slaves. It calls our attention to the intractable politics of the slavery issue in mid-nineteenth-century U.S. politics, and it helps us appreciate Lincoln's political skills even more. Via his circuitous route he was able to accomplish what the abolitionists, because of their intransigence, were not. This does not mean that the abolitionists' activities were wrong or unnecessary to the final victory. What it means is that effective political leadership in a democracy must make concessions to the realities of political power. Both the abolitionists and Lincoln made important contributions to the common goal of overcoming slavery—but they were different contributions.

One could argue that lying by presidents is much more closely connected to their public duties than sexual fidelity is and ought to be taken more seriously. This is a sound argument but does not easily lend itself to absolutism. My argument in this book is that we ought to evaluate presidential lies within the context of their motives and consequences. Thus some lies are justified, though most are not. Among those lies that are not justified, some are worse than others. Admitting that Ike lied in the U-2 affair does not seriously undermine his overall integrity and general probity. He was still a great leader and a near-great president. We do not have to whitewash him to appreciate his virtues.

Pointing out that Lyndon Johnson told a number of lies—from the trivial to the serious—does not vitiate his many contributions to civil-rights and social-welfare policies in the United States. In our overall evaluation of LBJ we must balance his contributions in social policy with his failures of leadership in Vietnam; we ought not to ignore one and focus only on the other.

It would be shortsighted to argue that no one who has been unfaithful to his or her spouse deserves to be honored as a political leader. To do so would be to argue that FDR, Ike, JFK, and LBJ should not be honored as political leaders. In order to honor them as political leaders, we do not need to honor them as paragons of virtue. To ignore their contributions because they have personal flaws of character is to throw the baby out with the bathwater.

To recognize and admit that some good presidents have had sexual affairs, however, does not mean that we have to approve or condone their behavior. The appropriate response is to try to understand their behavior within the context of their marriages and to judge them from an informed perspective. We can conclude that their behavior was understandable or unacceptable and factor these conclusions into our overall evaluation of the individual.

Certainly presidents have obligations as moral leaders and role models, and when they fail to fulfill their obligations as moral exemplars, they deserve blame. The immorality of the sexual misbehavior of John Kennedy,

Lyndon Johnson, and Bill Clinton is compounded by their position as president and their failures to fulfill their exemplary duties as president. These failures should dim their luster as national leaders but should not obviate their positive contributions as presidents.

My intention in this book is to encourage a realistic appreciation of presidential leadership. By pointing out some flaws in past presidents, I hope to present a more realistic standard against which we can judge contemporary presidents. Holding them up to unrealistic standards will not help us attract better leaders. On the other hand, evidence of flaws or unacceptable behavior in previous leaders (even great ones) does not constitute an excuse for misbehavior by current leaders. Thus Bill Clinton ought not to have used JFK's many affairs as an excuse or justification for his own sexual misbehavior.

We as citizens need to avoid the cynical perspective that all politicians are corrupt and conclude that presidential misbehavior makes no difference. On the contrary, our duty as citizens is to make difficult judgments about presidential character when we decide for whom we vote and whom we honor as past presidents. We do not need to investigate in historical detail what each president has done, but if we judge a president on the basis of some flaw or misbehavior, we ought to learn enough about the context of the behavior to have some confidence that our conclusions are justified. Of course, not all citizens will do this, but this is what we ought to aspire to when we make judgments about presidents (or any other human being).

CHARACTER AND POLITICAL SURVIVAL

To return to the line of reasoning posited in the introduction of this book, part of the explanation for the lack of pristine moral principles in presidents and their general human frailty is that they have survived a very brutal winnowing process. Sustaining a successful career in politics is not easy. People who are unwilling to cut corners, shade the truth, compromise, or renege on promises are not likely to arrive at the pinnacle of leadership in democratic politics. The U.S. political system is not likely to elevate the noblest individuals to the presidency.

Americans have always been ambivalent about political ambition. On the one hand, we deplore the pursuit of public office insofar as it seems to be the selfish seeking of personal power. On the other hand, we admire people who seek public office for the purpose of pursuing idealistic policies in the public interest. But we also admire those who would sacrifice public office because they want to remain true to their ideals (as Henry Clay said, they would rather be right than be president).[89] And we criticize those who seem to subordinate their ideals in order to win political office, that is, those who seem willing to compromise and who have no ideals they are willing to stand by in the face of possible defeat.[90]

More than a century ago Lord James Bryce wrote a book on American politics in which he titled one chapter "Why Great Men Are Not Chosen Presidents."[91] Among other reasons, Bryce pointed out that "eminent men make more enemies, and give those enemies more assailable points, than obscure men do. They are therefore in so far less desirable candidates. . . . The famous man has probably attacked some leaders in his own party . . . [and] has perhaps committed errors which are capable of being magnified into offences. . . . Hence, when the choice lies between a brilliant man and a safe man, the safe man is preferred."[92] In addition, the nominating and party system places more value on getting a winning candidate than on the governing abilities of the person once in office. The American voter "likes his candidate to be sensible, vigorous, and, above all, what he calls 'magnetic,' and does not value, because he sees no need for, originality or profundity, a fine culture or a wide knowledge." Thus, "the merits of a President are one thing and those of a candidate are another thing."[93] Bryce's insights of a century ago still ring true today.

We must also bear in mind that, despite popular stereotypes, the vocation of politics is not an easy one. It calls for sustained efforts to meld conflicting factions and interests into enough consensus to make important decisions about public policy. As Max Weber argued, "Politics is a strong and slow boring of hard boards. It takes both passion and perspective."[94] Weber also observed that "He who lives 'for' politics makes politics his life, in an internal sense. Either he enjoys the naked possession of the power he exerts, or his life has meaning in the service of a 'cause.'"[95] But more probably, successful politicians enjoy *both* wielding power and fighting for a cause.

Thus a political career is difficult and does not appeal to everyone, and the ones to whom it appeals tend to be more pragmatic than idealistic. We may admire idealists, but they do not last too long in democratic politics. In the judgment of Pendleton Herring, successful politicians are not likely to have moral standards greatly higher than those of the people whom they serve. According to Herring, "The differences within the community provide the strands with which the politician weaves a political fabric. If the product is often frayed and soiled, look to the threads as well as the fingers."[96] Herring observes, "Thus, while in the area of belief and discussion voters declare themselves in favor of efficiency and impartiality in the administration of the law, they react quite differently when tagged for parking. *The experienced politician is not disturbed by such inconsistencies. He takes life as he finds it. This is his value and his limitation*" (emphasis added).[97]

The function of a politician, according to Herring, is less to be a moral exemplar than to enable opposing factions to live together peacefully. Politicians "seek not the ideal but terms of agreement that reduce the chances of violence or coercion."[98] Thus Herring would have us be tolerant of some of the faults of our political leaders.

The realities of politics as a career are trying, and, as Stephen Hess observes, with few exceptions (Willkie and Eisenhower) in the twentieth century, the major parties have nominated only professional politicians to be president. Hess argues further that the one distinguishing characteristic of all successful presidential candidates is an overweening ambition to be president.[99] Indeed, if a potential candidate does not demonstrate the necessary "fire in the belly" to be willing to put up with arduous campaigns, that person is often dismissed as not serious. Even though most politicians have a goodly measure of ambition, the gap between the next highest offices, senator and governor, and the presidency is so great that only those with excessive ambition even attempt to run for the presidency.

It takes a combination of driving ambition combined with chutzpah to seriously pursue the presidency.[100] In addition, the right to wield power comes along with political achievement. It is also a biological reality that dominant male mammals are often the most attractive to females and are willing to use their power to obtain sexual gratification.[101] In fact, much of human society is organized around the necessity of curbing the sexual inclinations of aggressive men.[102] Taking these factors into account, it should not surprise us, though it may appall us, that sometimes powerful men act as if the normal rules of sexual restraint do not apply to them. This explanation for some presidential behavior certainly does not excuse it, but it may help us to understand it.

Rexford Tugwell, an adviser to FDR, speculated about the nature of successful politicians. According to Tugwell,

All were hearty, full-blooded types, vital, overflowing with energy, restless, driven by ambitions long before their compulsions had any focus:

They were unintellectual in the scientific sense.

They were strongly virile and attractive.

All were extroverts, enjoying sensual pleasures.

All were superb conversationalists; all knew the uses of parables.

All were insensitive to others' feelings except as concerned themselves.

All seemed to have thick skins because they were abused, but this was only seeming; all were hurt and all were unforgiving; and all were anxious for approval.

All were ruthless in the sense of not reciprocating loyalty; they punished friends and rewarded enemies.

All had thick armor against probings. Not even those nearest to them knew their minds.

All were driven by an ambition to attain power in the political hierarchy, and all allowed it to dominate their lives.[103]

Despite our understandable desire for presidents to be nice human beings, most of these characteristics seem to apply to most of our recent presidents.

Tugwell's observations raise the question of whether our presidents should be likeable people and ethical paragons as well as effective politicians. Most presidents are able to project an image of friendliness and intimacy, especially in our media-driven age. Appearing to be approachable and a "regular guy" whom we can "relate to" is very useful in American politics. But politicians who are able to project an "accessible" image often do not live up to that image in their private lives. The most striking example is Ronald Reagan, who was very effective at making acquaintances feel at ease but who was also emotionally distant from his closest advisors and even his immediate family.

Other presidents were also quite effective in relating to mass audiences. Franklin Roosevelt's fireside chats made him seem to be giving friendly, personal advice. Yet Roosevelt enjoyed setting his staffers in conflict with each other, and he was not always kind in his personal relationships. Bill Clinton was very effective in relating to audiences and convincing them that "I feel your pain." Yet his personal relationships with his staffers and friends were often tumultuous, and he ignored their feelings.[104] Thus effective presidents are often not "nice" people to be around, but the work they do is important enough to their staffers and families that their personality deficiencies are worth tolerating.

Ought our presidents to be moral and ethical paragons as well as effective leaders? As has I have argued, presidents are role models whether they like it or not. Societies need exemplars to look up to and provide inspiration for young and ambitious people entering public service. This moral-leadership role is a trust that presidents ought not to flout. Their example can have profound effects, for good or ill, over generations of American politics and even world leadership. Yet it is obvious that presidents often fail to live up fully to this leadership obligation. When they do not measure up, we are justifiably disappointed. They have failed in one of the important obligations of political leadership.

But as admirable as personal likeability and moral leadership are, the bottom line of the presidency is effective governance. Presidents must ensure that the machinery of government in the executive branch functions as effectively as possible and that relations among the three branches do not break down. We also expect policy leadership from our presidents. They must provide positive direction in both domestic and international arenas. Thus effective executive leadership is the *sine qua non* of a successful presidency. In order of priority, effective governance ranks first, moral leadership second, and personal appeal third. When our presidents do not excel at all three roles, we should keep in mind that not all roles are equally important.

This argument for a more realistic understanding of presidential character is not meant to justify cynicism or lower our standards for the moral behavior of presidents. The American separation-of-powers system is set up to be able to counter the exercise of arbitrary power and counteract an aggrandizing president. Congress and the courts also share responsibility for political leadership. But the system cannot run of itself; the *Federalist Papers* make it clear that virtue is still necessary because people are not angels. Our political system can correct for and survive an occasional seriously flawed president, but it cannot survive the *complete* lack of virtue in its leaders.

Luckily for us, we often find virtuous, if not flawless, presidents. To paraphrase Benjamin Franklin, we have a republic—if we can keep it. And keeping it means that we have to find virtuous presidents, even if they are not perfect.

NOTES

Chapter 1. Judging Presidential Character

1. William Safire, *Safire's New Political Dictionary* (New York: Random, 1993), p. 112.
2. Peggy Noonan, "Ronald Reagan," in Robert A. Wilson, ed., *Character above All* (New York: Simon, 1995), p. 202.
3. See the insightful analysis of Richard Reeves, "John Kennedy," in Robert A. Wilson, ed., *Character above All* (New York: Simon, 1995), p. 100.
4. James Davison Hunter and Carl Bowman, *The Politics of Character* (University of Virginia: Institute for Advanced Studies in Culture, 2000), pp. 13–19. The authors conclude: "On the one hand, there is no question that the American public recognizes democracy's need for strong moral character and its attendant virtues. . . . At the same time, large sectors of the American public lack discrimination and reveal a surprising level of confusion and contradiction in their thinking about character. Character seems to be a catch-all for everything—for anything—commendable or simply positive" (p. 53). See also James Davison Hunter, *The Death of Character* (New York: Basic, 2000).
5. Quoted by Michael Beschloss, "George Bush," in Robert A. Wilson, ed., *Character above All* (New York: Simon, 1995), p. 242.
6. See Greenstein's *Foreword* to Alexander L. George and Juliette L. George, *Presidential Personality and Performance* (Boulder: Westview, 1998), pp. ix–x. For Greenstein's analysis of President Clinton's personality see "There He Goes Again: The Alternating Political Style of Bill Clinton," *P.S.: Political Science and Politics* (June 1998): 179–81.
7. Robert Shogan, *The Double-Edged Sword* (Boulder: Westview, 1999), p. 11.
8. George and George, *Presidential Personality and Performance*, p. 9.
9. Niccolo Machiavelli, *The Prince and the Discourses* (New York: Modern Library, 1950), particularly chap. 18, pp. 63–66. See also Richard A. Posner, *An Affair of State* (Cambridge: Harvard University Press, 1999), chap. 4, "Morality, Private and Public," pp. 132–69; and J. Patrick Dobel, "Judging the Private Lives of Public Officials," *Administration and Society* 30, no. 2 (May 1998): 115–42; Deborah Rhode, "Moral Character in the Personal and the Political," *Loyola University of Chicago Law Journal* (fall, 1988): 1–19.
10. See Reinhold Niebuhr, *Moral Man and Immoral Society* (New York: Scribner, 1949), pp. 257–77.
11. Posner, *Affair of State*, pp. 133–69.

12. See J. Patrick Dobel, "Political Prudence and the Ethics of Leadership," *Public Administration Review* 58, no. 1 (Jan./Feb. 1998): 74–81.

13. See the insightful analysis of Andrew Stark, *Conflict of Interest in American Public Life* (Cambridge: Harvard University Press, 2000), pp. 142–47.

14. See Posner, *Affair of State,* p. 135.

15. This discussion is based on the formulation of Michael Josephson, *Making Ethical Decisions: What Are You Going to Do?* 3d ed. (Marina del Rey, Calif.: Josephson Institute of Ethics, 1995).

16. Quoted in *Time,* Sept. 14, 1998, in the "Verbatim" portion of the "Notebook" section.

17. Quoted in *U.S. News and World Report,* May 3, 1999, p. 8, in the "Washington Whispers" section.

18. Quoted in *U.S. News and World Report,* May 10, 1999, p. 10, in the "Washington Whispers" section.

19. "A foolish consistency is the hobgoblin of little minds, adored by little statesmen and philosophers and divines. With consistency a great soul has simply nothing to do." From Ralph Waldo Emerson, *Self-Reliance and Other Essays* (New York: Dover Publications, 1993), p. 24.

20. For a careful analysis of prudence in political life see Dobel, "Political Prudence and the Ethics of Leadership," pp. 74–81.

21. For a discussion of some of the psychological approaches to presidential character see James P. Pfiffner, "Judging Presidential Character," *Public Integrity* 5, no. 1 (winter 2002–2003): 7–24. Some treatments of psychological aspects of character include Harold D. Lasswell, *Psychopathology and Politics* (New York: Viking, 1960 [first copyright 1930]); Alexander L. George, *Presidential Decision Making in Foreign Policy: The Effective Use of Information and Advice* (Boulder: Westview, 1980); George and George, *Presidential Personality and Performance*; Stanley A. Renshon, *High Hopes: The Clinton Presidency and the Politics of Ambition* (New York: New York University Press, 1996); James David Barber, *The Presidential Character: Predicting Performance in the White House,* 4th ed. (Englewood Cliffs, N.J.: Prentice, 1992).

22. See especially Robert A. Wilson, *Character above All* (New York: Simon, 1995). Wilson asked eminent presidential biographers to write analyses of the character of a president. The chapters include Doris Kearns Goodwin on Franklin Roosevelt, David McCullough on Harry Truman, Stephen Ambrose on Dwight Eisenhower, Richard Reeves on John Kennedy, Robert Dallek on Lyndon Johnson, Tom Wicker on Richard Nixon, James Cannon on Gerald Ford, Hendrik Hertzberg on Jimmy Carter, Peggy Noonan on Ronald Reagan, and Michael Beschloss on George H. W. Bush. What is striking about these insightful essays is that though each writer focuses on presidential character, each has a different definition or approach to character. There is no consensus or common theme to the essays.

Chapter 2. The Nature of Presidential Lies

1. Earlier versions of Chapters 2 and 3 have appeared in James P. Pfiffner, "Presidential Lies," *Presidential Studies Quarterly* 29, no. 4 (Dec., 1999): 903–907; and "Presidential Character: Multidimensional or Seamless?" in Mark J. Rozell and Clyde Wilcox, eds., *The Clinton Scandal* (Washington, D.C.: Georgetown University Press, 2000), pp. 225–55.

2. Richard Stengel, "Lies My President Told Me," *Time*, Aug. 31, 1998, p. 48.

3. For an insightful analysis of the social uses of lying see David Nyberg, *The Varnished Truth* (Chicago: University of Chicago Press, 1993), especially chap. 1, "Truth Telling Is Morally Overrated," pp. 7–26.

4. St. Augustine, *The Essential Augustine*, ed. Vernon J. Bourke (New York: New American Library, 1964), p. 169.

5. *The Essential Augustine*, p. 170.

6. Immanuel Kant, "On a Supposed Right to Lie from Altruistic Motives," reprinted in the appendix to Sissela Bok, *Lying: Moral Choice in Public and Private Life* (New York: Vintage, 1978), pp. 285–90.

7. William J. Bennett, *The Death of Outrage: Bill Clinton and the Assault on American Ideals* (New York: Free Press, 1998), p. 42.

8. Immanuel Kant, *Fundamental Principles of the Metaphysic of Morals* (New York: Bobbs, 1949), p. 38 (italics in original).

9. Richard Nixon, *Six Crises* (New York: Doubleday, 1962), p. 353.

10. Nixon, *Six Crises*, p. 355.

11. Nixon, *Six Crises*, p. 355.

12. For an analysis of the incident, see Herbert S. Parmet, *JFK: The Presidency of John F. Kennedy* (New York: Dial, 1983), pp. 47–49. See also Fawn M. Brodie, *Richard Nixon: The Shaping of His Character* (New York: Norton, 1981), pp. 411–13.

13. The analysis of this incident is based on Seymour M. Hersh, *The Price of Power: Kissinger in the Nixon White House* (New York: Summit, 1993), pp. 60–75.

14. Hersh, *The Price of Power*, p. 74.

15. Hersh, *The Price of Power*, p. 74.

16. See Hamilton Jordan's account in *Crisis: The Last Year of the Carter Presidency* (New York: Putnam, 1982), pp. 264–68.

17. Jules Witcover, *Marathon: The Pursuit of the Presidency* (New York: Viking, 1977), p. 320.

18. See the analysis of Carter's statements in Bob Woodward, *Shadow* (New York: Simon, 1999), pp. 41–43. Woodward also says that Carter lied to congressional leaders about statements he had previously made to Woodward and Ben Bradlee. See pp. 49–52.

19. *Congressional Quarterly* (Oct. 16, 1976): 3009.

20. Both statements quoted in Witcover, *Marathon*, p. 336.

21. See the insightful and detailed biography of Carter by Betty Glad, *Jimmy Carter in Search of the Great White House* (New York: Norton, 1980).

22. David Von Drehle, "McCain Seeks Favor as a Happy Warrior," *Washington Post*,

Jan. 31, 2000, p. A6. See also Gloria Borger, "Confronting a Crusade," *U.S. News and World Report*, Feb. 14, 2000, p. 23.

23. Terry M. Neal, "McCain Reverses Flag Stance," *Washington Post*, Apr. 20, 2000, p. A1.

24. The lies considered here are "minor" only in the context of the other, more serious lies examined in this book. In other contexts, similar lies might not be considered minor. For instance, falsifying credentials on a resume when applying for a job is a serious matter, but in the context of his whole presidency, Kennedy's implication in his official biography that he graduated from the London School of Economics was relatively minor.

25. Marcus Cunliffe, *George Washington: Man and Monument* (New York: New American Library, 1982), pp. 6–7. Weems's biography of Washington went through forty editions by 1825, and forty more would subsequently be published.

26. Quoted in Nyberg, *The Varnished Truth*, p. 154. According to Nyberg, not only is the tale untrue, but it was plagiarized by Weems from a story by Dr. James Beattie, titled "The Minstrel," which had been published in London several years earlier.

27. Cunliffe, *George Washington*, pp. 6–7. According to the curators at Mount Vernon, the story is not true. "Quick Quiz," *Washington Post*, Feb. 2, 1999, p. VA6.

28. In the same section of the book, Weems quotes Washington's father instructing the young George about truth telling. "Truth, George . . . is the loveliest quality of youth. I would ride fifty miles, my son, to see the little boy whose heart is so *honest*, and his lips so *pure*, that we may depend on every word he says. . . . But, Oh! How different, George, is the case with the boy who is so given to lying, that nobody can believe a word he says! . . . Oh, George! My son! Rather than see you come to his pass, dear as you are to my heart, gladly would I assist to nail you up in your little coffin, and follow you to your grave." This seems to be a rather harsh imprecation for lying. This quote is taken from the website "The Papers of George Washington" (www.virginia.edu/gwpapers/documents). It is titled "The Fable of George Washington and the Cherry Tree." (The word *fable* seems appropriate and avoids the problem of misleading readers about the historical accuracy of the story.) The website took the quote from Mason Locke Weems's *Life of Washington*, a new edition with primary documents and introduction by Peter S. Onuf (Armonk, N.Y., and London: Sharpe), pp. 8–10.

29. Dallek was quoted by Michael Powell in "The Lost Art of Lying," *Washington Post*, Dec. 8, 1998, p. C1.

30. Lyndon Johnson, *Public Papers of the Presidents of the United States*, 1966 (Washington, D.C.: GPO, 1967), book II, p. 1278. Quoted in David Wise, The Politics of Lying (New York: Vintage, 1973). Wise analyzes Johnson's genealogy carefully to show how Johnson's claim was impossible (pp. 27–32). See also Robert Caro, *Means of Ascent* (New York: Knopf, 1990), p. xxvi.

31. Doris Kearns, *Lyndon Johnson and the American Dream* (New York: New American Library, 1976), p. 15.

32. Richard Reeves, *President Kennedy: Profile of Power* (New York: Simon, 1993), p. 280. Reeves cites page 35 of Sidey's oral-history statement at the Kennedy Library. Sidey later wrote, "Reeves was a bit off. Yes, Kennedy and I joked about it. Either

1000 or 1200 words is accurate enough for these things. I checked the 1200 words out with Evelyn Woods [the director of the institute]. She said it sounded ok.... He was a good leader" (personal letter to the author Apr. 16, 2001).

33. Reeves, *President Kennedy,* p. 54.

34. This incident is reported in some detail by Lou Cannon in his highly regarded book on Reagan as president, *President Reagan: The Role of a Lifetime* (New York: Simon, 1991), pp. 486–90. See also Benjamin Bradlee, "America's Truth-Ache," *Washington Post,* Nov. 17, 1991, p. C1, 4. George Shultz maintains that American newspapers "garbled" the story and that Reagan "said no such thing" (*Turmoil and Triumph,* p. 551). Reagan's account of the films (though not of the incidents just mentioned) are in *Ronald Reagan: An American Life* (New York: Simon, 1990), p. 380.

35. Michael Deaver with Mickey Herskowitz, *Behind the Scenes* (New York: Morrow, 1987), p. 177.

36. Ronald Reagan, radio address to the nation on the observance of Mother's Day, May 7, 1983. Reported in John White, *The New Politics of Old Values* (Hanover, Vt.: University Press of New England, 1988), p. 12.

37. I am grateful to my colleague Jim Burroughs for pointing this out and for bringing me copies of Medal of Honor citations from the U.S. Army Center of Military History. There was an interesting exchange of letters in the *Washington Post* concerning Reagan's Medal of Honor story. In response to a columnist calling Reagan's story a "whopper," Richard P. Hallion, the U.S. Air Force historian defended Reagan. He cited several factual accounts of Medal of Honor heroism and concluded that the columnist did "a disservice not only to former president Reagan . . . but also to the memory of the 52,173 Army Air Forces airmen who died in combat in World War II" (*Washington Post,* Oct. 21, 2000, p. A21). In response Lars-Erik Nelson wrote to the *Post* and pointed out that Reagan did not tell any of the factual stories: "In fact, no Medal of Honor citation during World War II—and I have read them all—matches Reagan's story." Nelson concluded that "Hallion himself does a disservice to genuine Medal of Honor winners. . . . As historian of the Air Force, Hallion must surely want to distinguish fiction from the real heroism shown during the war" (*Washington Post,* Oct. 28, 2000, p. A23).

38. Reported in White, *The New Politics of Old Values,* p. 13.

39. Walter Cronkite, *A Reporter's Life* (New York: Knopf, 1996), pp. 55–58.

40. The account of Reagan's often-used story is in Lou Cannon, *Reagan* (New York: Putnam, 1982), p. 36. In the account, which Cannon got from the *Rockford Morning Star,* Reagan said, "I finally wrote a story about it [the football incident he had just related] and sold it to a national boys' magazine. That sale just about turned the tide for me away from professional sports and coaching on the one hand and acting on the other." Cannon's account continues: "There are no contemporary accounts of any incident of this sort, and Dixon High lost to Mendota only once when Reagan was a member of the varsity team. In that game, when Reagan was a senior in 1927, Mendota won 24–0."

41. Mark Hertsgaard, *On Bended Knee: The Press and the Reagan Presidency* (New York: Farrar, 1988), p. 279.

42. See Lou Cannon, *The Role of a Lifetime*, pp. 518–20. During his 1976 campaign Reagan said that a Chicago woman "has eighty names, thirty addresses, twelve Social Security cards and is collecting veterans' benefits on four nonexisting deceased husbands. . . . Her tax-free cash income alone is over $150,000." But the woman was convicted in 1977 for having two aliases and receiving unauthorized benefits of $8,000. For another account of Reagan's welfare queen stories, see David Zucchino, *Myth of the Welfare Queen* (New York: Scribner, 1997), pp. 64–65.

43. Nancy Reagan, *My Turn* (New York: Random, 1989), p. 273. According to scholar John Sloan, Reagan was prone to self-deception: "In Reagan's mind, unpleasant facts could be avoided; contradictions could be denied; anecdotes could overcome facts; movie illusions could substitute for history; unpleasant realities could be blamed on a hostile press." John W. Sloan, *The Reagan Effect: Economics and Presidential Leadership* (Lawrence: University Press of Kansas, 1999), p. 99.

44. It is also ironic that Reagan's nickname was "the Gipper," whom Reagan played in the 1940 movie, *Knute Rockne—All American*. Rockne told the tear-jerking story of famed Notre Dame football player George Gipp, who on his deathbed asked Coach Rockne to "win one for the Gipper." The problem with Rockne's account, according to John K. White, was "*it never happened*" (italics in original). George Gipp was a gifted athlete, but he was "lazy, undependable, and not particularly well liked by his teammates." In addition, Rockne was not present at Gipp's deathbed. See White, *The New Politics of Old Values*, pp. 7–15. See also Michael R. Steele, *Knute Rockne: A Bio-Bibliography* (Westport, Conn.: Greenwood, 1983), p. 20; and Gary Wills, *Reagan's America: Innocents at Home* (New York: Doubleday, 1987), pp. 120–22.

45. Don Van Natta, Jr., *First Off the Tee* (New York: Public Affairs, 2003), pp. 182–224.

46. Woodward, *Shadow*, p. 498; Shepherd Campbell and Peter Landau, *Presidential Lies: The Illustrated History of White House Golf* (New York: Macmillan, 1996), p. 218.

47. Stephen Ambrose, "Eisenhower," *Miller Center Journal* 4 (spring, 1997): 12. Van Natta says that Eisenhower was an honest golfer but that he would occasionally take a mulligan or a gimme and that he "on occasion, used the club face to gently alter the lie of his ball." *First Off the Tee*, p. 74.

48. Reeves, *President Kennedy*, p. 24.

49. Reeves, *President Kennedy*, p. 24. See Robert E. Gilbert, *The Mortal Presidency* (New York: Basic, 1993), pp. 154–79.

50. Robert Dallek, "The Medical Ordeals of JFK," *Atlantic Monthly*, Dec., 2002, p. 60. See also Robert Dallek, *An Unfinished Life: John F. Kennedy, 1917–1963* (New York: Little Brown, 2003).

51. Dallek, "The Medical Ordeals of JFK," p. 60.

52. Dallek, "The Medical Ordeals of JFK," p. 49.

53. See the account by Richard Nixon in *RN: The Memoirs of Richard Nixon* (New York: Grosset, 1978), p. 663–65.

54. For an analysis of the stigma attached to mental illness in the United States and its effects, see Otto Wahl, *Media Madness: Public Images of Mental Illness* (New Brunswick: Rutgers University Press, 1995).

55. See Robert Bauman, *The Gentleman from Maryland* (New York: Arbor, 1986).

56. This account is based on Jane Mayer and Jill Abramson, *Strange Justice* (Boston: Houghton, 1994), pp. 11–22.

57. Personal conversation with Roger Wilkins, spring, 1998.

58. Robert T. Hartman, *Palace Politics: An Inside Account of the Ford Presidency* (New York: McGraw, 1980), p. 155. Hartman's account says that Ford said that a denial that his staff was working on a possible transition would have been the truth since Buchen was not on his staff at that time. This equivocal account calls into question whether Ford was completely in the dark about transition planning. See also the account by John Robert Greene, *The Presidency of Gerald R. Ford* (Lawrence: University Press of Kansas, 1995), pp. 23–25.

59. Quoted in Woodward, *Shadow*, p. 12. Woodward's account of these meetings is on pp. 1–12.

60. Elliot L. Richardson, *Reflections of a Radical Moderate* (New York: Pantheon, 1996), p. 210.

61. Quoted in David Von Drehle and Ceci Connolly, "GOP Homes in on Gore's Credibility," *Washington Post*, Oct. 8, 2000, p. 1, A12. See also Melinda Henneberger, "Is What We've Got Here a Compulsion to Exaggerate?" New York Times, Oct. 15, 2000, p. WK1, and Peter Keating, "Will the Biggest Liar Win?" *George*, May 2000, pp. 50–57.

62. Candidate for vice president Richard Cheney said that he was "puzzled and saddened" by Gore's misstatements. Cheney may have been genuinely puzzled, but it is doubtful that he was saddened. More likely, Cheney was delighted that Gore made the statements that put him in such a bad light. Was Cheney lying, or was he being ironic? See Michael Kinsley, "Lies the Press Likes," *Washington Post*, Oct. 10, 2000, p. A25.

63. During the campaign debates Bush said that in Texas he brought Democrats and Republicans together to pass a "Patients' Bill of Rights," when he had vetoed such a bill in 1995 and refused to sign the portion of a similar bill in 1997. See Molly Ivins, "Bush's Lies," *Washington Post*, Oct. 21, 2000, p. A23; Glenn Kessler, "Debaters' Messages: Not the Whole Truth," *Washington Post*, Oct. 18, 2000, p. A15.

Chapter 3. Serious Presidential Lies

1. Quoted by Paul Gray, "Lies, Lies, Lies," *Time*, Oct. 5, 1992, p. 34.

2. See the account by Kenneth S. Davis, *FDR: The War President, 1940–1943* (New York: Random, 2000), pp. 277–89. See also Richard M. Ketchum, *The Borrowed Years, 1938–1941: America on the Way to War* (New York: Doubleday, 1989), pp. 602–603; and Justis D. Doenecke, *Storm on the Horizon: The Challenge to American Intervention, 1939–1941* (New York: Roman, 2000), pp. 259–62.

3. James MacGregor Burns, *Roosevelt: The Soldier of Freedom, 1940–1945* (New York: Harcourt, 1970), p. 140.

4. Quoted in Ketchum, *The Borrowed Years*, p. 602.

5. Quoted in David M. Kennedy, *Freedom from Fear* (New York: Oxford University Press, 1999), p. 497.

6. Kennedy, *Freedom from Fear*, p. 247 (accounts of the incident, pp. 496–98); Burns, *Roosevelt*, pp. 139–41; Doris Kearns Goodwin, *No Ordinary Time* (New York: Simon, 1995), pp. 277–78; and Robert Dallek, *Franklin D. Roosevelt and American Foreign Policy, 1932–1945* (New York: Oxford University Press, 1981), pp. 285–89.

7. See the accounts by Davis, *FDR: The War President*, pp. 277–89, and Doenecke, *Storm on the Horizon*, pp. 259–62.

8. Stephen Ambrose, *Eisenhower: Soldier and President* (New York: Simon, 1990), p. 507.

9. See the account by Fred Greenstein, *The Hidden-Hand Presidency* (New York: Basic, 1982), p. 253.

10. Dwight D. Eisenhower, *Waging Peace, 1956–1961* (New York: Doubleday, 1965), p. 546.

11. Michael R. Beschloss, *Mayday: Eisenhower, Khrushchev and the U-2 Affair* (New York: Harper, 1986), p. 233.

12. Quoted in Beschloss, *Mayday*, p. 252.

13. Eisenhower, *Waging Peace*, p. 548.

14. James Bamford, *Body of Secrets* (New York: Doubleday, 2001), p. 52.

15. Eisenhower, *Waging Peace*, p. 549. See also Ambrose, Eisenhower, p. 510.

16. Beschloss, *Mayday*, p. 254.

17. Beschloss, *Mayday*, p. 257; Eisenhower, Waging Peace, p. 550.

18. Bamford, *Body of Secrets*, p. 43. Bamford cites the oral history of Richard M. Bissell Jr.

19. Eisenhower, *Waging Peace*, p. 546.

20. Bamford, *Body of Secrets*, pp. 58–59. Bamford cites White House top-secret memorandum "Discussion at the 445th Meeting of the National Security Council, May 24, 1960," p. 8.

21. Beschloss, *Mayday*, p. 314.

22. Beschloss, *Mayday*, p. 314. Ironically Richard Helms was at the hearing representing the CIA. Helms was convicted for perjury in 1977 for lying about CIA operations in Chile in 1970. Helms said of the U-2 testimony, "They were all sworn . . . knowing what they knew and what actually went on, if it isn't perjury, I don't understand the meaning of the word" (*Mayday*, p. 314).

23. When asked about the reason for Eisenhower's actions, General Andrew Goodpaster, one of his top aides, said that they had prepared a "cover story" based on the premise that the plane and pilot would have been destroyed if the mission went amiss. Their mistake, he said, was to use the cover story (conversation with the author, March 21, 2000, Washington, D.C.).

24. Beschloss, *Mayday*, p. 252.

25. See Greenstein, *The Hidden-Hand Presidency*.

26. Richard Reeves, *President Kennedy: Profile of Power* (New York: Simon, 1993), pp. 265–66.

27. Reeves, *President Kennedy*, pp. 265–66.

28. Reeves, *President Kennedy*, pp. 280–81.

29. Quoted in Stanley I. Kutler, *The Wars of Watergate* (New York: Knopf, 1990), p. 619. Also quoted in Fawn M. Brodie, *Richard Nixon: The Shaping of His Character* (New York: Norton, 1981), p. 504.

30. Quoted in Kutler, *The Wars of Watergate*, p. 347.

31. The selection from the tape is reprinted in Michael Nelson, *Congressional Quarterly's Guide to the Presidency* (Washington, D.C.: CQ, 1989): 1389. Also, see the discussion in Kutler, *Wars of Watergate*, pp. 534–35.

32. Kutler, *Wars of Watergate*, pp. 432–33.

33. On the probable violation of the Arms Export Control Act by the Reagan administrations see George Shultz, *Turmoil and Triumph: My Years as Secretary of State* (New York: Scribners, 1993), p. 11.

34. George Bush with Victor Gold, *Looking Forward* (New York: Doubleday, 1987), p. 240.

35. Shultz, *Turmoil and Triumph*, pp. 808–809.

36. Quoted in Shultz, *Turmoil and Triumph*, p. 809.

37. William S. Cohen and George Mitchell, *Men of Zeal* (New York: Viking, 1988), pp. 264–65. For another account of Bush's dissembling about his involvement in meetings about arms sales to Iran see independent counsel Lawrence E. Walsh, *Iran-Contra: The Final Report* (New York: Times, 1993), chap. 28, pp. 473–83.

38. Shultz, *Turmoil and Triumph*, p. 809.

39. Joint Hearings on the Iran-Contra investigation—testimony of Caspar W. Weinberger (Washington, D.C.: GPO, 1988), pp. 100–10, 139; quoted in Cohen and Mitchell, *Men of Zeal*, p. 265.

40. Shultz, *Turmoil and Triumph*, p. 815.

41. Quoted in John F. Harris and Bill Miller, "In a Deal, Clinton Avoids Indictment," *Washington Post*, Jan. 20, 2001, p. 1.

42. H. Sidgwick, *The Methods of Ethics*, quoted in Sissela Bok, *Lying: Moral Choice in Public and Private Life* (New York: Vintage, 1978), p. 154.

43. Quoted in Jeffrey Toobin, "Circling the Wagons," *The New Yorker*, July 6, 1998, p. 29.

44. Quoted in Jerrrey L. Katz and Andrew Taylor, "House Accuses Clinton of Perjury, Obstruction," *CQ Weekly*, Dec. 22, 1998, p. 3322.

45. Henry Hyde on Iran-Contra, 1987, quoted by Michael Powell, "The Lost Art of Lying," *Washington Post*, Dec. 12, 1998, p. C11.

46. For an argument that Clinton's lies did not constitute the "high crimes or misdemeanors" necessary for impeachment, see James P. Pfiffner, The Modern Presidency, 3rd ed. (New York: Bedford St. Martin's, 2000), chap. 8; and Pfiffner, "President Clinton's Impeachment and Senate Trial," in James P. Pfiffner and Roger Davidson, eds., *Understanding the Presidency*, 2nd ed. (New York: Addison, 2000).

47. Bok, *Lying*, p. 182.

48. For a plausible, though not conclusive, argument that the United States may have been deliberately provoking the North Vietnamese in order to create an incident that would build congressional support for military action, see Fredrik Logevall, *Choosing War: The Lost Chance for Peace and the Escalation of War in Vietnam* (Berkeley: University of California Press, 1999), pp. 200–205.

49. *Foreign Relations of the United States* (FRUS), Vietnam, 1964 V, 607–9; quoted by Robert Dallek, *Flawed Giant: Lyndon Johnson and His Times* (New York: Oxford University Press, 1998), p. 151.

50. Alexander M. Haig Jr., *Inner Circles* (New York: Warner, 1992), p. 122.

51. Quoted in Logevall, *Choosing War*, p. 203.

52. Robert S. McNamara, *In Retrospect: The Tragedy and Lessons of Vietnam* (New York: Times, 1995), p. 137. On Oplan 34A and U.S. knowledge of it, see Edwin E. Moise, *Tonkin Gulf and the Escalation of the Vietnam War* (Chapel Hill: University of North Carolina Press, 1996), pp. 101–105.

53. Gulf of Tonkin Resolution, reprinted in Robert J. Spitzer, *President and Congress* (New York: McGraw, 1993), p. 167.

54. Quoted in Moise, *Tonkin Gulf*, p. 226. The punctuation is taken verbatim from the Moise book. See also Michael Beschloss, *Reaching for Glory: Lyndon Johnson's Secret White House Tapes, 1964–1965* (New York: Simon, 2001), p. 191.

55. Moise, *Tonkin Gulf*, p. 243.

56. George W. Ball, *The Past Has Another Pattern* (New York: Norton, 1982), p. 379. For an analysis sympathetic to Johnson see Dallek, *Flawed Giant*, pp. 147–56; for a critical account see Stanley Karnow, *Vietnam: A History* (New York: Penguin, 1983), p. 367–75; Joseph Goulden, *Truth Is the First Casualty: The Gulf of Tonkin Affair* (Chicago: Rand McNally, 1969); Neil Sheehan, *A Bright Shining Lie* (New York: Vintage, 1988). See also Larry Berman, *Planning a Tragedy: The Americanization of the War in Vietnam* (New York: Norton, 1982), pp. 31–34; and H. R. McMaster, *Dereliction of Duty* (New York: Harper, 1997), pp. 107–108, 121–23.

57. Beschloss, *Reaching for Glory*, pp. 37–39. At this point Johnson wanted to resist Barry Goldwater's calls for more aggressive military action in Vietnam.

58. Goulden, *Truth Is the First Casualty*, p . 160. The context of this quote was that Johnson was implying that he was misled by the Pentagon.

59. Both quotes from David Wise, *The Politics of Lying* (New York: Vintage, 1973), pp. 65–66.

60. McMaster, *Dereliction of Duty*, p. 195.

61. McMaster, *Dereliction of Duty*, p. 195.

62. Quoted in Logevall, *Choosing War*, p. 273.

63. McMaster, *Dereliction of Duty*, p. 247.

64. McMaster, *Dereliction of Duty*, p. 261.

65. See Logevall, *Choosing War*, p. 315.

66. McMaster, *Dereliction of Duty*, p. 211.

67. Quotes from Beschloss, *Reaching for Glory*, pp. 214–16.

68. Quoted in Berman, *Planning a Tragedy*, p. 57.

69. Quoted in Berman, *Planning a Tragedy*, p. 57.

70. Quoted in McMaster, *Dereliction of Duty*, p. 260.

71. McMaster, *Dereliction of Duty*, p. 263.

72. McMaster, *Dereliction of Duty*, p. 291.

73. Berman, *Planning a Tragedy*, p. xii.

74. McMaster, *Dereliction of Duty*, p. 319.

75. McMaster, *Dereliction of Duty*, pp. 319–20.

76. McMaster, *Dereliction of Duty*, p. 330.

77. This analysis is based on Seymour Hersh, *The Price of Power* (New York: Summit, 1983), pp. 60–65.

78. Robert Seamans was Secretary of the Air Force and was not told of the bombing missions in Cambodia. His morning briefing indicated that the bombs were dropped in Vietnam. He signed documents about the location of the bombing targets based on his misunderstanding of the actual location of some of the targets (conversation with the author, September 4, 1991, Washington, D.C.).
79. Richard Nixon, *RN: The Memoirs of Richard Nixon* (New York: Grosset, 1978), p. 382.
80. Walsh, *Iran-Contra*, pp. 468, 519–20. See Davie Abshire's account of Reagan's changing story in *To Save a Presidency: The Curse of Iran-Contra* (forthcoming), chap. 13.
81. Lawrence Walsh, *Firewall: The Iran-Contra Conspiracy and Cover-Up* (New York: Norton, 1997), p. 4.
82. Walsh, *Iran-Contra*, pp. 469–70.
83. See Shultz, *Turmoil and Triumph*, p. 811.
84. *Washington Post*, July 16, 1987, p. A15.
85. *Washington Post*, July 16, 1987, p.A1, A15.
86. *Washington Post*, July 16, 1987, p. A1, A15.
87. *Washington Post*, July 16, 1987, p. A15.
88. On whether the arms to Iran were primarily for the release of the hostages, see Shultz, *Turmoil and Triumph*, pp. 813 and 824. In a meeting President Reagan said that the release of the hostages was not linked to the arms sales, but Poindexter said, "How else will we get the hostages out?" Shultz concluded that "In that flash of candor, Poindexter had unwittingly ripped away whatever veil was left to the rationale of a 'changed Iran' as the reason for our arms sales."
89. Theodore Draper, *A Very Thin Line* (New York: Hill, 1991), p. 33.
90. *Washington Post*, July 16, 1987, p. A17.
91. *Washington Post*, July 16, 1987, p. A17.
92. *Washington Post*, July 16, 1987, p. A1.
93. *Washington Post*, July 16, 1987, p. A1.
94. *Washington Post*, July 16, 1987, p. A17.
95. Draper, *A Very Thin Line*, p. 570.
96. *Washington Post*, July 16, 1987, p. A15.
97. *Washington Post*, July 16, 1987, p. A14.
98. *Washington Post*, July 16, 1987, p. A14; Draper, *A Very Thin Line*, p. 570.
99. See Leon Festinger, *A Theory of Cognitive Dissonance* (Stanford: Stanford University Press, 1957).
100. See David Nybert, *The Varnished Truth* (Chicago: University of Chicago Press, 1993), p. 86.

Chapter 4. Sexual Probity and Presidential Character

1. Lynn Martin, secretary of labor for George Bush, quoted by Michael Beschloss, "George Bush," in Robert A. Wilson, ed., *Character above All* (New York: Simon, 1995), p. 242.

2. William J. Bennett, *The Death of Outrage: Bill Clinton and the Assault on American Ideals* (New York: Free Press, 1978), pp. 21, 37.

3. For an analysis of the Clinton impeachment see James P. Pfiffner, *The Modern Presidency*, 3rd ed. (New York: Bedford/St. Martin's, 2000), pp. 218–30.

4. See Herbert Parmet, *George Bush: The Life of a Lone Star Yankee* (New York: Scribner, 1997), pp. 178–79, 239–49). See also Gil Troy, *Affairs of State* (New York: Free Press, 1997), p. 325.

5. Doris Kearns Goodwin, *No Ordinary Time* (New York: Simon, 1994), p. 19. See also Geoffrey C. Ward, *A First-Class Temperament: The Emergence of Franklin Roosevelt* (New York: Harper, 1989), p. 412.

6. See Blanche Wiesen Cook, *Eleanor Roosevelt*, vol. 1, 1884–1933 (New York: Penguin, 1992), pp. 228–32, 285–86. See also Ward, *A First-Class Temperament*, p. 413.

7. Goodwin, *No Ordinary Time*, p. 20. Eleanor most likely knew that FDR would probably not sacrifice his promising career for Mercer, so her "offer" may have been disingenuous. Another possible obstacle to a Roosevelt-Mercer marriage was Lucy's Catholicism; her religion did not, however, prevent her from having an affair with a married man.

8. James Roosevelt with Bill Libby, *My Parents* (Chicago: Playboy, 1976), p. 101. Although some have doubted that the romance between FDR and Lucy Mercer was sexual, their son James argues to the contrary, "there came to light during this time a register from a motel in Virginia Beach showing that father and Lucy had checked in as man and wife and spent the night" (p. 101). See also Ward, *A First-Class Temperament*, pp. 362–69.

9. Goodwin, *No Ordinary Time*, p. 377; and Ward, *A First-Class Temperament*, p. 415.

10. See Cook, *Eleanor Roosevelt* (vol. 1), pp. 314–17; Ward, *A First-Class Temperament*, pp. 709–15.

11. Hugh Gregory Gallagher, *FDR's Splendid Deception* (New York: Dodd, 1985), pp. 136–37; Ward, *A First-Class Temperament*, pp. 709–14.

12. Ward, *A First-Class Temperament*, p. 709.

13. Quoted in Ted Morgan, *FDR: A Biography* (New York: Simon, 1985), p. 256; see Ward, *A First-Class Temperament*, pp. 710–11.

14. See Gallagher, *FDR's Splendid Deception*, p. 131. Gallagher, though conceding that FDR was sexually potent, argues that FDR and Missy probably did not have a sexual relationship and maintains that FDR was apparently celibate from the age of thirty-six until he died. See pp. 130–44, particularly p. 138. Frank Freidel, in *Franklin Delano Roosevelt: The Triumph* (Boston: Little, 1956), reprints the technical report of the doctors who examined FDR when he was running for president in 1931. FDR underwent the examination to reassure supporters and opponents that he was healthy enough to be president. The panel of doctors concluded that FDR was capable of sexual relations: "No symptoms of *impotentia coeuendi.*" Their report is reprinted on pp. 210–11. The panel of doctors was headed by the director of the New York Academy of Medicine, who selected the panel of eminent physicians to examine FDR. The technical part of the doctors' report was first published by John Gunther, *Roosevelt in Retrospect* (New York: Harper, 1950), pp. 266–67.

15. Roosevelt, *My Parents*, pp. 104–105. James doubts that his father was capable of sex because of his polio. "From my observation, it would have been difficult for him to function sexually after he became crippled from the waist down from polio" (p. 104). But Hugh Gallagher, FDR biographer and fellow polio victim, has no doubt that the doctors' analysis was correct in concluding that FDR was capable of sexual function. According to Gallagher, from his medical understanding and personal experience, polio affects the muscles but not the organs essential for sexual performance. Nevertheless, Gallagher thinks that because of the general mores of the times, it is unlikely that FDR and Missy had a sexual relationship (personal communication with the author, March 1, 2001). See also Ward, *A First-Class Temperament*, pp. 712–14. Ward doubts that their relationship was sexual.

16. Goodwin, *No Ordinary Time*, p. 120.

17. Cook, *Eleanor Roosevelt*, vol. 2, 1933–1938, p. 38; Goodwin, *No Ordinary Time*, p. 121.

18. See James Roosevelt's account in *My Parents*, pp. 107–108. James was executor of FDR's will. Also Goodwin, *No Ordinary Time*, p. 246.

19. On Eleanor's relationship with Hickok see Cook, *Eleanor Roosevelt*, vol. 2, pp. 174–76, 192–212, and passim.

20. Goodwin, *No Ordinary Time*, pp. 221–22. See also Rodger Streitmatter, *Empty without You: The Intimate Letters of Eleanor Roosevelt and Lorena Hickok* (New York: Free Press, 1999).

21. Roosevelt, *My Parents*, p. 110. See also Cook's account of their relationship in *Eleanor Roosevelt*, vol. 1, pp. 430–35.

22. Roosevelt, *My Parents*, p. 102.

23. Goodwin, *No Ordinary Time*, p. 221.

24. Goodwin, *No Ordinary Time*, pp. 600–602.

25. Goodwin, *No Ordinary Time*, p. 629.

26. This analysis is based on her account of their affair in Kay Summersby Morgan, *Past Forgetting: My Love Affair with Dwight D. Eisenhower* (New York: Simon, 1976). Her earlier version of her wartime memoirs, without the explicit account of their affair, was Kay Summersby, *Eisenhower Was My Boss* (Englewood Cliffs, N.Y.: Prentice, 1948).

27. Merle Miller, *Ike the Soldier: As They Knew Him* (New York: Putnam, 1987), pp. 639–40.

28. Morgan, *Past Forgetting*, pp. 146–47, 269.

29. Wilson, *Character above All*, p. 65; Stephen E. Ambrose, "Eisenhower," in *Remarks Presented in a Miller Center Forum on March 30, 1996* (Charlottesville, Va.: Miller Center of Public Affairs, 1996), p. 14.

30. Quoted in Stephen E. Ambrose, *Eisenhower: Soldier and President* (New York: Simon, 1990), p. 211. The letters are reproduced in Miller, *Ike the Soldier*, pp. 644–46.

31. Miller, *Ike the Soldier*, pp. 644–45. See also Ambrose, *Eisenhower*, p. 211.

32. Morgan, *Past Forgetting*, p. 275.

33. Morgan, *Past Forgetting*, pp. 277, 280.

34. Merle Miller, *Plain Speaking: An Oral Biography of Harry S. Truman* (New York:

Berkley, 1973), p. 340. Truman and Eisenhower also disagreed about whether Truman had ever offered to back Eisenhower for the presidency. Evidently one or the other did not tell the truth. In Eisenhower's book, *Crusade in Europe* (New York: Doubleday, 1948), Eisenhower says that when Truman visited him in Germany at the end of the war he did. But Truman denied that he did any such thing. When asked by Merle Miller about a rumor that he had offered to support Eisenhower for president, Truman replied: "There's no reason for any debate about it. I saw him there in Frankfurt, and I told him how grateful the American people were for the job he'd done, and we talked about the fact that a lot of wartime heroes get into politics and get elected. And he said that under no circumstances was he going to get into politics at any time. And that's all there was to it. He said I said it, but I didn't. . . . And it was the same thing in 1948; he said I offered him the Presidency, which I didn't" (Miller, *Plain Speaking*, p. 338). Robert J. Donovan also reported that Truman offered to back Eisenhower for the presidency in 1948. See *Conflict and Crisis* (New York: Norton, 1977), p. 338. In diary entries dicovered in 2003, Truman said that in 1947 he offered to back Eisenhower for the presidency in 1948 if General MacArthur ran as a Republican. (Rebecca Dana and Peter Carlson, "Harry Truman's Forgotten Diary," *Washington Post* (July 11, 2003), p. 1. A10.)"

35. Ambrose, *Eisenhower*, p. 210.

36. Miller, *Ike the Soldier*, pp. 642–43. Miller also mentions Drew Pearson's account of rumors that General Patton had written to his wife about Ike's wish for a divorce (p. 642).

37. Peter Lyon, Eisenhower: *Portrait of the Hero* (Boston: Little, 1974), pp. 387–88. Lyon also says that the correspondence is not in Marshall papers, but this is in accord with Truman's account. Lyon characterized the rumor that Eisenhower had planned to divorce his wife as "idle malice" (p. 387). In his book he describes many aspects of Summersby's role in Eisenhower's wartime life, including horseback riding (p. 197) but does not believe that they had a "liaison" (p. 387). See also pp. 7–8, 12, 18, 21, 123, 133, 150, 156, 197, 277, 313, 340, 387–88, and 431.

38. Quoted in Gil Troy, *Mr. and Mrs. President: From the Trumans to the Clintons*, 2d ed. (Lawrence: University Press of Kansas, 2000), p. 64.

39. Ambrose, *Eisenhower*, p. 212–13.

40. "For the purpose of this deposition, a person engages in 'sexual relations' when the person knowingly engages in or causes . . . contact with the genitalia, anus, groin, breast, inner thigh, or buttocks of any person with an intent to arouse or gratify the sexual desire of any person." Quoted in Alan M. Dershowitz, *Sexual McCarthyism* (New York: Basic, 1998), p. 18.

41. Some accounts of Eisenhower's service in the war discount the rumors of a relationship with Summersby. Geoffrey Perret dismisses Summersby as a woman with romantic delusions and detached from the reality that Eisenhower was not in love with her and that her book, *Past Forgetting*, was written by a woman "dying of cancer and, in the grip of certain death, was reviewing a life that was a tale of failure and disappointment" (Geoffrey Perret, *Eisenhower* [New York: Random, 1999], p. 216). According to Perret "Eisenhower was using Kay, in a one-sided relationship that was exploitative and manipulative" (p. 217). This interpretation of

the nature of their relationship casts Eisenhower in a much less favorable light than do those who believe he had a romantic relationship with Summersby.

42. See the account by Seymour Hersh, *The Dark Side of Camelot* (New York: Little, 1997), pp. 326–40.

43. According to former Secret Service agent William T. McIntyre, once when Jackie unexpectedly decided to take a swim, the president "was in the pool with a couple of bimbos." The Secret Service agent on duty delayed her entrance to the pool until the president and his friends had left. Hersh, *Dark Side of Camelot*, p. 240. On Kennedy's sexual exploits in the White House swimming pool, see also Traphes Bryant with Frances Spatz Leighton, *Dog Days at the White House* (New York: Macmillan, 1975), pp. 22–24. See also Peter Collier and David Horowitz, *The Kennedys: An American Drama* (New York: Summit, 1984), p. 283.

44. According to historian Michael Beschloss, "His lawyers, his father, and his brother Robert evidently used financial payoffs, legal action, and other kinds of threats to silence women who had been involved with Kennedy and, for breach of promise or other reasons, threatened to go public." Michael Beschloss, *The Crisis Years* (New York: Burlingame, 1991), p. 614.

45. For an account of Kennedy's prepresidential relationships with women see Nigel Hamilton, *JFK: Reckless Youth* (New York: Random, 1992), pp. 358–59, 731–32, and passim. See also Collier and Horowitz, *The Kennedys*, p. 175.

46. Troy, *Mr. and Mrs. President*, p. 126; Richard Reeves, "John F. Kennedy, 1961–1963," in Wilson, *Character above All*, p. 93; Ben Bradlee, *A Good Life: Newspapering and Other Adventures* (New York: Simon, 1995), pp. 216, 394.

47. Seymour M. Hersh, *Dark Side of Camelot* (New York: Little, 1997), p. 31.

48. Both quotes from Hersh, *Dark Side of Camelot*, pp. 24 (Bradlee) and 299 (Exner).

49. Richard Reeves, *President Kennedy: Profile of Power* (New York: Simon, 1993), pp. 35, 42.

50. On the Kennedy–Pinchot-Meyer relationship, see Edward Klein, *All Too Human* (New York: Pocket, 1996), pp. 327–29; also Parmet, *JFK*, pp. 304–308.

51. Bradlee, *A Good Life*, pp. 268–69. For an account of Kennedy's affair with Myer, see her biography by Nina Burleigh, *A Very Private Woman: The Life and Unsolved Murder of Presidential Mistress Mary Myer* (New York: Bantam, 1998), particularly pp. 181–227. The Secret Service gate logs of her White House visits are reproduced on pages 329–30.

52. James N. Giglio, *The Presidency of John F. Kennedy* (Lawrence: University Press of Kansas, 1991), p. 267. For another list of Kennedy sexual partners see Jeffrey D. Schultz, *Presidential Scandals* (Washington, D.C.: CQ, 2000), pp. 345–48.

53. Historian Robert Dallek discovered evidence of the affair when he requested that an oral history account be released. See Dallek, *An Unfinished Life: John F. Kennedy, 1917–1963* (Boston: Little Brown, 2003), p. 476. Fahnestock's words come from Lloyd Grove, "The Reliable Source," *Washington Post*, May 16, 2003, p. C3.

54. Reeves, *President Kennedy*, p. 290; also Reeves, "John F. Kennedy," in *Wilson*, p. 93. Bobby Baker reported that Kennedy said to him, "You know, I get a migraine headache if I don't get a strange piece of ass every day." Hersh, *Dark Side of Camelot*, p. 389.

55. On the Kennedy-Campbell relationship, see Klein, *All Too Human*, pp. 244–48; Collier and Horowitz, *The Kennedys*, pp. 293–95, 412–13.

56. Beschloss notes that Kennedy did not know that Campbell had a relationship with Giancana when he began his affair, but he did not stop it when he found out (Beschloss, *The Crisis Years*, pp. 611–12).

57. See Hersh, *Dark Side of Camelot*, pp. 294–325, and passim. See Reeves, *President Kennedy*, pp. 288–92, and passim.

58. Reeves, *President Kennedy*, p. 290; Hersh, *Dark Side of Camelot*, p. 313.

59. Hersh, *Dark Side of Camelot*, pp. 389–90.

60. Beschloss, *The Crisis Years*, pp. 615–17; Hersh, *Dark Side of Camelot*, pp. 399–400.

61. For an analysis of some of Kennedy's affairs before he was president and while he was in the White House, see Parmet, *JFK*, pp. 110–30. For an amusing account of an encounter between JFK and Marlene Dietrich in the White House, see Kenneth Tynan, "The Journals of Kenneth Tynan: Entries from the Unpublished Private Journals of a Man with Passions" (*New Yorker* [August 7, 2000], pp. 49–50). For a photograph of Dietrich at the White House with Kennedy aide Dave Powers, see Barbara Leaming, *Mrs. Kennedy: The Missing History of the Kennedy Years* (New York: Simon, 2001), pp. 182–83.

62. Hersh, *Dark Side of Camelot*, pp. 237, 242.

63. Hersh, *Dark Side of Camelot*, pp. 229–30.

64. For a discussion of Kennedy's proclivity for womanizing, see Doris Kearns Goodwin, *The Fitzgeralds and the Kennedys* (New York: St. Martin's, 1987), pp. 836–38, 892–93. For a treatment of Jacqueline Kennedy's reaction to JFK's relationships with other women, see Sarah Bradford, *America's Queen: The Life of Jacqueline Kennedy Onassis* (New York: Viking, 2000), pp. 84–85, 104–105, 111–12, 154–56, 222–26, 380–83, and passim.

65. Hersh, *Dark Side of Camelot*, p. 23.

66. On the Kennedy-Monroe relationship, see Klein, *All Too Human*, pp. 308–12; Thomas C. Reeves, *A Question of Character* (Roseville, Calif.: Prima, 1997), pp. 317–27; Hersh, *Dark Side of Camelot*, pp. 102–106; Reeves, *President Kennedy*, pp. 315–16; Leaming, *Mrs. Kennedy*, pp. 196–201, 210–11 .

67. Hersh, *Dark Side of Camelot*, pp. 239, 241. One young staffer and enabler of Kennedy's sexual exploits, Fred Dutton, told Kennedy biographer Richard Reeves, "We're a bunch of virgins, married virgins, and he's like God, fucking anybody he wants to anytime he feels like it" (Reeves, *President Kennedy*, p. 291).

68. Hersh, *Dark Side of Camelot*, p. 396; Reeves, *President Kennedy*, p. 539; Reeves, "John F. Kennedy," p. 95.

69. Beschloss, *The Crisis Years*, p. 615; Troy, *Mr. and Mrs. President*, p. 125.

70. Bradlee, *A Good Life*, p. 484.

71. For an account of their relationship from Jackie's perspective, see Leaming, *Mrs. Kennedy*.

72. Jan Jarboe Russell, *Lady Bird: A Biography of Mrs. Johnson* (New York: Scribner, 1999), p. 168.

73. For accounts of Johnson's relationship with Alice Glass see Robert Caro, *The Path to Power* (New York: Knopf, 1982), pp. 480–92; Robert Caro, *Means of Ascent* (New

York: Knopf, 1990), pp. 25–26; Troy, *Mr. and Mrs. President*, pp. 146–47; Irwin
Unger and Debi Unger, *LBJ: A Life* (New York: Wiley, 1999). Biographer Paul K.
Conkin in *Big Daddy from the Pedernales* (Boston: Twayne, 1986) is skeptical of
accounts of LBJ's affair with Glass and argues that "the evidence is not conclusive
on the depth of his involvement or on the fact of sexual intimacy" (p. 98). But
most historical accounts accept their affair as established. See particularly Caro's
account of their relationship in *Path to Power*, pp. 476–92. Caro bases his account,
among other sources, on interviews with Glass's sister, Mary Louise Glass Young;
her friend Alice Hopkins; her friend Frank C. Oltorf; her friend Harold H. Young
(who married Glass's sister), and also a source who wanted to remain anonymous.
John Connally, who had personal knowledge of their affair, wrote about it in *In
History's Shadow* (New York: Hyperion, 1993), pp. 69–71.

74. Russell, *Lady Bird*, pp. 272, 129–40. After LBJ died, Glass wrote to ask for the return
    of the eagle, and Lady Bird sent it to her.

75. See Michael Beschloss, *Taking Charge* (New York: Simon, 1997), p. 137. See also
    Joseph Califano, *The Triumph and Tragedy of Lyndon Johnson* (New York: Simon,
    1991), p. 337. Califano was told of the affair by Harry McPherson and Horace
    Busby; see endnote number 25 on page 381 of *Triumph and Tragedy*.

76. Unger and Unger, *LBJ: A Life*, p. 82.

77. Robert Caro, *Master of the Senate* (New York: Knopf, 2002), pp. 144–45; Michael
    Beschloss quotes Lady Bird's account from her diary in *Taking Charge*, p. 268.

78. See Robert Dallek, *Flawed Giant: Lyndon Johnson and His Times, 1961-1973* (New
    York: Oxford University Press, 1998), pp. 186–87.

79. Russell, *Lady Bird*, p. 272.

80. Quoted by Dallek, *Flawed Giant*, p. 408.

81. Russell, *Lady Bird*, pp. 170, 172. On Johnson's crude behavior see Unger and Unger,
    LBJ: A Life, p. 371; Dallek, *Flawed Giant*, p. 186; Caro, *Path to Power*, p. 485; and Troy,
    Mr. and Mrs. President, p. 148. During the 1950s Johnson, though clearly attached to
    Lady Bird, would flaunt his sexual conquests. One afternoon, for instance, he went
    for a car ride with a young woman beside him and Lady Bird next to her in the front
    seat. According to a Johnson staffer who was in the back seat, Johnson had his hand
    under the woman's skirt while Lady Bird ignored his behavior. See Horace Busby's
    account of this incident in Russell, *Lady Bird*, p. 204, and in Caro, *Master of the
    Senate*, p. 437. According to journalist Hugh Sidey, Johnson "caressed other women
    in front of her [Lady Bird]" (Caro, *Master of the Senate*, p. 437).

82. Russell, *Lady Bird*, pp. 204, 212.

83. Troy, *Mr. and Mrs. President*, p. 139.

84. Russell, *Lady Bird*, p. 307. On LBJ's womanizing see Unger and Unger, *LBJ: A Life*,
    pp. 430–31; Troy, *Mr. and Mrs. President*, p. 134–51; Dallek, *Flawed Giant*, pp. 186–87.
    On Johnson's deliberate humiliation of Lady Bird, see Caro, *Master of the Senate*,
    pp. 224–28.

85. On Johnson's attitudes toward women and his wife see Merle Miller, *Lyndon: An
    Oral Biography* (New York: Putnam, 1980), pp. 444–46.

86. Russell, *Lady Bird*, pp. 129, 205. For an account of LBJ's cruelty to his wife, see
    Caro, *Means of Ascent*, p. 70.

87. Russell, *Lady Bird*, p. 235; Unger and Unger, *LBJ: A Life*, p. 431.

88. Russell, *Lady Bird*, p. 184. On their relationship see also Caro, *Master of the Senate*, pp. 650–54.

89. Russell, *Lady Bird*, pp. 143, 156. For an account of their radio and TV holdings see Unger and Unger, *LBJ: A Life*, p. 116–22.

90. Russell, *Lady Bird*, p. 280.

91. Russell, *Lady Bird*, p. 203; see also Dallek, *Flawed Giant*, p. 187.

92. Russell, *Lady Bird*, p. 12.

93. David Maraniss, *First in His Class* (New York: Touchstone, 1995), pp. 440–41. Maraniss's account was based on interviews with Armstrong, Morris, and Wright.

94. Michael Isikoff, *Uncovering Clinton: A Reporter's Story* (New York: Crown, 1999), p. 32.

95. Gennifer Flowers with Jacquelyn Dapper, *Gennifer Flowers: Passion and Betrayal* (Del Mar, Calif.: Emery Dalton, 1995). See the account of the Flowers tapes in Joe Conason and Gene Lyons, *The Hunting of the President: The Ten-Year Campaign to Destroy Bill and Hillary Clinton* (New York: St. Martin's, 2000), pp. 16–29. Flowers's account of their affair is in *Gennifer Flowers*.

96. Quoted in Conason and Lyons, *Hunting of the President*, p. 24.

97. See Conason and Lyons, *Hunting of the President*, pp. 25–26.

98. Clinton testimony in the Jones deposition, quoted in Isikoff, *Uncovering Clinton*, p. 327. For a skeptical account of the Willey episode see Conason and Lyons, *Hunting of the President*, pp. 271–72, 286–89. For Isikoff's account see *Uncovering Clinton*, 117–21 and passim.

99. See Isikoff, *Uncovering Clinton*, pp. 52–74, and especially pp. 162–63. Much more disturbing was the account by Juanita Broaddrick, who claimed that in 1978 Clinton, who was then attorney general of Arkansas, forcibly had sex with her in her hotel room. Broaddrick's public accounts of the incident were inconsistent, and the evidence about it was inconclusive. See Susan Schmidt and Michael Weisskopf, *Truth at Any Cost: Ken Starr and the Unmaking of Bill Clinton* (New York: Harper, 2000), pp. 121–22; and Jeffrey Toobin, *A Vast Conspiracy* (New York: Random, 1999), pp. 140–41, 383–84. For accounts of how political enemies of Clinton financed and organized investigations, media stories, and lawsuits against him, see Conason and Lyons, Hunting of the President; Toobin, *A Vast Conspiracy*. See also James B. Stewart, *Blood Sport: The President and His Adversaries* (New York: Simon, 1996).

100. This account is based on *The Starr Report: The Findings of Independent Counsel Kenneth W. Starr on President Clinton and the Lewinsky Affair* (New York: Public Affairs, 1998), pp. 48–84. According to Lewinsky, when the president told her on May 24, 1997, that he was ending their intimate relationship, he said that earlier in his marriage "he had had hundreds of affairs; but since turning 40 [in 1986], he had made a concerted effort to be faithful" (p. 83).

101. See the analysis of Richard A. Posner, *An Affair of State* (Cambridge: Harvard University Press, 1999), pp. 38–44.

102. Goodwin, *No Ordinary Time*.

103. New York: William Morrow, 1998.

104. Carl S. Anthony, *Florence Harding* (New York: Morrow, 1998), p. 98 (italics in original).

105. Quoted in David Remnick, "Is Sex Necessary?" *The New Yorker*, Feb. 2, 1998, p. 32.

106. George Stephanopoulos, "A Question of Betrayal," *Newsweek*, Feb. 2, 1998, pp. 50–51; Myers quote in Institute of Governmental Studies, University of California at Berkeley, "Jay Gatsby in the Oval Office," *Public Affairs Report* 39, no. 4 (July 1998): 7.

107. See Andrew Stark, *Conflict of Interest in American Public Life* (Cambridge: Harvard University Press, 2000), pp. 142–47.

108. Bradlee, *A Good Life*, p. 484.

Chapter 5. Character, Consistency, and Campaign Promises

1. For an analysis of how press coverage fosters the inaccurate assumption that presidents do not keep their promises and encourages voter cynicism see Kathleen Hall Jamieson, *Everything You Think You Know about Politics and Why You're Wrong* (New York: Basic, 2000), chap. 2, pp. 19–36.

2. Stephen L. Carter, *Integrity* (New York: Basic, 1996), pp. 35–36.

3. See the discussion in Garry Wills, *Certain Trumpets* (New York: Simon, 1994), pp. 11–22.

4. See James P. Pfiffner, "Ranking Presidents: Continuity and Volatility," *White House Studies*, Vol. 3, No. 1 (2003), pp. 23–34.

5. Reinhard H. Luthin, *The Real Abraham Lincoln* (Englewood Cliffs, N.J.: Prentice, 1960), p. 337.

6. Quoted in David Herbert Donald, *Lincoln* (New York: Simon, 1995), p. 206.

7. Quoted in David Zarefsky, "Consistency and Change in Lincoln's Rhetoric about Equality," *Rhetoric and Public Affairs* 1, no. 1 (spring, 1998): 32

8. Donald, *Lincoln*, p. 214.

9. Quoted in Lerone Bennett Jr., *Forced into Glory: Abraham Lincoln's White Dream* (Chicago: Johnson, 2000), p. 208.

10. Donald, *Lincoln*, p. 167.

11. "Although there were differences in emphasis from one audience to another, Lincoln's basic position remained the same for most of his political career—he favored economic equality, but not social and political equality, between the races. Lincoln adapted this basic position in different ways as the audience and the situation required, relying both on careful dissociations and on hedging devices. . . . His remarks in the Charleston debate are conveniently 'forgotten,' excused as a necessary adaption to local politics and not reflective of the Great Emancipator's 'true' sentiment." Zarefsky, "Consistency and Change in Lincoln's Rhetoric about Equality," p. 41. Note that in quoting Lincoln in the Charleston debate Zarefsky uses the words "perfect equality" rather than the words "social and political equality" (Zarefsky, p. 33). Donald quotes the Charleston speech as "social and political equality" (*Lincoln*, p. 221).

12. Luthin, *The Real Lincoln*, p. 569.

13. Quoted in Donald, *Lincoln*, p. 368.

14. Donald, *Lincoln*, p. 369.
15. Quoted in Luthin, *The Real Abraham Lincoln*, p. 198.
16. Donald, *Lincoln*, p. 167.
17. Luthin, *The Real Abraham Lincoln*, p. 335.
18. Donald, *Lincoln*, p. 221.
19. Bennett, *Forced into Glory*, p. 15. Italics in original.
20. Luthin, *The Real Abraham Lincoln*, p. 569, Donald, *Lincoln*, p. 167, Bennett, *Forced into Glory*, pp. 381–87, 456–60.
21. Donald, *Lincoln*, p. 166.
22. Allen C. Guelzo, "Lincoln and the Abolitionists," *Wilson Quarterly* (fall, 2000): 68.
23. Guelzo, "Lincoln and the Abolitionists," p. 68.
24. Garry Wills, "What Makes a Good Leader?" in James P. Pfiffner and Roger H. Davidson, *Understanding the Presidency*, 2d ed. (New York: Longman, 2000), p. 470.
25. Luthin, *The Real Abraham Lincoln*, p. 569.
26. Wills, in Pfiffner and Davidson, *Understanding the Presidency*, p. 471.
27. Quoted in Wills, *Certain Trumpets*, p. 16.
28. Garry Wills, "Honest Abe," *Time*, Oct. 5, 1992, pp. 41–42.
29. Bennett, *Forced into Glory*, last paragraph of preface (no page number).
30. Bennett, *Forced into Glory*, p. 24.
31. Donald, *Lincoln*, p. 15.
32. James MacGregor Burns, *Roosevelt: The Lion and the Fox* (New York: Harcourt, 1965), p. 8.
33. Burns, *Roosevelt: The Lion and the Fox*, p. 143.
34. Burns, *Roosevelt: The Lion and the Fox*, p. 144.
35. Ted Morgan, *FDR: A Biography* (New York: Simon, 1985), p. 368.
36. James MacGregor Burns, *Roosevelt: The Soldier of Freedom, 1940–1945* (New York: Harcourt, 1970), p. 9. On FDR's inconsistency and flip-flops, see of Wills's *Certain Trumpets*, p. 25.
37. Jeff Fishel, *Presidents and Promises* (Washington, D.C.: CQ, 1985). See also Gerald Pomper with Susan Lederman, *Elections in America* (New York: Dodd, 1976), pp. 162–63; Michael G. Krukones, *Promises and Performance: Presidential Campaigns as Policy Predictors* (Lanham, Md.: University Press of America, 1984); Ian Budge and Richard I Hofferbert, "Mandates and Policy Outputs: U.S. Party Platforms and Federal Expenditures," *American Political Science Review* 84 (1990): 111–32.
38. Fishel, *Presidents and Promises*, p. 33.
39. Carolyn M. Shaw, "Has President Clinton Fulfilled His 1992 Campaign Promises?" Paper presented at the 1996 annual meeting of the American Political Science Association (August, 1996). Cited in Jamieson, *Everything You Think You Know about Politics*, pp. 33, 249.
40. Knight-Ridder Newspapers found that Clinton tried to keep 106 of 160 promises (66 percent); the *St. Petersburg Times* judged that Clinton kept 105 of 134 promises. See Jamieson, *Everything You Think You Know about Politics*, pp. 33, 249.
41. David M. Kennedy, *Freedom from Fear: The American People in Depression and War, 1929–1945* (New York: Oxford University Press, 1999), pp. 79, 118–19, 147.

42. Burns, *Roosevelt: The Lion and the Fox*, p. 143.

43. Burns, *Roosevelt: The Lion and the Fox*, p. 167.

44. Quoted in Arthur Schlesinger Jr., *The Crisis of the Old Order* (Boston: Houghton, 1957), p. 457.

45. Burns, *Roosevelt: The Lion and the Fox*, p. 246.

46. Burns, *Roosevelt: The Lion and the Fox*, p. 323. See also Kenneth S. Davis, *FDR: Into the Storm*, 1937–1940 (New York: Random, 1993), p. 9.

47. Kennedy, *Freedom from Fear*, p. 147.

48. Burns, *Roosevelt: The Lion and the Fox*, p. 448.

49. Davis, *FDR: Into the Storm*, p. 620. The Irish mothers in Boston were not particularly likely to be sympathetic to having their newly drafted sons sent to Europe to protect England from Hitler's armies

50. Davis, *FDR: Into the Storm*, p. 620; see also Burns, *Roosevelt: The Lion and the Fox*, pp. 448–49.

51. Doris Kearns Goodwin, *No Ordinary Time* (New York: Simon, 1994), p. 187.

52. Goodwin, *No Ordinary Time*, p. 187.

53. Michael R. Beschloss, "Foreign Policy's Big Moment," *The New York Times*, Apr. 11, 1999, p. WK17.

54. Kennedy, *Freedom from Fear*, pp. 263–64.

55. Stephen E. Ambrose, *Eisenhower: Soldier and President* (New York: Simon, 1990), p. 285.

56. Richard Nixon, *RN: The Memoirs of Richard Nixon* (New York: Grosset, 1978), p. 298.

57. Jeffrey Kimball, *Nixon's Vietnam War* (Lawrence: University Press of Kansas, 1998), p. 82.

58. William Safire, "On Language: Secret Plan," *New York Times Magazine*, May 21, 2000, pp. 29–30; Nixon, *RN*, p. 298.

59. See Larry Berman, *No Peace, No Honor* (New York: Free Press, 2001).

60. Quoted in Fishel, *Presidents and Promises*, p. 126.

61. *Inaugural Addresses of the Presidents* (Washington, D.C.: GPO, 1989), p. 332.

62. For further analysis see James P. Pfiffner, *The Strategic Presidency: Hitting the Ground Running*, 2d ed. (Lawrence: University Press of Kansas, 1996), pp. 100–10. See also Herbert Stein, *Presidential Economics* (New York: Simon, 1984), pp. 235–306; David Stockman, *The Triumph of Politics* (New York: Harper, 1986); John W. Sloan, *The Reagan Effect: Economics and Presidential Leadership* (Lawrence: University Press of Kansas, 1999).

63. See Stockman's account, *The Triumph of Politics*, pp. 106–10; and Sloan, *The Reagan Effect*, pp. 110–14.

64. See Sloan, *The Reagan Effect*, p. 149. According to Sloan, "This disingenuous remark may have assuaged Reagan's conscience, but it was widely ridiculed."

65. *Washington Post* reporter David Broder observed that Reagan "treats knowledge as if it were dangerous to his convictions. Often it is." See Sloan, *The Reagan Effect*, p. 83.

66. In 1982 Reagan backed the Tax Equity and Fiscal Responsibility Act (TEFRA), and in 1983 he supported the recommendations of the Greenspan commission to raise taxes and cut benefits in order to reform the Social Security system.

67. See the analysis by Bob Woodward, "Origin of the Tax Pledge," *Washington Post*, Oct. 4, 1992, p. A1.

68. Richard Darman, *Who's in Control?* (New York: Simon, 1997), pp. 192–95.

69. Peggy Noonan, *What I Saw at the Revolution* (New York: Random, 1990), pp. 307–308.

70. Noonan, *What I Saw at the Revolution*, p. 307.

71. Darman, *Who's in Control?* pp. 192–93. The words "read my lips" came from the popular Clint Eastwood movie "Dirty Harry," in which the macho movie star threatened the bad guys using the phrase. Even though some thought that the same phrase in Bush's mouth would not ring true because he was not a macho character, they were countered by Republican media adviser Roger Ailes, who pointed out that the pledge was one of the few strong lines in the speech and that he would coach Bush to deliver it effectively.

72. For details, see James P. Pfiffner, "The President and the Postreform Congress," in Roger Davidson, ed., *The Postreform Congress* (New York: St. Martin's, 1992).

73. Darman, *Who's in Control?* p. 259.

74. Darman, *Who's in Control?* pp. 262–63.

75. Darman, *Who's in Control?* p. 265.

76. Marlin Fitzwater, *Call the Briefing!* (New York: Times, 1995), p. 214.

77. Darman, *Who's in Control?* p. 266.

78. For an argument that Clinton should have broken his promise to cut the White House staff by 25 percent, see James P. Pfiffner, "Cutting Staff No Easy Task for Clinton," *Maine Sunday Telegram*, Dec. 12, 1993.

79. For a discussion of Clinton's campaign promises see David E. Rosenbaum, "What He Promised, and What He Did," *New York Times*, July 25, 1999, p. WK4. Stanley Renshon has a maximalist list of his calculations of Clinton promises in *High Hopes: The Clinton Presidency and the Politics of Ambition* (New York: New York University Press, 1996), pp. 76–84.

80. The economic agenda for the Clinton administration is the main subject of Bob Woodward's *The Agenda* (New York: Simon, 1994). Much of my analysis is based on Woodward's account. See also the insightful review of *The Agenda* by Robert M. Solow, "Advise and Dissent," in *The New Republic*, Aug. 1, 1994, pp. 41–43. On the credibility of Woodward's book, see Bert Solomon, "Seems like a Messy way to decide. But it could be a whole lot Worse," *National Journal*, June 25, 1994, pp. 1532–33. Solomon's interviews with White House staffers found no major disputes with Woodward's account of the early Clinton administration.

81. See Woodward, *The Agenda*.

82. Woodward, *The Agenda*, p. 84.

83. Woodward, *The Agenda*, p. 94.

84. For an analysis of the politics of the first Clinton budget see James P. Pfiffner, "President Clinton and the 103rd Congress: Winning Battles and Losing Wars," in James A. Thurber, ed., *Rivals for Power* (Washington, D.C.: CQ, 1997).

85. R. W. Apple Jr., "Small Change," *New York Times*, Aug. 8, 1993, p. E1.

Chapter 6. Three Presidents in Crisis

1. See the perceptive analysis by David Gergen, *Eyewitness to Power* (New York: Simon, 2000), pp. 93–104.
2. Quoted in Stanley I. Kutler, *The Wars of Watergate* (New York: Knopf, 1990), p. 112. On May 16, 1973, in a conversation with Alexander Haig, Nixon said, "The Ellsberg thing was something that we set up. Let me tell you. I know what happened here and Al knows what happens. We set up in the White House a (*sic*) independent group under Bud Krogh to cover the problems of leaks involving, at the time, of the Goddamn Pentagon papers; right? . . . the plumbers operation." Tape transcript in Stanley I. Kutler, *Abuse of Power: The New Nixon Tapes* (New York: Free Press, 1997), p. 514.
3. Fred Emery, *Watergate* (New York: Times, 1994), p. 30.
4. See Kutler, *Abuse of Power*, p. 33.
5. Of the Huston plan, Nixon said, "Well, then to admit that we approved . . . illegal activities. That's the problem." Also, "I ordered that they use any means necessary, including illegal means, to accomplish this goal." Quoted in Kutler, *Abuse of Power*, p. xxi.
6. Leonard Garment, *Crazy Rhythm* (New York: Times, 1997), p. 297.
7. See Kutler, *Abuse of Power*, p. xxi.
8. The New York Times, *The White House Transcripts* (New York: Vintage, 1973), p. 146–47; March 21, 1973.
9. See Michael Genovese, *The Nixon Presidency* (New York: Greenwood, 1990), p. 190.
10. *The White House Transcripts*, quoted in Larry Berman, *The New American Presidency* (Boston: Houghton, 1987), p. 189.
11. Weinberger and Shultz argued in meetings with the president that selling arms to Iran might break the Arms Export Control Act. But Reagan said in retrospect, "I felt that as far as being the president that a thing of this kind to get back five human beings from potential murder, yes, I would violate that other—that law." Bob Woodward, *Shadow* (New York: Simon, 1999), p. 164. See also pp. 109–10, 137, 155.
12. See George Shultz, *Turmoil and Triumph* (New York: Scribner, 1993), p. 824. After reviewing the CIA analysis, Shultz concluded: "Khomeini was firmly in power, and Rafsanjani was carrying out the ayatollah's resolute policy of opposition to the United States; recent events in Iran suggested that no Iranian leader other than Khomeini has the power to initiate a rapprochement with the united States or even to offer such a suggestion for debate."
13. Quoted in William S. Cohen and George J. Mitchell, *Men of Zeal* (New York: Viking, 1988), p. xx.
14. See Shultz, *Turmoil and Triumph*, pp. 237, 239, 785. Shultz was angered that he was told by White House aides that the United States was not selling arms to Iran and that he was assuring our European allies of it at the same time that the United States was in fact selling arms to Iran. See pp. 783–924, passim.
15. See the chronology in Cohen and Mitchell, *Men of Zeal*, pp. xix–xxxi.
16. See Shultz, *Turmoil and Triumph*, p. 811.

17. See Theodore Draper, *A Very Thin Line* (New York: Hill, 1991), pp. 225–26, 247–48. See also Woodward, *Shadow*, p. 137. White House counsel Peter Wallison also reported to chief of staff Donald Regan that the shipments were likely violations of the act (Woodward, *Shadow*, p. 109).
18. See Schultz, *Turmoil and Triumph*, p. 804.
19. See the discussion of the law in Cohen and Mitchell, *Men of Zeal*, pp. 12–13, 279–88.
20. For an analysis of the Boland amendment and its application to the National Security Council staff see *Report of the Congressional Committees Investigating the Iran-Contra Affair* (Washington, D.C.: GPO, November 1987), pp. 41–42.
21. See Draper, *A Very Thin Line*, p. 33.
22. Shultz, *Turmoil and Triumph*, p. 811.
23. *Report of the Congressional Committees Investigating the Iran-Contra Affair*, p. 280.
24. See David Abshire's account of his experience in the Reagan White House, *To Save a Presidency: The Curse of Iran-Contra* (New York: Oxford University Press, forthcoming). On the internal Baker investigation, see Woodward, *Shadow*, p. 151. It included 13 interrogations of the president, a staff of 67 people in the White House, and examined more than 12,000 documents.
25. Dick Morris, *Behind the Oval Office* (Los Angeles: Renaissance, 1999), p. xxiv.
26. Stephen J. Wayne, "Presidential Personality: The Clinton Legacy," in Mark J. Rozell and Clyde Wilcox, eds., *The Clinton Scandal* (Washington, D.C.: Georgetown University Press, 2000), p. 217–18.
27. *Congressional Quarterly Weekly* (Dec. 22, 1998): 3324.
28. Richard Nixon, *RN: The Memoirs of Richard Nixon* (New York: Grosset, 1978), p. 1089.
29. Lawrence E. Walsh, *Iran-Contra: The Final Report* (New York: Random, 1993), pp. 445.
30. *Report of the Congressional Committees Investigating the Iran-Contra Affair*, pp. 21–22.

Chapter 7. Character Complexity

1. George Lardner Jr. and Michael Dobbs, "New Nixon Tapes Are Released," *Washington Post*, Oct. 6, 1999, p. A31.
2. Lardner and Dobbs, "New Nixon Tapes Are Released," p. A31.
3. Stanley I. Kutler, *The Wars of Watergate* (New York: Knopf, 1990), p. 107.
4. Stanley I. Kutler, *Abuse of Power* (New York: Free Press, 1997), p. 31. The expletive Nixon used was "cocksuckers."
5. Charles Krauthammer, "Nixon on the Couch," *Washington Post*, Oct. 15, 1999, p. A29.
6. Leonard Garment, "Richard Nixon, Unedited," *Washington Post*, Oct. 19, 1999, p. A31.
7. Michael Beschloss, "A Question of Anti-Semitism," *Newsweek*, Oct. 18, 1999, p. 30.
8. Quoted by Marcus Cunliffe, *George Washington: Man and Monument* (New York: New American Library, 1982), p. 1.

9. Seymour Martin Lipset, "The Conditions for Democracy in the United States and the Greatness of George Washington," typescript draft, second-from-last page in the manuscript (no page numbering). For an argument that Washington was more honored in his own time than recently, see Colleen J. Shogan, "George Washington: Can Aristotle Recapture What His Countrymen Have Forgotten?" In *George Washington: Foundation of Presidential Leadership and Character,* ed. Ethan Fishman, William Pederson, and Mark Rozell (Westport, Conn.: Praeger, 2001).

10. David Abshire, *The Character of George Washington and the Challenges of the Modern Presidency,* pamphlet (Washington, D.C.: Center for the Study of the Presidency, 1998).

11. Joseph Epstein, "George Washington: An Amateur's View," *The Hudson Review* 51, no. 1 (spring, 1998): 39.

12. Fritz Hirschfeld, *George Washington and Slavery: A Documentary Portrayal* (Columbia: University of Missouri Press, 1997), pp. 11–12, 20, 212, 220. Hirschfeld's book is an impressive collection of documents and analysis. Much of the analysis in this section is based on his book. For a similar, though slightly different, count of Washington's slave holdings, see James Thomas Flexner, *George Washington: Anguish and Farewell* 1793–1799 (Boston: Little, 1969, 1972), p. 113.

13. Washington was a "kind master," as slave owners went. But as Roger Wilkins points out: "There were kind masters, though kindness in the context of such a heinous criminal enterprise as American slavery must necessarily have a rather shallow meaning." *Jefferson's Pillow* (Boston: Beacon, 2001).

14. Hirschfeld, *Washington and Slavery*, p. 37.

15. Letter from Washington to Captain Joseph Thompson of the schooner Swift, dated July 2, 1766. Reproduced in Hirschfeld, *Washington and Slavery*, pp. 67–68. The letter is also printed in part in Flexner, *George Washington*, pp. 113–14.

16. However, as early as 1774 Washington wrote that if the Americans submitted to British domination, then "custom and use shall make us tame and abject slaves, as the blacks we rule over in such an arbitrary way." Quoted in Flexner, *George Washington*, p. 114. Note that the words "custom and use" imply that blacks are not inherently inferior to whites but that any perceived inferiority came from "custom and use" rather than race.

17. Flexner, *George Washington*, p. 115.

18. Hirschfeld, *Washington and Slavery*, pp. 21–29.

19. Wilkins, *Jefferson's Pillow*, pp. 44–45.

20. Flexner, *George Washington*, p. 118.

21. Flexner, *George Washington*, p. 118.

22. Flexner, *George Washington*, p. 121.

23. Flexner, *George Washington*, p. 121.

24. Hirschfeld, *Washington and Slavery*, pp. 172–78.

25. Quoted in Flexner, *George Washington*, p. 122 (italics in original).

26. Quoted in Flexner, *George Washington*, p. 113.

27. Letter from Washington to Oliver Wolcott Jr., dated Sept. 1, 1796. Reproduced in Hirschfeld, *Washington and Slavery*, p. 113. See also Wilkins, *Jefferson's Pillow*, pp. 82–83.

28. Letter from Washington to Major George Lewis, dated November 13, 1797. Quoted in Hirschfeld, *Washington and Slavery*, p. 70.

29. See Flexner, *George Washington*, p. 115.

30. Hirschfeld, *Washington and Slavery*, p. 200.

31. Letter from Robert Pleasants to George Washington, dated "Curles 12mo. [Dec.] 11th 1785," reprinted in Hirschfeld, *Washington and Slavery*, pp. 193–95.

32. Edward Rushton to Washington, an "expository Letter to George Washington on his continuing to be a Proprietor of Slaves." Quoted by Dorothy Twohig, "'That Species of Property': Washington's Role in the Controversy over Slavery," paper presented at a conference on Washington and slavery at Mount Vernon, October, 1994. From the Papers of George Washington website, posted by the University of Virginia, www.virginia.edu/gwpapers/articles/slavery/index.html (March 31, 2003).

33. See David McCullough, *John Adams* (New York: Simon, 2001), pp. 132–34, 330–31, and passim.

34. Max Farrand, ed., "The Records of the Federal Convention of 1787," 2:364, 369, 370. Quoted in Hirschfeld, *Washington and Slavery*, p. 174.

35. See Flexner, *George Washington*, p. 115; see also Joseph J. Ellis, *Founding Brothers: The Revolutionary Generation* (New York: Knopf, 2000), p. 96. Ellis argues that Madison, like Jefferson and others of the Virginia dynasty, "regarded any explicit defense of slavery in the mode of South Carolina and Georgia as a moral embarrassment. On the other hand, he regarded any effort to end slavery as premature, politically impractical, and counterproductive." Ellis refers to this position as "the Virginia straddle" (pp. 113–14).

36. Ellis, *Founding Brothers*, p. 90; Andrew Levy, "The Anti-Jefferson," *The American Scholar* 70, no. 2 (spring, 2001): 19.

37. Ellis, *Founding Brothers*, pp. 89–90. See also Gordon S. Wood, "The Greatest Generation," *The New York Review of Books*, Mar. 29, 2001, pp. 17–22. Wood states: "Not only were there more antislave societies created in the South than in the North, but manumissions in the upper South grew rapidly in the years immediately following the end of the War for Independence" (p. 21). Thus slavery was not universally accepted in the South in Washington's time.

38. Hirschfeld, *Washington and Slavery*, p. 182.

39. On Benjamin Franklin and slavery see Carl Van Foren, *Benjamin Franklin* (New York: Garden City, 1941), pp. 128–29, 774–75; John C. Van Horne, "Collective Benevolence and the Common Good in Franklin's Philanthropy," in J. A. Leo Lemay, ed., *Reappraising Benjamin Franklin* (Newark: University of Delaware Press, 1993), pp. 431–39; Claude-Anne Lopez, *My Life with Benjamin Franklin* (New Haven: Yale University Press, 2000), pp. 205–11.

40. Wilkins, *Jefferson's Pillow*, pp. 90–91.

41. Levy, "The Anti-Jefferson," p. 16.

42. Levy, "The Anti-Jefferson," p. 24.

43. Levy, "The Anti-Jefferson," p. 25. See also "The Deed of Gift," letter from the editor of *The American Scholar*, p. 2.

44. Hirschfeld, *Washington and Slavery*, p. 79.

45. John Bernard's memoirs, *Retrospections of America, 1797–1811*, quoted in Hirschfeld, *Washington and Slavery*, p. 73.

46. Quoted in Hirschfeld, *Washington and Slavery*, p. 209.

47. Hirschfeld, *Washington and Slavery*, pp. 209–11 (italics in original).

48. Hirschfeld, *Washington and Slavery*, pp. 213–22. John Adams's wife, Abigail, wrote to her sister Mary on December 21, 1800: "[S]he [Martha Washington] did not feel as tho [*sic*] her life was safe in their Hands, many of whom would be told that it was [in] there [sic] interest to get rid of her—She therefore was advised to set them all free at the close of the year." Quoted in Hirschfeld, *Washington and Slavery*, p. 214.

49. Hirschfeld, *Washington and Slavery*, p. 6.

50. Ellis, *Founding Brothers*, p. 263.

51. See Matthew Spalding and Patrick J. Garrity, *A Sacred Union of Citizens: George Washington's Farewell Address and the American Character* (Lanham, Md.: Rowman, 1996), p. 71.

52. Wilkins, *Jefferson's Pillow*.

53. Wilkins, *Jefferson's Pillow*, pp. 128, 138–39.

54. Robert F. Dalzell Jr., "George Washington, Slaveholder," *New York Times*, Feb. 20, 2000, p. A27.

55. Dalzell, "George Washington, Slaveholder," p. A27.

56. Joseph A. Califano Jr., *The Triumph and Tragedy of Lyndon Johnson: The White House Years* (College Station, Tex.: Texas A&M University Press, 2000), p. 10.

57. Quoted in Robert Dallek, "Lyndon B. Johnson," in Robert A. Wilson, ed., *Character above All: Ten Presidents from FDR to George Bush* (New York: Simon, 1995), pp. 105–106.

58. Dallek, "Lyndon B. Johnson," in Wilson, p. 106.

59. Robert Dallek, *Flawed Giant: Lyndon Johnson and His Times, 1961–1973* (New York: Oxford University Press, 1998), p. 188.

60. See Robert A. Caro, *The Years of Lyndon Johnson: The Path to Power* (New York: Knopf, 1995) and *Means of Ascent* (New York: Knopf, 1990).

61. Quoted in Dallek, *Flawed Giant*, p. 112.

62. For a fascinating analysis of the strategy and tactics of the passage of the Civil Rights Act of 1964, see Robert D. Loevy, "The Presidency and Domestic Policy: The Civil Rights Act of 1964," in James P. Pfiffner and Roger H. Davidson, eds., *Understanding the Presidency* (New York: Longman, 1997), pp. 232–43.

63. Dallek, *Flawed Giant*, p. 114.

64. Dallek, *Flawed Giant*, p. 120.

65. For an analysis of Republican gains in the South from the 1960s to the 1990s, see James P. Pfiffner, "President Clinton, Newt Gingrich, and the 104th Congress," in Nelson W. Polsby and Raymond E. Wolfinger, eds., *On Parties: Essays Honoring Austin Ranney* (Berkeley: Institute of Governmental Studies, 1999). Also James P. Pfiffner, "President and Congress at the Turn of the Century: Structural Sources of Conflict," in James Thurber, ed., *Rivals for Power*, 2d ed. (Lanham, Md.: Rowman, 2001), pp. 170–90.

66. Dallek, *Flawed Giant*, p. 219.

67. For a positive review of Johnson's policy achievements see John A. Andrew III, *Lyndon Johnson and the Great Society* (Chicago: Dee, 1998).

68. R. W. Apple Jr., "A Vietnam War Critic Now Has Praise for Johnson," *New York Times*, Nov. 27, 1999, p. A10.

69. George McGovern, "Discovering Greatness in Lyndon Johnson," *New York Times*, Apr. 12, 1999, p. WK17.

70. See John Sloan, *The Reagan Effect* (Lawrence: University Press of Kansas, 1999), pp. 80–81.

71. For an analysis of the initial Reagan policy agenda, see James P. Pfiffner, *The Strategic Presidency: Hitting the Ground Running*, 2d ed. (Lawrence: University Press of Kansas, 1996), pp. 103–110.

72. For an analysis of the problem of the domineering chief of staff see James P. Pfiffner, "The President's Chief of Staff: Lessons Learned," in James P. Pfiffner, ed., *The Managerial Presidency*, 2d ed. (College Station, Tex.: Texas A&M University Press, 1999).

73. Fred Greenstein, "Ronald Reagan, Mikhail Gorbachev, and the End of the Cold War: What Difference Did They Make?" in William C. Wohlforth, ed., *Witnesses to the End of the Cold War* (Baltimore: Johns Hopkins University Press, 1996). See also Frances Fitzgerald, *Way Out There in the Blue* (New York: Simon, 2000).

74. For an analysis of the causes of the Soviet Union's downfall, see Jack A. Goldstone, "Revolution in the USSR, 1989–1991," in Jack A. Goldstone, ed., *Revolutions: Theoretical, Comparative, and Historical Studies* (Belmont, Calif.: Wadsworth, 2003), pp. 261–70.

75. Erwin C. Hargrove, *The President as Leader* (Lawrence: University Press of Kansas, 1998), p. 171.

76. See David Maraniss, *First in His Class* (New York: Simon, 1995), pp. 153–54.

77. For an insightful and balanced evaluation of Clinton and his presidency, see David Gergen, *Eyewitness to Power* (New York: Simon, 2000), pp. 317–42. Gergen's perspective on Clinton is drawn from his personal service in the Clinton White House and enhanced by his service in the White House during the presidencies of Presidents Nixon, Ford, and Reagan.

78. For an astute analysis of Clinton and the character issue see Betty Glad, "Evaluating Presidential Character," *Presidential Studies Quarterly* 33, no. 4 (fall, 1998): 861–72.

79. Todd S. Purdum, "Facets of Clinton," *New York Times Magazine*, May 19, 1996, p. 36.

80. Purdum, "Facets of Clinton," p. 36.

81. Fred I. Greenstein, "There He Goes Again: The Alternating Political Style of Bill Clinton," *P.S.: Political Science and Politics* (June, 1998), p. 179.

82. Dick Morris, *Behind the Oval Office* (Los Angeles: Renaissance, 1999), p. xiv.

83. Stephen J. Wayne, "Presidential Personality: The Clinton Legacy," in Mark J. Rozell and Clyde Wilcox, eds., *The Clinton Scandal* (Washington, D.C.: Georgetown University Press, 2000).

84. There are at least two justifications for paying attention to polls. In a democracy what the people want ought to be relevant, if not determinative. Public opinion

helps set the boundaries of possible action in a polity that is responsive to the public.

85. See Stanley A. Renshon, "The President's Judgment," *PRG Report* 21, no. 1 (spring, 1998), p. 10. For Renshon's in-depth analysis of Clinton's character, see *High Hopes: The Clinton Presidency and the Politics of Ambition* (New York: New York University Press, 1996).

86. For an analysis of Clinton's 1993 budget proposals and the politics of their passage see James P. Pfiffner, "President Clinton and the 103rd Congress," in James A. Thurber, ed., *Rivals for Power* (Washington, D.C.: CQ, 1998), pp. 170–90.

87. Jonathan Alter, "An October Surprise," *Newsweek*, Nov. 2, 1998, p. 29.

88. Erwin C. Hargrove, "Public Purposes and Private Pursuits: Questions about Bill Clinton," *Presidential Studies Quarterly* 33, no. 4 (fall, 1998): 854. See Hargrove's insightful article on Clinton, "The Study of Political Leadership: Bill Clinton as a Test Case," *PRG Report* (fall, 1998): 12–14.

89. In a Senate speech in 1850 Clay said, "I would rather be right than be President." *Bartlett's Familiar Quotations* (New York: Little, 1980), p. 444.

90. See Andrew Stark, *Conflict of Interest in American Public Life* (Cambridge: Harvard University Press, 2000), pp. 142–47.

91. James Bryce, *The American Commonwealth*, 2d ed., vol. I (New York: Macmillan, 1891), pp. 73–80.

92. Bryce, *The American Commonwealth*, p. 74.

93. Bryce, *The American Commonwealth*, p. 75.

94. H. H. Gerth and C. Wright Mills, *From Max Weber: Essays in Sociology* (New York: Oxford University Press, 1946), p. 128.

95. Gerth and Mills, *From Max Weber*, p. 84.

96. Pendleton Herring, *The Politics of Democracy* (New York: Rinehart, 1940), p. 144.

97. Herring, *The Politics of Democracy*, p. 64.

98. T. V. Smith, *The Promise of American Politics* (Chicago: University of Chicago Press, 1936), p. 248. Quoted in Herring, *The Politics of Democracy*, p. 135.

99. Stephen Hess, *Presidents and the Presidency* (Washington, D.C.: Brookings, 1995), pp. 39–45.

100. Hess, *Presidents and the Presidency*, p. 44.

101. See Bobbi S. Low, *Why Sex Matters: A Darwinian Look at Human Behavior* (Princeton: Princeton University Press, 2000).

102. See Francis Fukuyama, *The Great Disruption* (New York: Free Press, 1999), pp. 92–111.

103. Rexford D. Tugwell, *The Art of Politics* (New York: Doubleday, 1958), pp. 242–43; quoted in Thomas E. Cronin and Michael A. Genovese, *The Paradoxes of the American Presidency* (New York: Oxford University Press, 1998), p. 38.

104. See, for example, George Stephanopoulos's memoir, *All Too Human: A Political Education* (New York: Little, 1999).

SOURCES FOR EPIGRAPHS

Chapter 1. Judging Presidential Character

"Liberty cannot be preserved without general knowledge among the people who have the right to that knowledge and the desire to know. But besides this, they have a right, an indisputable, unalienable, indefeasible, divine right to that most dreaded and envied kind of knowledge—I mean of the character and conduct of their rulers." (John Adams, 1765)

Source: Quoted in David McCullough, "Harry S. Truman, 1945–53," in Robert A. Wilson, *Character above All* (New York: Simon and Schuster, 1995), p. 59.

Chapter 2. The Nature of Presidential Lies

"It is only the cynic who claims "to speak the truth" at all times and in all places to all men in the same way. . . . He dons the halo of the fanatical devotee of truth who can make no allowance for human weaknesses." (Dietrich Bonhoeffer, "What Is Meant by 'Telling the Truth?'")

Source: Quoted in Sissela Bok, *Lying: Moral Choice in Public and Private Life* (New York: Vintage Books, 1978), p. 154.

"You know I am a juggler, and I never let my right hand know what my left hand does. . . . I may have one policy for Europe and one diametrically opposite for North and South America. I may be entirely inconsistent, and furthermore I am perfectly willing to mislead and tell untruths if it will help win the war." (Franklin D. Roosevelt, May 15, 1942)

Source: Quoted by Warren F. Kimball, *The Juggler: Franklin Roosevelt as Wartime Statesman* (Princeton, N.J.: Princeton University Press, 1991), p. 7. See also Geoffrey C. Ward, *A First-Class Temperament* (New York: Harper and Row, 1989), p. xii.

"When in doubt, tell the truth. It will confound your enemies and astound your friends." (Mark Twain)

Source: Widely attributed to Mark Twain.

"You don't know how to lie. If you can't lie, you'll never go anywhere." (Richard Nixon to a political associate)

Source: Stanley Kutler, *The Wars of Watergate* (New York: Alfred A. Knopf, 1990), p. 619.

Chapter 3. Serious Presidential Lies

"Men are so simple and so ready to obey present necessities, that one who deceives will
   always find those who allow themselves to be deceived." Niccolo Machiavelli
Source: Quoted in Sissela Bok, *Lying: Moral Choice in Public and Private Life* (New York:
   Vintage Books, 1978), p. 30.

"Nearly everyone will lie to you, given the right circumstances." (Bill Clinton, 1992)
Source: Quoted by Paul Gray, "Lies, Lies, Lies," *Time Magazine*, October 5, 1992, p. 34.

"'I did that,' says my memory. 'I could not have done that,' says my pride, and remains
   inexorable. Eventually—the memory yields." (Friedrich Nietzsche)
Source: Friedrich Nietzsche, *Beyond Good and Evil*, in *The Philosophy of Nietzsche* (New
   York: Modern Library, 1927, 1954), p. 451.

Chapter 4. Sexual Probity and Presidential Character

"What counts with a candidate for president is his character, and nothing shows it like
   his relationship with women. Here you have a man who is asking you to trust him
   with your bank account, your children, your life and your country for four years. If
   his own wife can't trust him, what does that say?" (George Reedy)
Source: Quoted in Ben Bradlee, *A Good Life: Newspapering and Other Adventures* (New
   York: Simon and Schuster, 1995), p. 483.

Chapter 5. Character, Consistency, and Campaign Promises

"I stick by my principles, and one of my principles is flexibility." (Everett Dirkson)
Source: Widely attributed to Senator Everett Dirkson.

Chapter 6. Three Presidents in Crisis

"I gave them a sword. And they stuck it in, and they twisted it with relish. And I guess if
   I had been in their position, I'd have done the same thing." (Richard Nixon)
Source: Quoted in "The Misty Road to Impeachment," *The Economist,* September 19,
   1998.

Chapter 7. Character Complexity

"If they sometimes lie in the strenuous task, it is regrettable but understandable. If they
   sometimes truckle, that is despicable but tolerable. If they are sometimes bribed,
   that is more execrable but still not fatal. The vices of our politicians we must
   compare not with the virtues of the secluded individual but with the vices of
   dictators. . . . People elsewhere get killed in the conflicts of interest over which our

politicians preside with vices short of crimes and with virtues not wholly unakin to magnanimity." (T. V. Smith)

Source: T. V. Smith, *The Promise of American Politics* (Chicago: University of Chicago Press, 1936), p. 248. Quoted in Pendleton Herring, *The Politics of Democracy* (New York: Holt Rinehart and Company, 1940), p. 135.

INDEX